ALYSSA

W9-BYM-828

IDA BAILEY ALLEN'S
COOK BOOK FOR TWO

IDA BAILEY ALLEN'S

Cook Book
for Two

GARDEN CITY BOOKS

GARDEN CITY, NEW YORK

A new, revised edition of FOOD FOR TWO

LIBRARY OF CONGRESS CATALOG CARD NUMBER: 57-6701

COPYRIGHT ©, 1947, 1957, BY IDA BAILEY ALLEN

ALL RIGHTS RESERVED

PRINTED IN THE UNITED STATES OF AMERICA

What — When — Where Do We Eat?

What twosomes eat depends mostly on personal preference, whim, cooking ability, and the food budget.

When twosomes eat depends on the time they return from business, a favorite TV show, or, if they do not go to business, mealtime may accommodate a free-time schedule.

Where twosomes eat, even in their own homes, depends on whether or not they are the imaginative type. The spring sun shining into the living room may suggest breakfast on trays beside the window. If it's chilly — and the open fire comforting — dinner will be near the fireplace. When the lilacs bloom, a picnic in the yard is imminent. In addition there's always the terrace, patio, or porch for a change of backdrop. Sometimes right in front of the TV set is the dining spot — watch while dinner grows cold! And occasionally dining out will be the choice.

Whether you are a bride and groom, a retired couple, two bachelors, or young women sharing an apartment together, you can enjoy good meals, often glamorous, without making a chore of it and without "busting" the budget. This book tells you how. If you will take a few moments to read the leading paragraphs of each chapter you will find answers to all your questions.

Yes, you can eat well and have fun doing it. Here's how.

Ida Bailey Allen

v

Contents

—Cooking terms—Baking for two—Baking time
table—Your food repertoire—Spécialité de la
maison—Time-table meals—Cooking ahead.

Stews, goulashes, curries and ragouts—"The innards"—Smoked meats and sausage—Poultry and
game—Oddments of meat and poultry—Using
canned meats—Cold cuts—Special for Gourmet
and Gourmette—Spectacular! Chicken baked in
foil—More ways with foil.

IDA BAILEY ALLEN'S
COOK BOOK FOR TWO

CHAPTER I

Your Kitchen Is Wherever You Cook

A REVOLUTION IS TAKING PLACE IN HOME COOKING.

More and more convenience and partly prepared foods are appearing in the supermarkets.

Cooking has become easier, almost a dainty process.

It has even become movable! Sometimes in the kitchen or kitchenette; in chafing dishes on a buffet table; with electrical equipment on the terrace or piazza; on a barbecue or grill in the garden or back yard; at the fireplace. Whatever place you cook is your kitchen. And preparing food has become a creative, highly respected art.

Stay-at-home wives, young and older, are discarding house dresses and cover-all aprons. The replacement? Swirls, colorful sunbacks, play suits with button-on skirts.

Young married wives have discovered that husbands are tired of looking at women in business clothes. So the moment they come home, off goes the suit, and on with the swirl, the toreador pants or shorts and shirts, *espadrilles* or loafers, and a ribbon band for the hair. One young husband I know prefers to see his wife in a velvet tea gown.

You will enjoy the freedom of this new cooking era. All you have to do to make it easy is to plan the cooking arrangements for convenience, wherever you cook.

The Size and Arrangement of the Kitchen

Much is being said and written about the right size for a kitchen. Some authorities advocate a large kitchen with a living room or nursery end. Others advocate a small kitchen workshop. Each has advantages. For the family of two, I advise a small kitchen with a dinette alcove or eating bar, or a kitchenette with adjacent dining facilities. Any family of two or more, whether living in a summer camp, a trailer or on a houseboat will find the kitchen facilities adequate if the equipment and supplies are carefully arranged for space saving, and if there is no unnecessary accumulation of articles that do not belong in the kitchen. A small kitchen of this type is surprisingly convenient. In fact, you can easily cook in it for more than two persons if you clear up as you work.

Kitchenettes

The kitchenette is now a recognized part of the modern apartment. It may be built into the wall of a room, with doors or folding screens which open and reveal a built-in sink, refrigerator, cupboards and shelves. Or it may be a large renovated closet with space enough for not more than a two-burner stove and grill, a few shelves and a cupboard. Or, in its humblest version, the kitchenette may be even improvised in a screened-off corner of a single room.

No matter how limited the space, it can be efficiently equipped and made capable of producing wholesome and appetizing meals. Wherever you cook is your kitchen.

The Improvised Kitchenette

Suppose you are going to improvise a small kitchenette in a closet or corner of the room. Observance of fire laws demands first consideration.

No flame-burning stoves are allowed in closets or small rooms without window ventilation to the out-of-doors. Hence, an electric table stove or grill is the only choice for the unventilated room or closet.

If electric or gas equipment can be legally operated

(check this with your landlord), the table or cupboard on which the cooking unit rests, and the surrounding walls to a height of 12 inches, should be lined with sheet metal or zinc. This is a necessary precaution against fire hazards.

Space Savers

Contrivance makes convenience. Small shelves provide many inches of extra storage space. They can be built or purchased and screwed into place. A corner bracket shelf may take care of spice containers. A narrow "mezzanine" or recessed shelf, two or three inches in width, can be made to fit beneath wider overhanging shelves, or fastened directly above or beneath an overhanging cupboard. If shelves are not already installed, it may prove more economical to buy separate wooden or steel cupboards. A knife rack and a set of hooks on a brace for utensils can be attached to the wall conveniently near the preparation table. Spring hooks prevent cups from slipping off, and together with ordinary utensil hooks they may be screwed beneath shelves or along the edge of the work table. A drop-leaf shelf may be put on the back of a door or other convenient wall space.

For storing extra vases, casseroles, and large pots or supplies not in everyday use, shelves may be built high to utilize space near the ceiling. Build up if you can't spread out. A folding aluminum step-ladder will be needed.

If a basin or sink with running water is available, the washing-up equipment should be centered around it. A can with a tight fitting cover should be provided for waste.

Electric Equipment

Shop before buying cooking equipment. If this is to be electrical, check the type of current available at your home to find whether it is AC or DC. Some equipment operates on only one of these currents, some on both. Electric equipment will operate only on the current for which it is designed. Be sure, too, that all the electrical appliances you plan to buy can be operated at one and the same time without overloading the wires. And before purchasing be certain there is a suitable place to store the equipment when not in use.

If a regulation small range is not available, you will find many possible substitutes. For instance, broilers and table stoves that broil, toast, boil, fry, and operate on three heats. There is a three-unit cloverleaf table stove consisting of three electric plates which fold together when not in use, each plate maintaining a different degree of heat. Augment either of these with an electric roaster or a separate electric oven or ovenette, and you can prepare any foods a family of two may fancy.

Useful additional equipment includes a plate warmer, a toaster, and a waffle iron. You will probably look with longing on an electric mixer, but its cost is justified only if you do considerable cooking; instead, buy a small portable electric beater.

The Furnishings

The most helpful time- and step-saving article you can acquire is a small wheeled table that can be used in the kitchen if there is room, and that doubles as a hospitality wagon whenever there are guests. Look around before purchasing this. Several designs are available. They cost from seven or eight dollars up to forty-nine. Or a light weight portable bar can be used instead. Or at a fraction of the cost you can buy a small wooden table with a lower shelf, and equip it with castors so it can be rolled wherever it is to be used. In case there is no room to stand a hospitality wagon, portable bar or rolling table, look up an all-purpose folding table that will fold into compact space and is strong enough to hold a heavy load. Or use the time-honored card table. In any case, provide some extra working surface. The inconvenience of trying to cook in cramped quarters with no surface on which to work is one of the reasons many would-be twosome cooks give up and "eat out."

The Refrigerator

A good refrigerator is the most important article of kitchen furnishing; an automatic refrigerator if it can be operated—and there are types that operate by electricity, gas and kerosene—or an adequate, well-insulated refrigerator cooled by ice. When you buy a new automatic refrigerator be sure to get a model with a freezing drawer or cabinet, in which quick-frozen foods may be stored. Whatever type refrigerator you have, it must be really cold to safeguard the freshness of food. Forty-five degrees Fahrenheit is what is known as the "safety-zone." The only accurate way to check this is to keep a refrigerator thermometer in the refrigerator at all times and consult it daily. If it is near or above 50 degrees it is not safe to keep fish, raw or cooked; fresh meat; or any custard or made cream desserts or cake in it more than a few hours, and no leftovers should be kept over twenty-four hours. The percentage of families using accurate thermometers in their refrigerators is very small. Yet it is the only way to find out whether or not the family food is safeguarded. Start out right. Add a refrigerator thermometer to your list of kitchen "musts."

Lighting and Color Schemes

Nothing is more dreary than to try to cook in a room that does not have enough light. Besides you can't tell whether dishes are really clean, the lettuce well washed, or even if the pie in the oven has a nice brown crust. So have lights over the sink and the stove or cooking unit.

And here's a thought!—use a flash light when you look into the oven.

There's just one thing left to complete a little kitchen or kitchenette—the color scheme. Work out a color scheme you like and that is becoming to you. Why not? Aren't you the star in the kitchen setting? Cover the walls with enamel, one of the plastic paints or washable wallpaper. Use curtains that need no laundering. Cover the floor with linoleum and keep it waxed. Choose utensils, canisters and earthenware that harmonize and are decorative as well as utilitarian; then arrange them for convenience, keeping in mind their decorative value. Yes, indeed, whether a package kitchen or a substitute, it can be made efficient and attractive.

Cooking Utensils

Choose cooking utensils that are of good quality, easy to clean and care for. They should be steady, and not have handles that jut out unnecessarily, or knobs that stand up on top to make storage difficult. They should have rounded corners and edges, and few hard-to-clean crevices.

Here are lists of near-minimum equipment you will require to prepare and clear away the meals for two suggested in this book. I would like to start out with a pressure cooker, which can well be the central unit of the equipment. If this seems beyond the starting budget, get the following utensils first, and save up for the pressure cooker. Used intelligently it will soon more than save its cost by making thrifty foods delicious, and bills small, not to mention that all-important saving of food values and cutting of cooking time by two-thirds.

If you are a career woman, a pressure cooker is an absolute time saving necessity no matter how small the family. Full information about pressure cookers and how to use them will be found in "PRESSURE COOKING," by Ida Bailey Allen.

Utensils Needed for Food Preparation, Cooking and Baking

1 set standard measuring spoons
2 standard measuring cups
1 nest 4 mixing bowls
1 small flour sifter
1 pastry blender
1 rotary egg beater
1 wooden mixing spoon
1 rubber scraper
1 rolling pin
1 vegetable cutting board
1 biscuit cutter
1 set round aluminum racks for cake-cooling, etc.
1 long-handled metal spoon
1 long-handled slotted metal spoon
1 cooking tongs
1 long-handled 2-tined kitchen fork
1 bread knife
1 meat knife
1 paring knife
1 peeling-corer knife
1 food chopper (aluminum)
1 narrow spatula—¾" wide
1 wide spatula—2½" wide
1 potato masher
1 good can opener
1 jar opener
1 bottle opener and cork screw
1 small tea strainer
1 medium large strainer
1 four-sided grater

1 fruit reamer (for juice)
1 vegetable brush
1 nylon pastry brush
1 small ladle
1 kitchen scissors
1 funnel
1 drip coffee-maker, 4 to 6 cups
1 china teapot, 4 cups
1 tea kettle, 3 quart
1 double boiler, 1½ quart
1 frying pan, 9" (iron)
2 round bottomed individual frying pans (stainless steel)
1 Dutch oven, 4½ quart, cast aluminum or electric
1 saucepan with cover, 1¼ pint
1 saucepan with cover, 1 quart
1 saucepan with cover, 2 quart
1 saucepan with cover, 3 quart
1 set medium-sized muffin pans
2 layer cake pans, 8" aluminum
1 shallow square or oblong cake pan (aluminum)
1 loaf pan, 8½" x 4½" x 2½" glass ovenware
1 pie plate, 9" glass ovenware
1 covered casserole, 1½ quart glass ovenware or earthenware
6 custard cups, glass
1 shallow roasting pan with rack (10" x 15") aluminum
1 four-quart pressure cooker

ADDITIONAL MISCELLANEOUS EQUIPMENT INCLUDES:

1 oven thermometer
1 safety zone refrigerator thermometer
1 pair rubber gloves
1 large tray
1 small tray
1 bread box (or use a large covered utensil)

6 pint-sized square refrigerator dishes
4 quart-sized oblong refrigerator dishes
2 quart jars for refrigerator use
2 pint jars for refrigerator use
Canisters for flour, sugar, coffee and tea

1 dishpan
1 rubber covered dish drainer
1 rubber sink stopper
1 spray for kitchen faucet
Salt and pepper shakers
1 towel rack with folding arms
1 paper-towel rack
2 dish cloths
1 dish mop and 1 dish brush ·
1 long-handled dish mop for wiping up floor spills

4 thick pot holders or 2 holders and 1 pair oven mitts
6 dish towels
1 hammer
1 medium-sized screw driver
1 box assorted nails
1 pair pliers
1 yard stick
2 asbestos mats
1 kitchen timer
1 Fire Extinguisher

Jay-Walking Cooks

In spite of the miles of words that have been printed about kitchen efficiency; in spite of the thousands of hours speakers, radio and TV commentators have given over to the subject, we still have among us many jay-walking cooks. And they are not all inexperienced newcomers—not by any means. Some have been cooks for a lifetime. Why is this? First let's think through that term "jay walker." A jay walker is a person who without thought crosses the street without regard to traffic or light signals. Psychologically a jay walker is absent-minded. Absent-mindedness, or failure to concentrate on the work being done, is the reason there are so many jay-walking cooks.

Once your cooking facilities have been laid out for efficient work, stick to the plan. If, after a thorough tryout, this doesn't work, adjust it if necessary.

Before starting to prepare a meal or special dish be sure the ingredients are in the house. Don't stop in the midst of your work to jay walk to the store for the missing article.

Read through the recipe, and take out at one time whatever ingredients may be needed from the refrigerator. Don't double-track.

If necessary to open the stepladder to reach a high shelf, be sure to get down every article you need with the one operation.

Use a tray in setting the table, or clearing it, instead of jay walking back and forth with a dish in each hand.

J. M. T. for Kitcheneers

If you are a business woman, career girl or industrial worker, the letters J. M. T. are familiar to you. They stand for Job Methods Training. Firms often give courses in J. M. T. to make production faster on the part of employees and the work less fatiguing. As yet J. M. T. courses in cooking and housekeeping are not available in most sections of the country. But where they have been given, startling time-savings in cooking and housekeeping have been effected.

Be your own critic, your own guide in J. M. T. If the preparation of a meal takes longer than you feel it should, review the arrangement of your kitchen or its substitute. Check up the placement of utensils. Then check yourself honestly to find out if your motions are really slow or wasteful, and how they can be speeded up.

Even apparently small operations count. Slow paring, because knives are dull. (Remedy—sharpen them.) Slow scouring because you're afraid you'll chip your nail polish. (Remedy—use rubber gloves.) Or you may find out the real reason you are slow is because you resent having to cook at all. In this case try the good old-time remedy of being thankful that you have a home and two people in it.

The Well-Dressed Table

The smart table does not require costly Spode and Wedgwood to satisfy good taste. Happily enough, inexpensive table settings, provided they are well chosen, are in equally good taste, especially if selected to harmonize with the setting in which they will be used.

With a family of two the number of dishes must usually be limited. But guests will be expected and little dinners for four can be handled as skillfully as meals for two, if one has four of a kind to go around. Or if there are more guests, there's always buffet service to use. However, if there is enough money and sufficient space, it pays to purchase china and glass for six, to allow for breakage.

Minimum Table Equipment for a Couple and Two Guests

4 cereal dishes
4 dinner plates
4 dessert plates, luncheon size
4 salad plates
4 bread-and-butter plates
4 cups and saucers
4 after-dinner cups and saucers
1 plate for bread and rolls
1 large platter
1 small platter
2 vegetable dishes
4 cream soup dishes or onion soup bowls with matching plates
4 shirred egg dishes
4 large pottery ramekins

1 sugar bowl, covered
1 cream pitcher
2 extra pitchers for syrup or sauce
4 sauce dishes
1 large cake plate
1 large sandwich plate
1 glass relish dish
1 glass dessert bowl
4 water goblets
1 water pitcher
4 tomato juice glasses
4 iced tea glasses
4 sherbet glasses
4 wine glasses

Accessories: These include salt and pepper shakers of glass or pottery, in bright or subdued colors to complement the china. White or colored candlesticks, appropriately used only at the evening table, look best in low glass, pottery, or brass holders to match the bowl used for a flower arrangement. Ash trays should be inconspicuous and should harmonize in color and material with the glass, silverware or flower bowl. Individual nut dishes may be as gay as desired. The bowl to hold flowers or fruit may be of glass, pottery, burnished copper, brass, or woven reed if fruit is used, to harmonize with the rest of the table setting. A basket is nice for bread and rolls. And be sure to have an attractive teapot.

Wood: A wooden salad bowl, with wooden salad fork and spoon, is used at the table when the salad is to be mixed and served from one large salad bowl. Sets of wooden-handled knives and forks, showing the natural wood grain, or in bright cheerful colors, are smart on the informal table. Plastic salad sets are attractive.

Service Trays: One can scarcely have too many trays. For passing beverages use cocktail trays that will not stain. Trays of assorted sizes, from very small to large utility size, are particularly helpful when serving without a maid.

Wherever You Eat Is Your Dining Room

Many twosomes are likely to dream of the dining room they will have some day, forgetting that in the meantime they will have to eat, perhaps thousands of meals, in a substitute. No matter whether this is a one-room apartment, whether it has a dinette, or whether there is a streamlined kitchen with a special table arrangement or bar for serving meals, it is *your* dining room. And it must be spotlessly clean and surrounded by good order. So——

Clean up and wash utensils as you cook.

Keep trash in the waste can, not on the floor.

If you are to breakfast in a one-room apartment, pull the cover up over the bed, and put away the bathrobes and slippers before serving. Pick up newspapers or the day's accumulation of disorder before serving dinner.

Be sure the room is well aired and lighted.

Set the table or bar neatly with sparkling glass and shining silver. Use a spotless cloth or table mats, even if they are paper. Have the table completely set for the meal. Don't be a "table hopper."

Remember you are hostess at all times. Look the part— tidy hair, a fresh dress, or pretty apron. Being hostess to a twosome can be the most important job in the world.

Yes, good eating is possible everywhere, with or without a real kitchen, with or without a large income, provided ingenuity, interest, and old-fashioned love sauce the meals.

CHAPTER II

What Makes Foods Taste Good

IT TAKES MORE THAN COOKING TO MAKE FOOD TASTE good. First of all comes a cheerful cook, with patience to shop for quality foods, conscience to keep them hygienically clean until used, and enough love and interest in their preparation and service to insure meals that look and smell and taste good. For appearance plays a prominent part in stepping up the palate to the real enjoyment of food, and causes beneficial stimulation of the entire digestive system. And nothing contributes more to good living than good digestion.

Rules for Judging Good Quality in Food

All fresh food should look fresh and clean.

Fruits should look plump and colorful. If possible they should be tree-ripened or garden-fresh.

Vegetables should look crisp and plump.

Leafy and green vegetables should be bright green and unwilted. Vegetables kept under refrigeration, iced or water-sprayed are fresher and have higher vitamin content than vegetables exposed to sun and heat.

If garden-fresh fruit and produce is not obtainable, look for and buy foods transported by air freight if you can afford them. They come from the farm to the table in minimum time, and are almost as fresh as when just gathered.

Milk should be pasteurized, in containers and refrigerated. Don't buy loose milk.

Eggs should be clean.

Cheese should be fully covered and protected from dust.

All meats, game and poultry should look well filled out, and should smell fresh. If in doubt take a sniff. The meat man may sniff at you, but he can't refuse your request.

Fish should look plump, not flabby, have clear eyes and red gills. If there is a strong smell, don't buy it.

Quick-frozen foods should be solidly frozen when purchased. They cannot be refrozen. Buy brands processed by reliable firms.

Canned foods must be selected after reading the labels, as many canned foods are graded, and the contents of the cans are fully described. Whenever possible buy canned foods in large cans instead of several small ones. This saves considerable money. When the can is opened pour the unused portion into a glass jar or refrigerator dish, cover, and refrigerate until needed.

Glassed foods can be partly judged for quality by the "look-see" method.

The contents of all packaged foods is fully described on the label. Read all that's printed. It describes what the food is, and the exact amount your money is buying.

Do not buy any ready foods that are unwrapped and exposed to dust and air. This means bread, rolls, cake, cookies, candy, nut meats, etc. They are germ-laden, and unfit for food when they are so exposed.

Do not purchase foods from dirty stores, or from sales people who do not look neat and clean, whose hands are dirty, or who show traces of illness, particularly wounds or eruptions on the hands. Disease can easily be transmitted to you by persons who handle your food.

The Care of Food After Marketing

The care of food after it reaches your home is as important as the care it received from the producers in shipping and in the store. All market orders should be promptly checked, and fresh foods needing refrigeration should be put away at once. A refrigerator must be kept hygienically clean, and this is possible only when the bottles and containers stored in it are clean.

Paper wrappings or bags should not be left on foods put in the refrigerator. This is not sanitary, and takes up unnecessary space. Instead use waxed paper, aluminum foil, or put the food in covered glass refrigerator dishes. As far as possible all foods should be covered, to prevent escaping flavors from merging with other foods.

Many fresh foods can be trimmed and made ready for subsequent use before refrigerating. This saves not only time, but storage space. Refrigerate in polyethelene bags.

Salad Plants: Wash, drain well, and pack into the hydrator or a covered glass or enamelware pan.

Root Vegetables: Potatoes, turnips, onions and beets do not need refrigeration. They should be kept in a cool place; the best one can do in a small apartment is to use a vegetable bin, effective because it permits circulation of air around the vegetables, which prevents "sweating" and quick spoilage. Or use a carton in which holes have been punched. It is not practical to keep on hand more than a week's supply.

Fruit: Wash and refrigerate.

Milk and Cream: Rinse the bottle or container with cold water before refrigerating.

Butter or Margarine: Store in covered dishes. Store a stick of butter in a butter dish that can go-to-table.

Cheese: Keep in covered glass dishes. If a piece of

'cheese is quite large, wrap it in waxed paper; put a tea-spoonful of vinegar in the bottom of the dish, and put the protected cheese on this. The presence of vinegar retards the formation of mold.

Eggs: Remove from the carton and put in a refrigerator dish. Do not wash unless necessary as this makes the egg shells porous. Air can then enter and cause deterioration. Keep refrigerated or in a cool place.

Meat or Poultry: Wrap in waxed paper; place in the coldest part of the refrigerator. If to be kept more than 24 hours, wrap in a polyethelene bag, place in the freezing unit and freeze; it may then be kept even 2 or 3 weeks.

Chopped Meat: Wrap loosely in waxed paper; use within 12 hours. No other meat spoils so quickly.

Canned, Jarred and Bottled Foods: Arrange these on special storage shelves. Put those to be used toward the end of the week at the bottom. Group the different kinds so you may see at a glance the stock on hand. Keep a small supply ahead.

Groceries: These include flour, sugar, baking powder, cereals, etc. Many can be kept in the original containers, if they are carefully opened so the tops can be pressed down to keep the contents clean. If this has not been done, cover with waxed paper secured with a rubber band. All-purpose flour and sugar keep best in canisters. All canisters should be clearly labelled. Write or type the name of the food on a gummed label, stick it in place, then cover with white shellac, to make it water proof and keep it in place. Baking powder, cocoa, baking soda, salt, etc. are kept in the original containers. To save space, small packages of odds and ends such as bouillon cubes, can be kept together in one canister. Store bottles of flavoring extracts away from the light. If there are several and they are inclined to topple over every time you touch one, stand them all in a square glass dish or small paste-board box.

Herbs and Spices: Valuable space in cupboards can rarely be spared for herbs and spices. But as they are ingredients that should be used often, put up a special shelf so they can be reached easily. This can be decorative as well as convenient. Don't—please—store them on a top shelf; you'll climb up for them only for special cooking, while both herbs and spices are seasonings for everyday foods. Keep the containers tightly closed.

Coffee: If purchased in a can or in a resealed vacuum jar, the coffee may be kept in it. If in a bag, turn into a canister with a snug-fitting cover to protect the flavor from the oxidizing effects of air and light. Do not store near the stove as heat causes the fine coffee oils to become rancid. Keep soluble coffee cool, too.

Tea: Keep in a tightly closed canister to protect the flavor.

Cooking the Food

A well arranged kitchen or well thought out substitute; foods of good quality; a well planned menu; standardized recipes that are reliable; good seasoning, a cheerful cook —these are the requirements that produce good eating. And the idea of a cheerful cook is not a bit of pollyanna, but a scientific fact. Experiments with lighthearted or downhearted women baking cakes proved that the lighthearted women baked better, lighter cakes. The reasons are self-evident. The lighthearted women concentrated on the recipe, were careful to measure accurately, worked rapidly and beat the cake batter with enthusiasm, in anticipation of a perfect loaf. The downhearted women were distracted; they made mistakes in measuring, were careless in putting the cakes together, worked slowly and beat the batter scarcely at all, for whether the cake would be good or not seemed unimportant. Yes, to be a good cook you must have enthusiasm.

Add imagination and you have the qualifications needed to become a cook supreme.

Flavoring and Seasoning

Flavor is first of all the natural taste of a food in itself, as the flavor of an orange or strawberries. A "flavoring" is something added to impart a nicer taste. And while the word flavoring is usually connected with the making of desserts, cakes and other sweets to which a flavoring extract is added, it can really be used as a synonym for the word "seasoning," traditionally connected with savory dishes of meat, poultry, game, fish, and vegetables. However, remember that the art of seasoning is not to produce one startling predominant taste, but to accentuate the natural flavor of the food itself. Call it what you will, flavoring or seasoning, a variety of the needed ingredients used sparingly yet with imagination, will make dull foods interesting and fine foods more glamorous. Start your selection with essentials and add others from time to time for more adventures in flavor.

Flavor Seasonings

There are 4 types of these flavorings or seasonings:—

1. Flavoring extracts: Made with a basis of an extracted natural flavor, or with a "test-tube" flavor made synthetically. These synthetic flavorings contribute fine taste, are harmless to good health, and as they take up little space and do not deteriorate, are a real asset in cooking for two. Start with the usual vanilla, lemon, almond and orange. In addition there are liquid cinnamon, nutmeg and clove, strawberry, raspberry, pineapple, banana, black walnut, cocoanut, mint, maple, rum and sherry. Others are on the way.

2. Salts: Including plain, iodized, onion, celery, garlic, and several herb-seasoned varieties including savory, basil, tarragon, thyme and marjoram salts. Nice to add a whiff of seasoning to canapés or salads. Buy seasoned salt, too.

3. Spices of all kinds: The essentials are cinnamon, paprika, clove, nutmeg, ginger, white and black pepper and poultry seasoning. In addition there are allspice, bay‧ leaf (whole leaves or powdered), chili powder, curry pow‧ der, saffron, mustard, caraway, celery seed, cumin seed, poppy seed, cardamom seed and mace, all worthy of spe‧ cial study and use.

4. Meat Condiments: Such as table-mustard, catsups of all kinds, chili sauce, chutney, horse-radish, Worcester‧ shire and other sauces to serve with meat or fish.

5. Special Vinegars: Including wine vinegar and vinegars flavored with tarragon, garlic, basil, eschalot, herbs 'n' spice, or herb vinegar. These give the gourmet touch to salads, sauces, and some meat, fish or vegetable dishes.

6. Special Seasonings: Include garlic, dried celery leaves and stalks, and dried onion flakes. There is a new-comer—liquid smoke for that charcoal-cooked flavor. Dried and fresh mushrooms are invaluable seasoners. And if meat stock or gravy tastes flat, reach for a bouillon cube, a little meat extract or gravy seasoning or hickory salt.

7. Herbs: These include sage, thyme, marjoram, basil, mint, rosemary, savory, tarragon, dill (leaves and seeds), juniper, oregano, dried parsley. Sets of herbs in easy-to-use jars and with full directions for use on the labels, may be purchased at various prices. One space-saving set comes in a hand-made pine rack that fits on the window sill and holds the jars in an easy-to-read position. Or accumulate your own set of herbs, seasonings and flavorings, and ar-range them on a special shelf in a convenient place. Al-ways be sure the covers or bottle tops are screwed on tight.

How to Use Herbs for Two

1.   Go easy at first. In a dish for two, start with a scant ¼ teaspoon of any powdered herb, or a scant teaspoon of

dried herb, or a scant half tablespoon of minced fresh herb. Increase the quantity next time if you like.

2. If a dried herb is not cooked in the food (as in making a soup), it should first be steeped 5 minutes in a very little hot liquid to cover, then added with the liquid. This releases aromatic oils and insures the full rich flavor. Use milk as the steeping liquid for a hot sauce; vinegar or lemon juice in salad making; bouillon or water for soups or gravies. Or lightly sauté the herb in fat if called for in the recipe.

3. There are two classes of herbs; fine herbs (*fines herbes* in France), which are delicate in flavor and are added close to the end of cooking, or raw when the dish is finished. These include **parsley, chervil, savory** and **burnet**. Herbs of stronger flavor are cooked for a longer time. These include **sage, thyme, dill, basil, mint,** etc.

4. A robust or strong herb can be blended with the fine or more delicate-flavored herbs.

5. **Marjoram, savory** or **tarragon** are good in almost any dish from hors d'oeuvres to salad.

6. **Tarragon** has an affinity for salads, fish and eggs.

7. **Sage** is good with pork, cottage cheese and stuffings. Don't use too much.

8. **Basil** is pungent, so use it lightly. Especially good with tomatoes, vegetable juices, meats, vegetables, rice, spaghetti and sauces.

9. **Thyme** is suited to soups, eggs, cheese, meats, poultry and game.

10. **Mint** is good in pea soup, tomato soup, with lamb, fresh pork or ham, tomatoes or squash, in tossed salads, and with almost all fruits.

To Keep Fresh Herbs

Chives, parsley, mint, fennel or any other herb should be sprayed well with cold water, drained on paper towels, then placed in a glass jar, covered, and refrigerated. They keep fresh and crisp several days.

To Use: Mince or cut up with the kitchen scissors.

Wines and Liqueurs in Cooking

Small amounts of wine add delectable flavor to certain cooked foods. The use of wines in cookery warrants a book in itself. However, there are four things to remember:

1.   Use dry wines or sherry with savory dishes and sauces.

2.   Use only light wines with light-colored ingredients.

3.   Use either white or red wine with dark-colored ingredients.

4.   Use sherry, sweet wines or liqueurs in desserts and sweet sauces.

Nose and Eye Appeal

Foods that smell good and look attractive, satisfying and abundant are real whets to appetite. When ingredients are good, foods cooked to a nicety (and never burned), and the fats used are fresh, any dish smells good in itself. Add a touch of spice or herbs and it has more nose appeal. Couple this with an arrangement that is neat and colorful, and you achieve eye-appeal as well—foods that are real "appeteasers."

Take the Temperature

That is, they will be "appeteasers" if the temperature is right. All cold foods should be served cold, in cold dishes. All hot foods should be served hot, if possible in heated dishes. All soups and hot beverages should be as near boiling-point as possible.

Garnishing and Serving

Don't over garnish; a little decoration goes a long way. And remember, the serving dish is the background-frame for the food. So choose a design that is simple, or one with a plain, banded, or bordered edge.

Be sure that no gravy or food is spilled on the edge of any dish. And don't, please, stick your thumb in the food when you pass the dish, or handle a glass from the top.

Be sure coffee or tea are not slopped over into the saucer.

As to the garnishes, they should always be edible and of contrasting color. Often the vegetables in the meal for two can be served as a garnish on the platter with the meat, poultry, fish or eggs.

Garnishes for Hot Meats: Parsley, cress, chicory, celery or finnochio tips, mushrooms, raw carrot sticks. Onion rings, sautéed or stuffed apples, or cooked pineapple or bananas are used with pork.

Fish: Choose a fresh green garnish and/or something tart. For instance, cress, fresh tarragon, lettuce, celery, chicory, red radishes, strips of green peppers or pimientos, cole slaw, fresh or broiled tomatoes. For that tart touch wedges of lemon or lime, or use pickles or olives.

Cold Meat or Fish Platters: Choose any fresh salad green or herb, sliced or small stuffed tomatoes or avocados, halved stuffed eggs, cole slaw, sliced cucumbers, radishes, scallions, carrot sticks, drained pickled beets or pineapple.

Desserts: Clear the table before they are presented; serve them with importance in attractive dishes. If the dessert looks uninteresting and calls for a garnish, choose a contrasting color. A little decoration goes a long way, for instance, for two persons a single shredded candied cherry, a date halved lengthwise, two whole nut meats or some chopped nuts, a little cut candied grapefruit or orange peel, plain or toasted coconut, a few chocolate chips, or a candy topping, such as crushed peanut brittle, chocolate crunch, or whole chocolate almonds or fruit drops.

Serving Food for Two

One of the best whets to appetite is that feeling of security fostered by an appearance of abundance. The old term M I K (more in the kitchen) is even more important today than it was in the days of our mothers when it was a household byword. In serving food for two, however, it is not always practical to have M I K. Perhaps there's no kitchen at all. So plan to make the platters and serving dishes of food look ample. Let them apparently contain a little more than one thinks he can eat.

The dreariest food sight I can remember is that of a 3-pound roast of beef served on a platter large enough for a 12-pound turkey. There were four persons at the table, and while the 3-pound roast really provided enough meat, it looked so little, so poverty-stricken skidding around on the big platter, that everyone felt uncomfortable. The moral? Make a dish look ample. If it's meat or fish, serve the vegetables with it, and add an edible garnish. If it's a made salad in a bowl that is too large, first line it with greens. If it's a cooked vegetable, try to use a dish that is the right size. If it's a pudding or custard served in the baking dish, don't choose a 1 or 2 quart casserole for two persons, as the pudding will look lost in it. Instead use a pint-sized dish, or individual baking dishes.

And one thing more. Serve the meal with a smile, with gaiety and self assurance. Present it with importance. For good food is important to good living.

CHAPTER III

Quick-Frozen Foods

QUICK-FROZEN FOODS ARE A GREAT HELP TO THE FAMILY OF two, if there is safe refrigeration, with an ice cube compartment, freezer drawer or tray, or if there is a separate freezing unit in which to store the foods until used. This is even more important for the twosome than for a larger family, for most quick-frozen foods are sold in packages which serve three to four persons. As the small family often needs only half a package there must be some adequate freezing unit in which to store the remainder until needed.

If there is no such unit available, the entire contents of the package must be cooked and the unused portion stored in a covered dish in the refrigerator. Frozen foods cannot be kept in a defrosted state, as they spoil more quickly than fresh foods because the freezing process softens the tissues. This is an asset when it comes to cooking, however, for it is the reason why quick-frozen vegetables and fish cook more rapidly than fresh; and it is one of the reasons why quick-frozen meats are more tender than so-called "fresh meats."

Garden Fresh

Most of us have eaten more quick-frozen foods than we realize during the past few years. For many quick-frozen fruits, vegetables, fish and sea foods, have been generally used by institutions, hotels, restaurants, dining cars and planes. When you ordered a "garden fresh" vegetable plate containing green peas, or a cut of "fresh cherry" pie, 100 to 1 the peas or the cherries were quick-frozen. However, that phrase garden-fresh was not a misnomer, for quick-frozen fruits and vegetables are frozen on the location where they are grown, as soon as they are gathered. That is why the flavor is superior; why they taste "garden-fresh," or "tree-ripened," and why analyses and experiments show their vitamin content is practically the equivalent of that of fresh produce. This freezing process is very rapid; at zero temperature it might almost be termed flash freezing. This is the reason why no large ice crystals form; and why there is no time for disintegration, or deleterious chemical change. The product is literally congealed "as is."

Buying Quick-Frozen Foods

The obligations of the processor and the storekeeper to safeguard foods by keeping them completely frozen ceases as soon as they are purchased. From that time on it's up to you. If buying them in quantity, with a lapse of more than 1 hour before the time of purchase and the time they reach your home, better get a fabrikoid covered, fibre-glass-lined bag with a zipper top in which to transport them. Fibre glass is an insulator which keeps in the cold and retards the entrance of heat for several hours. All frozen foods keep safely up to 4 to 6 hours, and brick ice cream will keep firm for about 2 hours, if the fibre-glass-lined bag is kept at normal temperature. Don't expect it to do a job if you stand it near the radiator of a train, or in a warm spot in your car.

But what if you don't own such a bag? Then turn to the time honored newspaper method. Put the frozen food packages together—to conserve all possible cold—then wrap in several folds of slightly damp newspaper, and tie securely. Follow this with at least two separate wrappings of dry newspapers. Unless they are to be used at once, pop them into the freezing chamber the minute you get home.

How Long Will They Keep?

In the ice cube chamber of an automatic refrigerator quick-frozen foods will keep a week. In a freezing drawer or locker, they will keep indefinitely with the exception of frigid doughs, which must be used within 2 weeks.

Defrosting the Refrigerator

All refrigerators should be defrosted every week. And quickly washed out with water containing 1 tablespoon of household ammonia to 2 quarts, wiped with a clean damp cloth or sponge and then wiped dry with a clean cloth. This must be done so fast that quick-frozen foods do not have time to thaw; meantime don't let them stand in the kitchen without protection. Better wrap them in folds of newspaper, and set them outside if the weather is cold. To defrost the refrigerator quickly, disconnect it or set at defrosting point, then fill the ice-cube trays with boiling water. Put these back in the ice chamber and close the refrigerator door. Defrosting will be complete within 30 minutes.

Thawing Quick-Frozen Foods

Thawing and defrosting mean exactly the same thing when applied to quick-frozen foods.

If defrosting foods to use in 4 to 6 hours, place on the bottom of the refrigerator. If to be used in 2 to 3 hours, defrost at room temperature. Poultry and thick cuts of meat or thick fish fillets need about 6 hours in the refrigerator, and at least 3 at room temperature to defrost.

However this time is lessened if you own a range equipped with a defrosting unit, which defrosts frozen foods in a matter of minutes by means of a special fan built into the barbecue grill. This unit eliminates possibility of loss of vitamins due to over-thawing and over-exposure to light, and full flavors are conserved, because the process is very quick.

If you don't have such a defrosting unit, improvise and turn an electric fan on the foods to be defrosted; it cuts the time in half. But be sure to keep the foods covered by the original containers, or if they are merely cellophane wrapped, roll in paper to keep out light, because exposure to light impairs vitamin efficiency.

In case quick-frozen fruit comes in a sealed cellophane bag, it can be immersed in a bowl of cold water from the tap to hasten defrosting, but cover it to keep out light. And never, never defrost quick-frozen meat, poultry, fish or any other unprotected frozen food directly in water, as this washes out both flavor and nutrients.

Protect the Vitamins

No matter how vitamin-rich quick-frozen foods may be, they will not retain their vitamins unless properly prepared. In this respect they correspond to fresh foods. Frosted fruits and fruit juices should never be allowed to stand exposed to the air after defrosting. Keep cold and tightly covered and use as soon as possible. Cook vegetables, meats, fish and sea food by the quickest method, preferably pressure cooking, fully explained in my book "PRESSURE COOKING." Or if this is not practical, steam boil them, or broil if this method is suitable. It must be kept in mind that frozen food, after thawing, needs less cooking than fresh—another reason nutritive values are retained.

And Now the Budget

Whether or not quick-frozen foods become a constant source of supply for your table should be determined by where you live, your refrigeration, whether or not you have a garden and whether you are gainfully employed so your time has specified monetary value. If living in crowded quarters it is a great convenience to purchase quick-frozen food with all waste removed; and when the first class quality of the food itself is taken into consideration, the higher cost is justified, especially if you are an employed homemaker and timesaving is imperative. But if you are a homemaker at leisure, you will save money by buying seasonable fresh fruits and vegetables, meats, fish and poultry, and by making your own specialty dishes. In this case, the expenditure of your time and energy means money saved, and therefore earned.

Points on Preparing or Cooking Quick-Frozen Foods

Quick-Frozen Vegetables

All quick-frozen vegetables must be cooked for they are frozen almost in the raw state. They may be cooked without defrosting, with the exception of corn-on-the-cob, which will still be frozen in the center after cooking unless first thawed. If vegetables are frozen in a solid piece, separate into halves, or cut into six chunks with a heavy sharp knife first dipped in hot water. The cooking heat can then penetrate to the center of the vegetable. Cut beans, corn and many other vegetables can be pushed apart with a fork. If there is time, better partly defrost broccoli or asparagus, so the stalks can be separated for uniform cooking. Complete defrosting often results in loss of vitamin C, shrivelling and therefore loss of flavor. Pressure cooking is a perfect way to cook frozen vegetables. In this case follow the directions that come with your pressure cooker, or as given in my book, "PRESSURE COOKING." For usual cooking, follow directions given on the package. Use as little water as possible; because of this add less salt than when cooking fresh vegetables. Cover closely and boil gently. Do not overcook. Watch the clock. Use the resulting liquid as a sauce, and serve the vegetable in sauce dishes so every drop will be used. Season as for fresh vegetables or serve with a sauce from the liquid. To make this add an equal amount of whole milk or light cream to the vegetable liquid; thicken with 1 tablespoon each flour and butter blended together, bring to a rapid boil, season and serve with the vegetable. All types of cooked quick-frozen vegetables may be used in place of fresh cooked vegetables in any of the made dishes, hors d'oeuvres or salads given in this book.

Broccoli, asparagus, brussels sprouts and cauliflower are especially good with vinaigrette, simulated Hollandaise or cheese sauce. And frozen vegetables are suited to the quick preparation of garden plates with a small portion of a more substantial quick-frozen food to balance. Add a good soup or hors d'oeuvre salad, an interesting bread, and a beverage, with a simple dessert or service of fruit and cheese, and an excellent satisfying meal is ready in quick time.

Quick-Frozen Meats

The flavor of meats is the same whether thawed or cooked in a frozen state. Large roasts or thick pieces of meat should be at least partly defrosted, to allow uniform cooking of the center and to prevent loss of juice and consequent shrinkage. However, thin cuts of meat, as steak, chops, or cutlets up to 1½ inches in thickness, need to be partly or completely defrosted. Hamburg steak or chopped meat must be completely defrosted for broiling, sautéing, or making into meat loaf. But if to be used in making a spaghetti sauce, quick stew or chili, cut the frozen meat into large cubes, and defrosting will take place as the meat cooks. When meats are cooked unthawed, allow from 10 to 15 per cent longer than when fresh.

It is impossible to brown meat cooked in the frozen state, so if a browned exterior is desired, brush the meat with fat after cooking and quickly brown in a hot oven, grill or barbecue unit.

Quick-Frozen Poultry or Game

This group includes chicken for roasting, broiling or frying, duck, turkey, pheasant and reindeer, as well as turkey cut in sections for more advantageous use by the family of two.

All quick-frozen poultry should be thawed before cooking, making possible any necessary singeing and the removal of pin-feathers. Then cook according to any of the recipes given in this book for preparing fresh poultry or game. Smoked turkey or chicken merely need defrosting. If to be served hot, brush plentifully with melted butter, and heat in a covered dish or pan in a slow oven.

Quick-Frozen Fish

Unless to be fried, quick-frozen fillets, small fish or frog's legs, may be broiled, boiled, steamed, poached or baked, in the frozen state. If fish is to be pressure-cooked, cut thick sections in halves or thirds to insure uniform cooking. In any case, use as little water or other liquid as possible. If a browned surface is desired, baste plentifully with butter or margarine toward the end of the cooking. All juices should be saved to make a sauce to serve with the fish.

Quick-Frozen Shellfish

If to be fried or boiled, shellfish should first be defrosted; this includes oysters, clams, shrimp, lobster and scallops. But if they are to be plain cooked and served creamed, à la Newburg, or in a stew or chowder, defrosting is not necessary. The juices should be saved to use as part of the liquid in making the sauce. Frozen minced clams do not need defrosting for chowder, but they must be defrosted for use when devilled, in clam cakes, or in clam and potato pie; in other words, whenever the pieces of clams must be separated before adding to a mixture. Oysters must be entirely defrosted (but left chilled) to serve raw. If to be fried, creamed, cooked Rockefeller or escalloped, they should be sufficiently defrosted to be easily separated.

Quick-Frozen Fruits

The wide variety of quick-frozen fruits and juices almost encircles the globe. All are appealing, good for you and quite reasonable in price, especially if combined with other fresh fruits in season. Quick-freezing is a superb method of capturing true fruit flavors. In using do not open the package while defrosting, as the action of oxygen on the fruit causes it to turn dark or oxydize. Use as soon as defrosted. If combined with fresh fruits, remember that most fruit is combined with sugar syrup before freezing, so go easy on the sugar. It can be used as a sauce, breakfast fruit, in shortcakes, cream tarts, fruit cups, pies, and piecakes; in other words just as fresh fruit is used. For making pies and other baked foods it should be partly defrosted. For dessert suggestions see Chapter *XIII* in this book.

Half Defrosted

Peaches, apricots, mixed fruits, raspberries, strawberries and other quick-frozen fruits are delicious served as an ice when a little more than half defrosted. This takes an hour and a half at room temperature.

Quick-Frozen Fruit Juices

These are prepared from tree-ripened fruit, and are delectable in flavor. They come in both concentrated and natural form. For the family of two the concentrated juice is the best buy. Open the can, estimate and remove the amount needed, close the can, fasten a double piece of waxed paper over the top with a rubber band, and return the can to the freezing unit. Add the required amount of water to the removed portion. Stir until defrosted and serve at once. Juices are also available in jars.

Custom Made Specialties

The list of quick-frozen specialties is long and interesting, including all types of savory dishes, from inexpensive New England codfish balls to costly dishes of world-renowned chefs. There are pâtés, shrimp cocktail, hors d'oeuvres, soups, entrées such as shrimp creole, lobster Newburg, interesting French, Hungarian, Italian and other popular foreign foods along with chicken à la king, roast or fried chicken, and chicken in gravy, pot roast of beef in gravy, roast lamb, Swiss steak, meat loaf, hamburgers, corned beef hash, "franks and kraut," and a host of other American favorites.

To prepare, follow directions on the package. In general, if the food is in a cream sauce, heat without defrosting in a double-boiler. If it is meat in gravy, use a small, heavy sauce pan, and slow heat; as fast as the food defrosts, loosen the pieces with a fork.

These specialties have the advantage of being quickly readied for service, but they are prepared for the mass taste, and so they suggest "restaurant cooking." They cost more than it does to prepare the dishes at home, and unless supplemented by or combined with other inexpensive ingredients, are likely to overtax the budget. Imagination and ingenuity will suggest many ways of stretching these food specialties by combining them with less costly ingredients. Here are some suggestions:

Quick-Frozen Meat and Poultry Dishes

Pot roast and gravy, flaked after defrosting, and served shortcake-fashion between split hot biscuit or plain or French toast.

French meat loaf, sliced and served with alternating slices of fried canned scrapple and tomato sauce.

Swiss steak with a thick blanket of fried onions and green peppers, balls of rice and grilled tomatoes.

Chicken croquettes surrounded with mixed vegetables, and sliced raw or grilled tomatoes.

Stuffed cabbage with tomato and green pepper sauce and mashed potato.

Hungarian goulash with tomato sauce, fried onions and fine noodles.

Franks and kraut with mashed potato, tomatoes and lettuce.

Meat balls in spaghetti sauce with plenty of spaghetti; an extra can of tomato sauce, and topped with thin slices of sharp cheese to be melted under the grill.

Vegetable chow mein combined with oddments of veal, or poultry.

Chicken à la king served shortcake-fashion between and on toast, in a rice ring, over mashed potato, or combined with ½ package of frozen peas.

Sliced turkey in gravy served on sliced sautéed cornmeal mush or scrapple, with cut string beans seasoned with brown butter.

Quick-Frozen Breads, Cakes and Pastries

These are technically known as *frigid doughs*. They may be kept in the frozen state about 2 weeks. As they contain very little moisture they can be baked without defrosting. However this takes considerable time; in fact, one saves both time and money by using a prepared mix and baking the foods by the usual method. But if you hanker for a good pie, and have no place or equipment to roll out the crust, a warm, freshly baked, or reheated quick-frozen pie tastes mighty good, or buy frozen rolled piecrust.

To Bake Frigid Doughs: Place in a very hot oven, 450 degrees to 475 degrees, F. for 20 minutes. Then reduce the temperature to 375 degrees, F. and bake until golden brown —about 1 hour for pies, 40 minutes for breads, cup-cakes and muffins. If the baking food browns too fast, cover with a clean sheet of parchment or brown paper.

Guest Dinners from Frozen Foods

Are quick and easy to prepare. They can be in the glamor class if enlivened with individualized seasonings and garnishes, and if one or two fresh foods are included.

FRIED CHICKEN DINNER
Grapefruit (fresh) with Frozen Strawberries
Fried Chicken (frozen) Sherry Cream Sauce (p. 172)
Whipped Potato (frozen) Mixed Vegetables (frozen)
Tossed Lettuce-Avocado Salad
Ice-Cream Fruit Platter (p. 246) Demitasse

ROCK CORNISH GAME HEN DINNER
Shrimp Bisque (frozen) Croutons
Rock Cornish Game Hen with Wild-Rice Stuffing (frozen)
Corn Kernels Sauté (frozen)
Tossed Salad of Mixed Greens
Warm Blueberry Pie (frozen) à la Mode Demitasse

CHAPTER IV

How to Become a Good Cook

YOU CAN'T BE A HOP-SKIP-AND-JUMP COOK AND EXPECT TO produce fine meals. But anyone can become a good cook if the same intelligence, care and interest is applied to food preparation as is used in a favorite sport, hobby or recreation. And good cooking can be carried out even under difficult conditions, if instead of allowing irritation to set in as a disturbing factor, we use our wits, ingenuity and patience.

However, no novice at cooking can turn out good food without using standardized recipes and accurate measurements. This is the only way to be sure of uniformly good results. Just why it is that many cooks pride themselves on cooking without following a recipe, and with guess-work measuring, is something I have never understood. A dressmaker uses a pattern to cut cloth; a manufacturer uses a die or model to stamp out parts; a baker follows a formula and weighs ingredients. Home cooking certainly is worth the success-insurance brought about by accuracy in measuring.

Read the Recipe

If you would be a good cook, learn to read a recipe. Don't merely glance at the ingredients; instead read them all the way through to be sure you have or can obtain them. After that, read the recipe directions through to the last sentence. Then, if there is in your mind a clear picture of the way you should proceed and how the finished dish should look, you are ready to start.

The Procedure: Be sure the necessary utensils or workable substitutes are at hand. Then assemble the ingredients; if the oven is required, set the oven control at the right temperature; if there is no oven control, use an oven thermometer; if there is no oven thermometer, use the flour-browning test for temperature described on page 45.

All Measurements Are Level

Level measurements are necessary because it is easy to over-estimate the quantity of ingredients when using rounded or heaping measurements. In this case, many extra ounces are often used, and the finished result is poor or a downright failure.

How to Measure

The recipes in this book have all been standardized by standard or level measurements. You will get accurate results each time you prepare a dish if you measure level and use a standard measuring cup, marked off into quarters, halves and thirds, and a set of 4 measuring spoons standardized to measure ¼, ½, 1 teaspoon and 1 tablespoon. There should be no varying luck in cooking. Accurate measurements signify only good luck.

To Measure Dry Ingredients

"All measurements are level," means that dry ingredients are heaped into the utensil, then levelled off with a knife. Flour should be sifted and spooned lightly into a cup, then levelled off. Coarse flour, like whole wheat, is not sifted before measuring. Instead stir it thoroughly with a spoon. To measure a fraction of a cupful of any dry ingredient, fill the cup to the level desired and indicated on the side of the measuring cup.

If you do not have a set of standard measuring spoons, use a silver tablespoon and a teaspoon. Do not use mixing spoons or soup spoons. In this case, to measure 1 teaspoon-

Liquid and Dry Measures

2 tablespoons	1 fluid ounce
3 teaspoons	1 tablespoon
4 tablespoons	¼ cup
8 tablespoons	½ cup
16 tablespoons	1 cup
8 fluid ounces	1 cup
16 fluid ounces	1 pint
2 cups	1 pint
4 cups	1 quart
2 pints	1 quart
4 quarts	1 gallon

Dry Weight

½ cup shortening	¼ pound
1 cup shortening	½ pound
2 cups shortening	1 pound
1 cup granulated sugar	½ pound
2 cups flour (white)	½ pound
1 ⅞ cups rice	1 pound
1 cup cornmeal	5 ounces
1 cup dry bread crumbs	2 ounces
1 square cooking chocolate	1 ounce
4 tablespoons grated chocolate	1 ounce
1 cup grated cheese	¼ pound

ful or tablespoonful of any ingredient, fill the spoon and level off with a knife. To measure ½ spoonful, level off, divide the contents lengthwise in halves and scrape off the unused portion. To measure ¼ spoonful, fill the spoon, level off, divide in halves lengthwise, then crosswise and scrape off the unused portion.

To Measure Liquid Ingredients or Liquid Fats: Fill the spoon or cup to the point where it is full without running over.

To Measure Solid Fats: The fat should be at room

temperature. Pack solidly into the spoon or cup to the mark indicated.

To Measure Half an Egg: Beat the egg to a froth; pour into a cup and use half the amount.

To Measure ½ Package of Prepared Mix: Measure the whole amount and use ½ of this.

Cooking Terms

Before you can read a recipe with understanding and gain an accurate mental picture of the way the dish is to be put together and how it should look when finished, it is necessary to know the meaning of cooking methods and terms. Methods applying to the preparation of fish, meat, poultry and vegetables are described in the chapters discussing these subjects. Here is the list of alphabetically arranged cooking terms with which you should be familiar. Don't try to learn them all at once. Take it easy as you find the terms mentioned in the recipes.

Alternate Food: Used in place of another and having about the same nutritive value.

Appetizer: Savory tidbits served as a first course to tempt the appetite.

Aspic: A jelly with a consommé or vegetable juice base for molding meats, fish, chicken and vegetables.

Au gratin: Baked dishes prepared with a sprinkling of crumbs on top.

Bake: To cook in the dry heat of an oven.

Bake-Fry: To brush plentifully with fat, or cover with fat-moistened crumbs, place in a well-greased pan and bake brown in a very hot oven.

Barbecue: To cook meat in the oven or grill, basting with barbecue sauce.

Baste: To moisten cooking meat, poultry or fish by spooning over at stated intervals small amounts of liquid and/or fat as designated.

Beat: To mix and blend with a rapid rotary stroke with a spoon, whisk or electric mixer.

Bite-Size: A pleasant mouthful. Equivalent of the French term "bonne bouchée."

Blanch: To plunge fruit, vegetables or nuts into boiling water, then into cold, for the purpose of removing the skins easily, or reducing strong flavor.

Boil: To cook food in a liquid maintained at boiling temperature, that is, 212 degrees, F. at sea-level. Decrease of temperature 1 degree, F. for each 500 feet of elevation. The liquid must "gallop" or actively bubble.

Bouillon: A clear meat soup; also applied to thin tomato or clear vegetable soup.

Braising or Pot-Roasting: Cooking meat gently in a small amount of liquid in a heavy covered utensil on top of the stove.

Breaded: Covering (croquettes, cutlets, etc.) with beaten egg and fine bread or cracker crumbs to seal in the food juices when frying or deep-fat frying.

Broil: To cook under or over strong direct heat generated by gas, electricity, coal, charcoal, or wood.

Canapés: Small savory pieces of food or food mixtures served on a piece of toast or on a crisp cracker.

Caramelize: To melt granulated sugar slowly over a low heat until golden brown.

Casserole: A heavy earthenware baking dish. "En casserole" (in a casserole) is the French term applied to food served at the table in the same baking dish in which it is cooked.

Chop: To cut into small pieces with a knife, chopping knife and bowl, or a food chopper.

Congeal: To solidify as in the making of gelatin or ice cream.

Cook and Stir: To stir constantly while cooking.

Cordon Bleu: A blue ribbon awarded in France for high attainment in cooking.

Cream: The verb "to cream" implies beating or blending shortening thoroughly by means of a spoon or electric mixer, until it is a light, creamy consistency.

Crisp: To reheat crackers or any cereal in the oven; or to freshen vegetables by placing in a hydrator in the refrigerator; but never by soaking in cold water.

Croustades: Hollowed-out, very thick, full-slice cubes of de-crusted bread toasted or fried, and used for holding creamed mixtures. Croustades may take the place of patty or pastry tart shells.

Croutons: Small cubes of bread toasted, baked or fried brown in fat to serve as a garnish for soups.

To Crumb: To cover all over with fine dry crumbs.

Cube or Dice: To cut into small cubes like dice.

Curdle: When milk sours, the solids in the milk curdle or separate. Acid combined with milk or egg mixtures will cause the mixture to curdle or separate. Egg and milk mixtures heated at too high temperature will separate or curdle.

Cut-In: To blend or cut firm shortening into flour by means of two knives, or by the back and edge of a spoon, or by a pastry blender.

De-crust: To cut off crusts from bread.

Deep-Fat Frying: The cooking of food in a kettle of hot fat deep enough to completely cover and surround the food.

Dot: To place bits of butter, margarine or cheese over the surface of food to be baked or broiled.

Double-Boiler: A two-pot utensil consisting of a pot to contain a food mixture that fits into another pot to be half-filled with boiling water; used for reheating or cooking food below boiling point.

Dredge: To coat food by sifting flour over it.

Dust: To sift a very little flour or salt, etc. over food.

Eggs: 1. *To Break Eggs:* Tap the egg on a hard surface; break the shell apart gently to retain the yolk in one portion of the shell, while the white drops and drains into a dish below.

2. *To Beat until Egg Whites are Frothy:* The whites are light and thick, but will not quite hold their shape.

3. *To Beat Egg Whites Stiff:* Chill all utensils if possible; then beat the whites with a hand or electric beater until they are light and hold their shape when the bowl is tipped.

En Brochette: (*French:* Translated "on a skewer.") To roast or broil small pieces of meat or vegetables speared onto skewers.

Entrée: In America a main dish; in France a light food preceding the main course.

Escalloped: Usually applied to vegetable or meat mixtures in a cream sauce base, with crumbs scattered on top, and heated in the oven in an uncovered dish or casserole.

Fold: To incorporate ingredients gently into a mixture by the use of an over and over rotary motion, until evenly distributed.

French Fry: To fry in sufficient hot fat to submerge the food.

Fricassee: Combined sautéing and stewing of poultry, meat or fish.

Fry: To cook in hot fat.

Garnish: The verb "to garnish" means to decorate a food; the noun "garnish" is applied to any edible tidbit that decorates the dish to which it is added.

Glacé: Food cooked in a sugar syrup to produce the appearance of a crystallized surface is glacéed; glazed has a similar meaning but the food is not sweetened and may have been cooked in butter and sugar to produce a shiny surface. Fruit tarts coated with melted jelly are termed "glazed."

Gourmet (Pronounced gour-may): A man who has a discriminating taste for and a keen appreciation of fine foods.

Gourmette: The feminine counterpart of gourmet.

Grill (Same as broiled): Sliced vegetables, meat, poultry, game, fish or fruit cooked under the broiler.

Hors d'Oeuvres: A savory dish of relish foods served as the first course of luncheon, dinner or supper.

Jardinière: Cooked meat or fish garnished with assorted diced vegetables.

Julienne: Vegetables cut before cooking into match-like strips, as Julienne potatoes; also cheese or meat cut after cooking.

Knead: To mix and work heavy dough with the hands or a mixer.

Marinate: To let meat, fish or a salad mixture stand in a marinade, that is, a savory vinegar sauce, or in French dressing to season.

Mask: To cover all over, as with mayonnaise or a thick sauce.

Meat Sauce: A highly seasoned commercial sauce for flavoring stews and gravy, meats or fish.

Meringue: A topping of stiffly beaten egg whites, usually sweetened, baked or used raw.

Mince: To chop very fine.

Oddments: Fragments of food.

To Oil Pans: Rub the pans lightly with any good unsalted shortening or cooking oil. They should not be thickly oiled unless designated in the recipe.

Onion Juice: To obtain, cut a slice from the top of a medium-sized onion (be sure to leave on the skin to protect the hands); then with a teaspoon scrape up the juice from the surface. When it is exhausted, cut off another slice and scrape up more juice.

Oxidation: Action of oxygen in the air on food, causing "rust" and impairing vitamins and vitality.

To Pan: Cook slowly in a frying or saucepan in a small amount of fat and liquid.

Pan-Broil: To cook meat on top of the stove without fat, in a heavy, heated unoiled frying pan.

Pan-Fry: Fry in a frying pan with a small amount of fat.

Parboil: To boil a few minutes to remove excess salt from smoked meat, or undesirable flavor from vegetables.

Parslied: Sprinkled with finely minced parsley.

Planked: Cooked and broiled meats, fish and vegetables served on a thick, wooden "steak" plank.

Poached (Eggs or Fish):   Eggs cooked by breaking into boiling water, then cooking just below boiling point, or fish fillets simmered in water, stock or milk.

Powder: To chop or rub herbs or other ingredients until extremely fine.

Pressure Cooking: To cook in live steam in a pressure cooker.

Purée: The pulp of cooked fruit or vegetables forced through a food mill or purée sieve. Also a type of thick soup.

Ragout: A thick stew of meat or poultry.

Ramekins: Individual pottery or glass baking dishes.

Reheat Rolls: Sprinkle with water, place in a pan, cover and oven-heat ten minutes; or steam in a double-boiler.

Riced: Cooked potatoes or other vegetables pressed through a potato ricer which shapes the vegetables like grains of cooked rice.

Roast: To cook meat, fowl or game in the hot dry heat of an oven.

Roll: To spread and flatten a heavy dough mixture by means of a rolling pin, as in making piecrust.

Sauté: Like pan frying, means to fry in a frying pan in a small amount of fat.

Scald: To bring milk, or other liquid, to steaming point; or to plunge vegetables, fruits, nuts or other food, into boiling water for the purpose of removing the skins easily.

Sear: To apply intense, quick heat to meat to brown the surface and seal in the juices.

Shirr: To break eggs into a shallow baking dish, season with butter, salt and pepper and bake.

Shred: To cut into thread-like or ribbon-like pieces.

To Sieve: To rub through a sieve, as a vegetable purée.

Sift: To restore lightness or break up lumps by passing dry ingredients through a sieve.

Simmer: To cook gently in liquid just below boiling point. The bubbles rise to the surface but do not break.

Slash: To make 4 to 6 small sharp slits in the top crust of a pie to release steam, while baking.

Soufflé: A light mixture containing whipped egg whites, baked, and dependent upon the egg whites to raise and make it light.

Spécialité de la Maison (French):   Specialty of the house. Any food exceptionally well cooked, by a restaurant or home cook.

Steam: To cook meat, fish, fruits or vegetables by means of steam generated by boiling water in a kettle beneath.

Steam-Boil: To cook food of any kind closely covered, with a very small amount of water.

Steam-Fry: To add a very small amount of water to the fat for frying food, then cover until the water evaporates. This steams the food. Frying follows in the fat already in the pan. Fries foods more quickly with less fat.

Steep: To make an infusion by the application of boiling water (or other liquid), for the purpose of drawing out juices or essential oils from the food, as steeping tea; or herbs for seasoning.

Stew: To cook food in a small amount of liquid slowly and below boiling-point.

Substitute Food: A food used in place of another, but not having the same nutritive value.

Try Out: To cook out fat from salt pork, beef suet, etc.

Vinaigrette: Vegetables or fish or meat served in a vinaigrette sauce, a form of French dressing.

Waterless Cooking: Same as steam boil.

Whip: To beat with a rapid motion to enclose all the air possible, by means of a spoon, hand beater or electric beater.

Baking for Two

We often hear the phrase, "So and so is a good baker," —as though being able to bake good biscuits or cake is the ultimate in cooking. But it takes equal care and skill to be a cooking success in any department. There is no mystery about baking—not if the recipe is standardized, the measuring accurate, and the oven temperature controlled. Recipes for baking pies, cakes, cookies, desserts and hot breads for two are clearly detailed in the various chapters of this book. When baking in quantities for two, smaller baking utensils are needed than for a full-sized family.

In every household where baking for two is done, there should be a small pie plate, a small loaf pan (half the usual size), a small tube cake pan, a small biscuit cutter, a set of tiny muffin or cupcake pans, two eight-inch layer cake pans and a set of individual ring moulds for baking cakes or gingerbread served with whipped cream in the center.

Large ramekins may be used for baking bread puddings,

soufflés, deep-dish pies, meringue puddings and betties; shirred egg dishes are excellent for individual pies, prune whip, etc. A plentiful supply of clean toothpicks for testing cakes for doneness, cake pan linings, and paper cups for the "panless" baking of cup cakes is essential.

When to Heat the Oven

Set the oven regulator and start the heat as soon as you are ready to put the mixture together. Allow from 10 to 15 minutes to heat.

If there is no oven control and you are using a portable thermometer, put it in the oven before applying heat; if you are using a portable oven, use the oven thermometer in the same way. If you have no thermometer, and are using the Browned Flour Oven Test, allow the oven to get to what you estimate is the required temperature, then put in the flour to make sure, and adjust the heat accordingly.

If the oven is not well-lighted, it's a big help to use a flashlight when the time comes to look at the baking food.

Baking Temperatures
(Oven Control or Oven Thermometer)

Slow Oven	325–350 degrees, F.
Moderate Oven	350–375 degrees, F.
Moderately Hot Oven	375–400 degrees, F.
Hot Oven	400–450 degrees, F.
Very Hot Oven	450–500 degrees, F.

Browned Flour Oven Test

Slow oven: 1 teaspoon flour sprinkled on a tin or aluminum plate turns light-brown in 5½ minutes.

Moderate oven: 1 teaspoon flour sprinkled on a tin or aluminum plate turns light-brown in 3½ minutes.

Moderately hot oven: 1 teaspoon flour sprinkled on a tin or aluminum plate turns light-brown in 3 minutes.

Hot oven: 1 teaspoon flour sprinkled on a tin or aluminum plate turns light-brown in 1½ minutes.

Baking Time Table

Bread and Biscuits

	TEMPERATURE	TIME
Baking Powder Biscuits . . .	400–425 deg., F.	12–15 min.
Biscuit Shortcake	375–400 deg., F.	25 min.
Muffins (small)	375 deg., F.	15–20 min.

Cakes

Plain Loaf (medium size) .	350 deg., F.	45 min.
Plain Layer	375 deg., F.	20 min.
Gingerbread	350 deg., F.	30 min.
White (egg whites) . . .	325–350 deg., F.	30–40 min.
Sponge (no shortening) . .	325 deg., F.	50–60 min.
Cup Cakes (small) . . .	375 deg., F.	15–20 min.

Cookies

Drop	375 deg., F.	10–12 min.
Rolled	375 deg., F.	10–12 min.
Ginger Molasses	350 deg., F.	10–12 min.

Custards and Puddings

Large Custard (1 pint) . .	350 deg., F.	50 min.
Individual Custard . . .	350 deg., F.	25–35 min.
Fruit Betty	375 deg., F.	20–30 min.
Meringue for Pie Topping .	325 deg., F.	12 min.

Pastry

Pie Shells	375 deg., F. 12 min.
Tart Shells	375 deg., F. 8–10 min.
One-crust Fruit Pies . . .	400 deg., F. for 10 min., then
	375 deg., F. for 30 min.
Two-crust or "deep" Pies .	400 deg., F. for 10 min., then
	375 deg., F. for 40 min.
Custard and Pumpkin Pies .	400 deg., F. for 10 min., then
	350 deg., F. for 35 min.

If small cake or loaf pans are used, the baking time should be reduced about ¼. Temperature remains the same.

Roasting

This must be done as carefully as baking. Full directions for roasting various kinds of meat and for using a meat thermometer will be found in Chapter IX of this book.

Stop—Look—Listen!

If you are inclined to be forgetful, better set the alarm clock or timer as a reminder when the food should be baked. Don't "test" the food you are baking until you are reasonably sure it is done. Then **Test**—don't **Trust!**

Your Food Repertoire

To become a good cook takes practice. When learning to play an instrument, studying voice, learning to paint or dance, or speak a new language, one starts with fundamentals and masters one thing at a time. This same principle applies to cooking.

If starting to learn to cook for two, plan a menu including one new dish to be learned, and depend on prepared foods for the balance of the meal. You will soon have learned how to cook enough dishes to make quite a food repertoire. But don't stop at that point. Continue to master a new-dish-a-day, and within a year you could almost be a candidate for the cordon bleu.

First of all, learn to make good coffee and tea; to toss an excellent salad bowl; to boil flaky potatoes and bake mealy ones; to cook frozen vegetables just enough but not too much; to broil or pan fry meat and fish; to cook bacon and sausages; and boil, poach and scramble eggs. Learn to prepare whole oven and broiler meals. Master biscuits, griddle cakes and waffles.

Work out a group of simple desserts. Study seasonings, and find out just what to add to heat-and-eat canned or quick-frozen foods, to make them individually yours. Then branch out as you like. This book contains all the instruction you need.

Spécialités de la Maison

Practice until you can cook a few foods superbly well, and make these "spécialités de la maison"—specialties of your house—that your guests will anticipate and enjoy. These do not need to be fancy dishes. Any interesting hors d'oeuvres, flaky hot biscuits, waffles, Welsh rabbit, sherried chicken, Chef's salad bowl, raspberry bavarian pie, or Viennese coffee are all worthy to be classed as spécialités de la maison.

Learn to look and feel dainty as you work; wash up the utensils as they are used. These two habits will soon drive out any subconscious fear that cooking is a "messy" job!

Readying Meals on Time

From the very first, plan to get all the foods for the meal prepared for service at one and the same time. And allow enough, but not too much time for preparation. If you are a stay-at-home cook, most of the preliminary dinner preparation may be done in the morning while breakfast is being cleared away and the kitchen ordered. If you are a career girl, plan simple dinners easily readied in half an hour.

In any case, write out the menu. Note the rotation in which the foods should be started to insure a finished meal all at once. Start first the dish that takes longest to prepare and cook. Then prepare the dishes in the time sequence you have figured out. They should all be ready when the dish first started is cooked. In other words, the preparation of a meal is a continuing process. Instead of waiting for one dish to be done before starting another, after putting it together leave it to cook with the necessary occasional supervision, and start each dish in logical sequence. But foods cannot always be left to their own devices. Each must be supervised. You cannot have a single-track mind and be a good cook. To be really successful you must learn to do several things at once. I have a special name for this rotation cooking.

It is what I call "Timetable Meals." The menu is your destination. The first dish to be started is where you board the train. To illustrate:

A Day of Timetable Meals

Starred recipes are in this book.

BREAKFAST
Grapefruit
French Toastwiches*
Coffee

7:15 Heat water for coffee
7:16 Prepare grapefruit
7:20 Set table
7:23 Make French toastwiches
7:29 Make coffee
7:30 Serve breakfast

LUNCHEON
Smoky Fish Chowder* with Melba Toast
Fruit Salad with Lemon-Honey Cream*   *Tea*

11:35 Make fish chowder
11:45 Make salad
11:50 Make Melba toast
11:52 Make lemon-honey cream
11:55 Set table
11:59 Make tea
12:20 Serve luncheon

DINNER

Spinach Soup (canned)   *Crisp Crackers*
Broiled Shoulder Lamb Chops* Buttered Macaroni Rings
Mashed Squash   Rolls   Celery
Prune and Orange Cup   Coffee

5:25 Put squash to cook
5:30 Open and heat soup
5:35 Prepare prune and orange cup
5:40 Cook macaroni rings
5:43 Set table
5:48 Broil lamb chops
5:50 Prepare celery
5:53 Heat rolls
5:55 Make coffee
6:00 Serve dinner

At first it may seem impossible to keep up with Time-table routines. But soon you will discover why you lose time, and learn to work more rapidly with fewer unnecessary interruptions and less waste motion. Many career women are studying J. M. T.—Job Methods Training. If the same type of self supervision is applied to a step-and-motion-saving arrangement of the kitchen and to the preparation of meals, unbelievable time and energy savings will be effected.

Cooking Ahead

In some cases it is a good plan to cook food ahead of time or have it ready for immediate cooking or heating. The real answer lies with available refrigeration. If the refrigerator is cold enough for safe preservation of flavor and freshness and large enough to hold the food, and if you are reasonably sure you will be at home to eat it before it spoils, then it will prove time-saving to prepare enough at one time for two meals. But no more. For when the same food appears more than twice in succession, boredom appears at the table. It is a better plan to skip a day between repetitions.

Foods that may be cooked ahead include cooked cereals; apple and fruit sauces; dried fruits; boiled, roasted, pot-roasted and fricasseed meat or poultry; potatoes, macaroni, spaghetti or rice; baked beans; cooked salad dressing and French dressing, certain cakes, cookies and pastry tart shells.

Partially preparing foods ready to cook is often helpful. For instance, poultry can be made ready to cook; a pot roast browned; a stew partly prepared. This can often be done in the evening ready for quick completion for dinner the next day.

Frozen meat or fish to be defrosted should be placed on the lower shelf of the refrigerator several hours in advance. They should never be defrosted the last minute by running water over them. This washes out valuable nutrients.

One caution: Fresh vegetables and fruits should not be pared, peeled or diced in advance, as the action of the oxygen of the air, on the cut surface, impairs the vitality of the vitamins. And they should never be prepared ahead and left to stand long in cold water, in which case they are as dead, nutritionally speaking, as though drowned.

CHAPTER V

Appetizers, Hors d'Oeuvres and Soups

THERE IS NO BETTER WAY TO DRESS UP A PLAIN DINNER than to serve an appetizer, hors d'oeuvres or soup. Costs little in time or money and adds a lot.

Appetizers are really liquid whets to the appetite—fruit juices, tomato and vegetable juices, cocktails or dry sherry all come under this heading. Hors d'oeuvres are savory tidbits.

Fruit cups, grapefruit and other fresh fruits are also classed as appetizers when served as a first course. With the exception of fruit or fruit juices, all appetizers should be served with crisp plain or cheese crackers, potato chips, corn chips, canapés or crisp seeded or nutted sticks.

Canapés

These delicious little tidbits are made with a basis of small crisp crackers or toast, bread or rounds of pastry. One caution—if the topping is inclined to be moist first spread the canapé base with soft butter; this supplies a coating so the moisture will not be absorbed and the canapés will stay crisp.

Decorate each canapé with a slice of olive, or use sliced red radish, bits of pimiento, polka dots of black olives, sieved hard-cooked egg yolks, a toasted nut meat, bit of sweet pickle, minced parsley, water cress leaves, etc. Takes only a few seconds, and makes the canapés look, oh, so professional!

Whether serving for two or twenty, canapés are always more enticing when attractively arranged. Put a paper doily on the plate, and if there are to be canapés only for two, heap water cress, lettuce, celery, crisp scallions, or radishes in the middle of the plate to make it look satisfyingly full. Never, please, allow any serving of food to look skimpy.

All measurements are level

CANAPÉ SPREADS

*For bread, toasts, crackers, large potato chips
or pastry rounds*

1. Southern Canapés: Blend cream cheese with a little butter and Smithfield ham spread.

2. Sardine Canapés: Blend mashed sardines in tomato sauce with cream cheese.

3. Shrimp Canapés: Combine minced shrimp, chopped olives, minced hard-cooked eggs and mayonnaise. Add a touch of mustard and tarragon vinegar.

4. Pecan Cheese Canapés: Combine equal parts bleu cheese, cream cheese and butter with a few minced toasted pecans.

CANAPÉ TOASTS

These can be made up in advance, ready to slip under the broiler and serve piping hot. Cut the crusts from white bread and toast on one side. Cut in squares. Cover with the spread; just before serving heat till bubbling under the grill.

1. Cheese-in-Wine: Spread canapé toasts with cheese-in-wine (page 101). Then grill.

2. Crab Tartare: Spread canapé toasts with minced crab meat in sauce tartare with a touch of mustard; then grill.

CANAPÉS FROM FISH PASTES

All of the fish pastes make tasty canapé toppings: Sardine, anchovy, lobster, bloater paste, etc. As they are highly concentrated, blend with an equal amount of cream cheese, butter or margarine.

For variety add minced pickled onion or stuffed olives; spread on crisp crackers, or finger-lengths or rounds of bread. Top with a dot of pimiento or slice of red radish.

Canapé Tray Service

When canapés are to be arranged on trays to serve at a party, the vegetable nibblers or other pleasant bites to be served with them, can act as a garnish. For instance, sprigs of water cress or parsley, curled celery hearts, crisp finnochio, carrot sticks, tomato wedges, radish roses, black or stuffed olives in stemmed glass dishes, or Savory Cream Cheese Balls.

Savory Cream Cheese Balls: Select small red radishes. Trim off the leaves, stems and roots, and cover each radish with cream cheese seasoned with salt and pepper and mixed with a little Roquefort or bleu cheese and plain butter. Roll in minced parsley or chives and chill.

"Pick Cookery"

This is the term used to describe the service of dainty tidbits on special cocktail picks or toothpicks, such as stuffed olives, rolled in bacon and broiled; cheese balls (page 55); a "dice" of sharp cheese slipped onto the pick and topped with a pearl-sized pickled onion; Chinese fried shrimp (page 114); or nice bites of smoked turkey to be dunked in Russian dressing. In fact in today's cookery

"Pick" and "Dunk" are the star twins of hors d'oeuvres. Wherever a pick-prepared appetizer appears, a dunking sauce is sure to be near. Appetizers speared on picks are served sometimes in large shallow bowls; but they are most attractive when thrust into a big grapefruit, or small perfect head of cabbage, or even enormous apples, and used as the center of a party hors d'oeuvres tray, with canapés circling around.

CHEESE BALLS ON PICKS
(*Makes 1½ dozen*)

¼ *teaspoon salt*   *Few grains pepper*
  Whites 2 eggs   ½ *cup grated Parmesan cheese*
              Deep frying fat

1. Add the salt to the egg whites and beat stiff.
2. Add the pepper to the cheese and fold into the egg whites. Shape with a teaspoon into balls the size of large marbles.
3. Drop into deep fat hot enough to brown a piece of bread in forty seconds (375 degrees, F.). Fry golden brown. Drain on crumpled paper towels. Serve hot on picks.

SMOKED TURKEY "PICKS"

Cube smoked turkey and slide onto the picks, with a cube of sharp cheddar cheese and a small stuffed olive to top it off.

HOT LUNCHEON MEAT "PICKS"

Canned luncheon meat   *Slices of sharp cheese*

Cut luncheon meat into ½-inch slices. Broil on one side until brown, then cut in quarters. Fit on inch-square slices of cheese; top with an anchovy or halved stuffed olive, broil until the cheese melts and serve on picks.

Hors d'Oeuvres Groups

In this next hors d'oeuvres group, the tray may be passed, or the foods may be arranged as for a small buffet, the guests serving themselves, which is, of course, the easiest way.

Another chic, simple and inexpensive arrangement is in matching oblong or oval glass dishes. They hold generous amounts if necessary; or if the service is for four or six, line the dishes with lettuce leaves to take up the empty spaces. Arrange them in a smart row or design on a tray or table with a fork or dessert or soup spoon for the service of each.

SNACKS NORWEGIAN STYLE
(For any number)

Norwegian fish balls   *Cold scrambled eggs with chives*
Mayonnaise   *Lettuce*
Sliced tomato   *Norwegian smoked sardines*
Herring tidbits   *Strips of toast*
Crisp rye crackers

1. Dice the fish balls, mix with mayonnaise, and heap in the centre of a big platter or tray.
2. Surround with half slices of tomato, each topped with a herring tidbit.
3. Circle this with lettuce leaves containing cold scrambled eggs, and border with the sardines on toast.
4. Serve with crisp rye crackers.

SMALL SMÖRGÅSBORD
(Serves any number)

Herring salad (ready to eat   *Egg and anchovy canapés*
in jars)   *Radishes*
Minced ham and chives   *Tiny meat balls*
canapés

1. Chill the salad and arrange on lettuce for serving.
2. Make the canapés, using white bread for the ham, dark bread for the minced egg and anchovies. Blend each spread with butter. Arrange on matching plates, with radishes for a garnish.
3. Meantime make the meat balls. Serve hot or cold, with picks for the eating.

Serve-at-the-Table Appetizers

These include fruit; fruit or fish cocktails; appetizer salads; oysters or clams on the half shell; and very small servings of highly seasoned fish, as crab meat au gratin, or oysters casino. To make an impression try one of these. Here are a few samples.

AVOCADOS, AIR-LINE STYLE
(2 servings)

1 *avocado*	1 *tablespoon sugar*
1 *tablespoon butter*	1 *tablespoon Worcester-*
1½ *tablespoons tomato*	*shire sauce*
catsup	¼ *teaspoon salt*
1 *tablespoon water*	*Dash tabasco sauce*
1 *tablespoon wine vine-*	
gar	

1. Chill the avocado. Cut in halves lengthwise and remove the seed.
2. Combine and heat remaining ingredients.
3. Pour hot into the chilled avocado halves and serve at once. Garnish with parsley, lettuce or cress.

SHRIMP COCKTAIL SUPRÊME
(2 servings)

¼ cup chili sauce
¼ teaspoon Worcestershire
½ teaspoon lemon or lime juice
Few grains cayenne

2 tablespoons mayonnaise
2 tablespoons sour cream
½ pound fresh cooked shrimp or ½ (5-ounce) can shrimp

1. Combine chili sauce, Worcestershire, lemon juice, and cayenne.

2. Add the mayonnaise, fold in the cream, and chill.

3. Place 4 or 5 chilled cleaned shrimp in a nest of shredded lettuce in each cocktail glass; pour over the prepared sauce just before serving.

Lobster Cocktail: Follow the preceding recipe, substituting for the shrimp flaked canned or fresh cooked lobster meat.

QUINTETTE OF DIPS

Use with potato chips, corn crackers, Indian shrimp chips, cooked shrimp, hot codfish balls, vegetable nibblers.

Clam Dip: To 1 cup commercial sour cream add 1 (4 ounce) jar minced clams, 1 teaspoon lemon juice, ½ teaspoon Worcestershire and 2 dashes Tabasco.

Avocado Dip: Make as above using ½ cup smooth-mashed avocado pulp instead of clams. Add garlic salt to taste.

Cheese Dip: Blend 1 (3-ounce) package cream cheese, 2 ounces Blue cheese, ⅓ cup each commercial sour cream and mayonnaise and ½ tablespoon lemon juice. Also nice with sections of fresh pears or apples.

Remoulade Dip: Combine ¼ cup home-made or commercial remoulade sauce, ¾ cup mayonnaise and 1 tablespoon minced chives. Try this with raw oysters; with shrimp; or with codfish balls, frozen fish bites or sautéed scallops or shrimp kept hot in a chafing dish.

Snappy Onion Dip: Add 1 package dehydrated onion soup to 1 cup commercial sour cream. Season with 2 dashes Tabasco and ¼ teaspoon Worcestershire. Refrigerate 1 hour.

ANTIPASTO
(2 servings)

4 *thin slices salami*	2 *sardines*
1 *halved pimiento*	4 *red radishes or scallions*
½ *cup cole slaw shredded*	*Olives*
fine	2 *lemon wedges*
Celery and/or finocchio	*Oil and wine vinegar*

1. Arrange individually. Put the salami and pimiento on each side of the plate; heap the center with cole slaw and place the sardines on top.

2. Garnish with the radishes, scallions, vegetables, olives and lemon wedges. Pass oil and wine vinegar.

Smart Soups

Soups can be prepared on time-saving schedules from 10 minutes up. Besides, they add real nourishment and make a meal seem more important. They are an economy, too. When you eat soup first, you do not need so much meat and meat costs—and costs!

It's worth while to become acquainted with the excellent prepared soups and chowders on the market, canned, quick-frozen and dehydrated. There's a heat-and-eat soup to fit any occasion.

Make good use too of canned consomme, bouillon cubes, and beef extract in place of clear soup stock. Garnish each serving with something substantial, as a chef does. You'll find it both easy and quick to provide good soups for two.

For thick soups or oyster stew, when you have guests, get out your mother's tureen and serve from the table. Saves time and looks hospitable. For the two of you choose French onion-soup bowls for substantial soups. For light soups use regular soup plates, bouillon or cream soup cups. Once form the habit of serving soup and you'll rarely go without it.

If you'll experiment you'll discover many more enticing soup combinations. As to individualizing ready-made soups, put your imagination to work. Experiment with a pinch of this herb, a dash of that condiment, and you'll soon turn into a soup specialist.

Picker-Uppers for Canned, Dehydrated or Quick-Frozen Soups

Asparagus Soup: Dilute with canned chicken soup.

Beef Soup: Add a dash of curry powder.

Black Bean Soup: Add sherry; or sprinkle with chopped hard-cooked egg; or serve with a thin slice of lemon.

Celery Soup: Combine with chicken soup. Serve with fried croutons.

Chicken Gumbo Soup: Pour over mounds of rice.

Chicken and Noodle: Add a little sautéed onion and green pepper.

Clam Chowder: Add one small can tomato sauce.

Corn Chowder: When hot, drop in a few small oysters and simmer two minutes.

Green Pea Soup: Serve with soured cream and/or minced mint.

Green Turtle Consommé: Add ½ cup of heated thin

cream to a cup of consommé and for a delectable Boula, also add 1 cup of canned pea soup purée (no water).

Mulligatawney Soup: Sprinkle with fried croutons.

Mushroom Soup: Add a little dry sherry.

Oyster Stew: Add minced celery, a little butter and serve with butter-fried croutons.

Pepper-Pot Soup: Add a dash of Worcestershire and tiny drop herb-seasoned dumplings (page 144).

Petite Marmite: Add diced breast of chicken and diced soup meat, French fashion, and serve topped with round toasts covered with cheese and grilled.

Printanière Soup: Serve with grated cheese.

Sea Food Chowder (Canned or Quick-Frozen): Add rich hot milk and tiny dices of cooked carrot, or finely minced cress heated in butter.

Spinach Soup: Serve with cubes of diced fresh tomato; add nutmeg.

Split Pea Soup: Add sliced skinless frankfurters, sliced oddments of sausage or luncheon meat; sprinkle with diced crisp bacon and/or fried croutons.

Tomato Soup: Heat with a crushed bayleaf. Serve with soured cream and/or chopped chives.

Vegetable Soup: Sprinkle with grated cheese.

Yankee Bean Soup: Dilute with an equal quantity of rich milk instead of water; or add a touch of basil vinegar.

Concentrated or Not

There are two kinds of canned soups, that which is ready to heat and serve, and the concentrated type, to which must be added an equal amount of water or liquid drained from cooked vegetables. In either case the average-sized can turns out 4 small servings, 3 good-sized servings, or 2 servings sufficient to fill honest-to-goodness soup bowls

and turn the soup into a substantial dish. A real asset if
it's lunch or supper. or when the main course at dinner is
a bit scant.

If a whole can of soup is not used, put the remainder
in a glass jar and refrigerate to use the next day or two.
It can always be stretched by adding a bouillon cube and
water, or by combining with another kind of soup, also
left over. For instance:

> *Spinach + Tomato*
> *Celery + Chicken*
> *Split pea + Tomato*
> *Yankee bean + Tomato*
> *Chicken gumbo + Vegetable*
> *Cream of mushroom + Chicken*

Quick Minestrone: Vegetable soup + consommé +
leftover canned tomato, + leftover vegetables, + spaghetti; + dried lima beans or garbanza beans and a touch
of basil or marjoram. And lots of grated cheese. A good
soup to clear out the refrigerator. And very good to eat.

DINNER SOUPS FROM CANNED CONSOMMÉ OR BOUILLON CUBES
(For Two)

French Onion Soup: Steam-fry 1 cup sl.redded onions
in butter. Add to 2 cups boiling consommé, or water with
2 bouillon cubes. Serve topped with squares of toast covered with sharp cheese and grilled.

Mushroom Soup: Make as above, substituting ½ cup
mushrooms for onions. Add a touch of nutmeg.

Spinach Soup Casino: Heat ¼ cup cubed fresh tomato in 1 tablespoon butter. Add ½ cup cooked spinach.
Finish as French Onion Soup.

Asparagus Soup: To 2 cups boiling consommé, or
2 cups boiling water and 2 bouillon cubes, add ¼ cup

leftover asparagus tips. Heat and serve strewn with croutons and chopped hard-cooked egg.

Treasure oddments of vegetables; they are grand for these soups.

Fresh Vegetable Nibblers

Crisp, well-prepared raw vegetables are among the best relishes. Serve on a relish tray at a party, or on a bed of ice, or standing in a deep bowl of ice cubes like a little garden; or without ice in a small relish dish for the family of two. Plain, or herb salt is used with them, or dunk if you like in Russian dressing.

To Prepare: Wash and scrub thoroughly in cold water. Roll in damp paper towels and chill and crisp in the refrigerator.

Brussels Sprouts: Remove yellowed leaves; wash, cut in halves and crisp.

Carrot, White Turnip or Raw Beet Sticks: Peel the vegetables; cut in narrow strips 2½ inches long.

Cauliflower Fleurettes: Break cauliflower into small natural sections.

Celery: Separate the hearts but retain the leaves. Cut long stalks into 4-inch lengths; peel off the strings; fringe the stalk ends, as you used to fringe paper for May baskets when you were a little girl. Stand 10 minutes in cold water to curl, then drain and crisp in a covered dish in the refrigerator.

Cucumbers: Peel, cut in halves crosswise, then into strips.

Finocchio (Fennel): Prepare like celery.

Radishes: Cut off the root ends. Keep one or two leaves for a handle.

Scallions: Cut off the green leaves to within 3 inches

of the end. Cut off the rootlets. Slash up the white end.

Mushrooms: Wash, dry; cut in quarters.

Water Cress: Use long stalks.

FRESH FISH CHOWDER
(Serves 2 to 3)

¾ *pound cod, haddock, flounder or other fish fillets*

1 *tablespoon minced onion*

1 *tablespoon butter or margarine*

1 *pint boiling water*

1 *cup sliced potatoes*

½ *teaspoon salt*

¼ *teaspoon pepper*

1 *cup milk*

2 *tablespoons flour*

¾ *tablespoon butter or margarine (extra)*

1. Cut fish into cubes. Fry the onion in the butter until yellowed. Pour in the boiling water, add the potatoes, cover, and simmer 20 minutes.

2. Add the salt, pepper and fish. Cook 10 minutes longer.

3. Add the milk, bring to boiling point; thicken with the flour blended with the remaining butter. Cook and stir until slightly thickened.

4. Serve in large bowls with toast or pilot crackers.

SMOKY FISH CHOWDER
(Serves 2 to 3)

½ *pound finnan haddie*

1½ *tablespoons butter*

¼ *cup sliced onion*

1¼ *cups hot water*

½ *bay leaf*

1 *cup sliced white potato*

¼ *teaspoon paprika*

⅛ *teaspoon black pepper*

1 *pint whole milk*

1 *tablespoon flour*

Salt to taste

1. Flake the finnan haddie into bite-size pieces.

2. Melt the butter in a quart saucepan. Cook the onion

in it until yellowed. Add the water, bayleaf, finnan haddie and potato.

3. Cover, and slow boil until the finnan haddie and potato are both tender, about 15 minutes. Add seasonings.

4. Add the milk and bring to boiling point. Thicken by slowly stirring in the flour stirred smooth in 2 tablespoons extra milk. Add salt to taste.

5. Serve with hot toast or pilot crackers.

QUICK SHRIMP BISQUE
(Serves 2 to 3)

1 *tablespoon butter*
1 *tablespoon raw rice*
½ *good-sized onion chop-*
   .ped
1 *cup water*
1½ *cups canned tomato*

½ *teaspoon curry powder*
Salt and pepper to taste
1 *(5-oz.) can shrimp cut*
   in quarters or ½ pound
   cooked fresh or frozen
   shrimp, diced

1. Melt the butter; add the rice; fry gently until yellowed.

2. Add the onion, water, tomato, the curry powder mixed smooth with 1 tablespoon of water, and salt and pepper to taste. Simmer 20 minutes.

3. Then add the shrimp and simmer 5 minutes longer.

4. Serve as a main dish.

Quick Cream of Vegetable Soups

Use as a basis a can or jar of puréed vegetable (sold for baby feedings). There is quite a choice including spinach, carrot, squash, string bean and green pea. Add 1½ cups milk. Stir until very hot. Season to taste with salt, pepper, celery or onion salt and/or a dash of meat condiment. To thicken, cream together ½ tablespoon each butter and flour. Add 1 tablespoon of the soup. Stir smooth; return to the soup in the saucepan and continue to stir until boiling. Serve with crisp crackers, croutons, or savory canapés.

Soup Meals

Restaurants and hotels are making a real success of soup luncheons because their customers get enough to eat—a big bowlful of substantial peasant-type soup, such as split pea, black bean, minestrone, pepper pot or corn chowder, served with bread or toasted rolls and butter, cole slaw or a green salad, a substantial dessert or candy, and a choice of coffee or tea. Soup meals like these are equally successful at home if—and here's the rub—*if* they are equally substantial. Usually they are not. Remember when serving a soup meal, to balance the lacking food values in the soup by the dessert. For example, if the soup is made from vegetables, have a dessert made with eggs, or serve fruit and cheese. Eggs and cheese supply the lacking precious protein. On the other hand, if the soup is made of legumes, that is, dried peas, beans or lentils, or if it contains fish, meat or milk (all proteins), a dessert might be apple brown betty or apricot compôte.

When enough soup is provided and the menu is balanced, soup meals satisfy.

Cold Soups

For the family of two we turn commercial again. There's canned madrilène and consommé printanière to be served jellied. There's vichysoisse, plus the whole family of cream soups that can be diluted with milk or a little cream and served ice-cold in cups. Very nice accompanied by hot or cold canapés.

Tricks with Toppings

Jellied Madrilène: Sprinkle with grated cucumber or minced chives.

Jellied Consommé: Sprinkle over minced hard-cooked egg and cress or cubes of avocado.

Jellied Printanière: Top with a little cream cheese rubbed through a sieve.

Relishes

Relishes are usually placed on the table with the first course, and so are classed among hors d'oeuvres. It's a temptation when cooking for two to omit relishes, and other nice little touches, with the thought, "We're only two, so it doesn't matter." Remember those little restaurant dinners you enjoyed, when the waiter brought a glass boat containing celery hearts, radishes and olives for two? This cost little in time or effort, but it started dinner with a luxury touch. It pays equal dividends to serve relishes at everyday home dinners. Here is an assortment of reminders.

Raw Relishes

Celery hearts	Caulifleurettes
Finnochio stalks	Halved Brussels sprouts
Radishes	Green pepper in strips
Carrot straws	Lettuce hearts
Turnip straws	Tomato wedges, etc.

Pickled Relishes

Sweet pickles	Green, black or stuffed olives
Sour pickles	Water-melon pickle
Bread and butter pickles	Pickled beets
Tomato dill pickles	Pickled carrots
Quartered dill pickles	Pickled beet relish
Piccalilli	Pickled pears
India relish	Pickled grapes

Pickled crab apples, etc.

Condiments

Mustard (plain or fancy)	Chutneys of all kinds
Tomato catsup	Horse-radish
Chili sauce	Meat sauces

Worcestershire sauce, etc.

All pickled relishes keep indefinitely if covered with pickling vinegar and covered tight. Olives should be covered with water containing ½ teaspoon of salt to ½ cup.

It is a pleasant touch to present mustard, catsup, chili sauce and horse-radish in special serving jars rather than in the original containers. In any case, they should be spotlessly clean. Chutney looks enticing in a deep glass dish; jelly, jam or conserve in one of the covered glass jars that come for the purpose.

For Gourmet and Gourmette

BUTTERED CRABMEAT

(*Serves 4 to 6*)

Nice to prepare electrically at the table while guests longingly look on. Flake ½ pound fresh, canned or defrosted quick-frozen crab meat. Take out all the shell. Heat 3 tablespoons butter in a round-bottom frying pan. When bubbling, stir in the crab meat; add a dash of salt, pepper and Worcestershire, and 1 tablespoon dry sherry. Stir with a fork until very hot. Serve on crisp crackers as a hot hors d'oeuvre.

CHAPTER VI

Breads, Sandwiches and Toasts

THERE'S NO GAINSAYING THE FACT THAT MEALS ARE MORE satisfying when bread is served. More nourishing too, for good bread is an essential energy food. In planning for two, bread is often a bit of a problem, as part of the loaf is frequently wasted. So unless you eat "in" regularly, better buy rolls. In this case, either reheat or split and toast them, for cold rolls are often poor fare. Coffee cake now and then is good for variety. So are brown n' serve rolls.

As to loaf bread, buy small loaves. If the bread gets a bit stale, heat it and serve hot. Or use the last of the loaf for French Toast or Toastwiches, Chopped Beef Toasts (page 87), or Meat or Poultry Toast Cakes (page 164). If only 2 or 3 stale slices are left, they will be just enough for a Savory Cheese Pudding (page 98), or Bread and Butter Pudding (page 231); or use in making croutons, or cheese-topped toasts for vegetable or French onion soup (page 62). Then there are toast points, those little triangles of toast used by chefs the world over to decorate and help out small servings of chops, steak, etc. As to finger-lengths of toast, when placed under crisp sausages they make even 4 look ample. Oh yes, those last slices of bread can be very useful.

TO REHEAT SLICED YEAST BREAD

Lightly butter or margarine the slices. Pile 4 together. Place in a pan, cover, and heat in a grill (low heat), or for 10 minutes in a slow oven.

TO REHEAT FRENCH BREAD

Cut the loaf diagonally in 6-inch long pieces; then cut almost through to the bottom to make thick slices. Spread a little softened butter or margarine on the cut surface, and heat 5 minutes in a moderate oven (375 degrees, F.). Or cover and heat in a grill (lowest heat).

GARLICKED FRENCH BREAD

If you are a garlic fiend, season the butter with garlic before spreading. Just let a peeled halved section of garlic stand in the butter required in the preceding recipe, and the deed is done. Spread on French bread; heat as above.

TO REHEAT ROLLS OR MUFFINS

Place in the top of a double boiler; then cover, set over boiling water and steam 10 minutes. Or wrap in aluminum foil, and oven heat 10 minutes.

TO REHEAT COFFEE CAKE

Better heat in the oven or under the grill (low heat). This will make the sugar topping bubble and caramelize a bit, as with Boiled Frosting. Tastes very good.

CROUTONS

Baked or Grilled Croutons: Spread slices of bread with butter or margarine. Cut in small dice. Bake or grill until golden brown. Stir occasionally.

Fried Croutons: Cut bread in small dice. Fry golden brown in butter or margarine.

ENGLISH MUFFINS OR CRUMPETS

Be sure to tear these apart, instead of cutting them, so the irregular interior will more easily hold the amount of butter or other spread needed to make them taste their best.

Toasted English Muffins or Crumpets: Butter or margarine generously. Toast under the grill and serve with jam, jelly or compôte.

Cheesed English Muffins or Crumpets: Butter or margarine, cover with snappy-flavored American cheese and grill until the cheese bubbles. Top with a slice of crisp bacon if you like. Or first put on a thin slice of ham, then the cheese, and grill.

"Pizza"—a frank imitation: Butter or margarine split English muffins; lay on paper-thin slices of tomato; dust with garlic salt. Top with anchovies and dabs of Bel Paese or any other creamy cheese. Grill and serve very hot. Nice with red wine.

NEW ENGLAND TOAST—MY FAVORITE

Light spread white bread with soft butter or margarine. Place spread-side up in a broiler (moderate heat), and toast until golden. Then turn to toast the other side. The butter soaks into the bread, and the grilling produces a delectably rich semi-toasted, semi-fried flavor and texture.

FRIED BREAD

Try frying half slices of white bread in a little bacon fat, to serve with scrambled eggs. Very tasty and a good "stretcher" of bacon.

BACON ROLLS

Halve and toast long rolls. Butter lightly and put together with crisp hot bacon.

All measurements are level

Quick Hot Breads

It's a grand plan to make hot breads by big family recipes if they can all be eaten. But when cooking for two this does not work out, because the last of the batch goes begging. But there are three solutions to this vary-the-bread problem: Buy muffins or biscuits from the baker; use good prepared mixes; or buy muffins of the frigid dough, quick-frozen type. If bought from the baker, muffins or biscuits must be reheated. If made from a mix, they can be baked in almost the same time it takes for reheating; they cost less, and are apparently home-made —and how men love that! If frozen they may be baked "as is" which takes 40 minutes. Or they may be baked in 20 minutes after defrosting, which takes about 2½ hours; so allow time when planning to bake them.

Cupboard space is often at a premium, and a package or two of prepared mix takes up less space than flour, baking powder, and other ingredients needed in making orthodox hot breads. So in this book I have gone all out for the mixes.

One package makes enough for two meals. Try a variety. One week buy a package of corn muffin mix and one of waffle mix. Next week, try popover mix and a bran muffin mix, and so on. Use them within a week or so. Always keep on hand a package each of pancake and biscuit mix. Prepare the mixes carefully, according to the manufacturer's directions; watch the oven temperature, and serve the breads hot and attractively. Be sure to try the quick yeast roll and coffee cake mixes. You'll be surprised and pleased.

PANCAKES

Choose a good plain wheatcake or buckwheat pancake mix, and follow the directions on the package. Make the pancakes small. If cooked at the stove, butter each hot off the griddle and stack in piles of three. If there are just two persons to eat, fry the cakes at the table on the electric stove and serve with warm buttered syrup, *i.e.*, any syrup you like heated with butter, and possibly a trace of cinnamon. Or try them in any of these ways:

With sweet cream and brown sugar—a New England custom.

Spread with sour cream and jam of your choice.

Butter or margarine, then sprinkle and top with brown sugar and pop into the oven until the sugar and butter melt.

BERRY PANCAKES

To each cup of prepared pancake mix add $\frac{1}{4}$ cup of fresh or defrosted quick-frozen blueberries and cook as directed.

FRENCH STYLE PANCAKES OR CRÊPES

Make the pancake batter thinner than usual by using a little more liquid. Spread the pancakes with butter and jelly or jam. Roll up, place fold-side down, and serve dusted with sifted powdered sugar. Crêpe mix is good.

TO COOK PANCAKES

Use a thick iron griddle or frying pan, or a magnesium griddle that transmits heat evenly. Put it over a moderate heat. When you think it is hot enough, drip 2 or 3 drops of water on it. If the drops steam and dance, fry the pancakes. Brush over the utensil with vegetable fat or oil. Drop on the pancake batter 1 tablespoon at a time. Turn in about 2 minutes, or as soon as the cakes are full of bubbles. The frying procedure is the same when the smooth plate of an electric grill is used. It's a good idea and easier to put pancake or waffle batter in a wide-mouthed pitcher and pour it out. Looks professional, too.

In case you prefer to mix your own pancake batter, here is the recipe.

MIX YOUR OWN PANCAKES
(Serves 2 to 3)

1½ *cups flour*	½ *tablespoon sugar*
2 *teaspoons baking powder*	1 *egg*
	1 *cup milk*
½ *teaspoon salt*	
2 *tablespoons melted shortening*	

1. Sift together the dry ingredients.

2. Beat the egg light, add the milk and pour into the first mixture.

3. Add the shortening, and beat until the mixture looks bubbly.

Cook as directed.

Waffles

Here again take your choice. Make your own waffle batter or use a good mix. In any case it's fun to bake the waffles at the table. If you have a double-decker waffle iron this is quick and easy. You can serve waffles often; not only for breakfast, but for dessert. And try crisp waffles for lunch or dinner under creamed chicken or diced meat in gravy, or use cheese or nut waffles for lunch. Different and delectable.

The New Waffle Iron

Better start the new waffle iron off right. Put a tablespoonful of water in each compartment; heat the iron and continue to heat until the water dries out. This is called "tempering," and it makes for more even cooking and less sticking.

To Cook Waffles

If using an old-fashioned iron on a gas or kerosene stove, or coal range, grease the iron with vegetable oil. (Use your nylon pastry brush for this.) The waffles are then really fried. But if using an electric waffle iron, no grease should be used, as the waffles are actually baked. They will not stick if sufficient shortening is used in the batter, and if the waffle iron is hot enough. Better bake one small test waffle to be sure.

Waffles Accompaniments Summed Up

Hot buttered honey or syrup, add rum if desired.
Sifted powdered sugar and cinnamon.
Hot butterscotch, chocolate or buttered rum sauce.
Maple syrup and chopped nut meats.
Half scoops of ice cream with crushed, fresh sweetened, or defrosted frozen fruit, or hot chocolate or butterscotch sauce with or without chopped salted almonds.

WAFFLES
(Serves 2 to 3)

1½ *cups flour*	¼ *teaspoon salt*
2½ *teaspoons baking*	2 *eggs*
powder	1 *cup milk*

⅓ *cup melted shortening*

1. Sift together the dry ingredients. Beat the egg yolks and add the milk.

2. Stir into the flour mixture; add the shortening and fold in the egg whites, whipped stiff.

3. Transfer by generous tablespoonfuls to a heated

waffle iron; close the iron and cook the waffles three to five minutes, according to thickness.

Cheese Waffles: Follow the preceding recipe. After putting the batter in the waffle iron, sprinkle with grated sharp American cheese. Bake and serve with butter instead of bread; nice with a tossed salad.

Nut Waffles: Follow the recipe for waffles. Sprinkle the waffle iron with coarsely chopped nut meats. Pour in the batter and bake as directed. Serve with buttered syrup or honey, jelly, jam and cream cheese, or with butterscotch or buttered rum sauce (page 243).

Ham Waffles: Add ½ cup minced or devilled ham to the waffle batter. Add 2 tablespoons extra milk and cook. Serve with butter and syrup if you like. (I don't like.)

Savory Waffle Shortcake: Put 2 waffle sections together and top with creamed ham, chicken or turkey, or home-made, canned or quick-frozen chicken à la king.

Welsh Rabbit Waffles: Top with snappy Welsh rabbit, home-made or purchased in jars.

Waffle Savories: Top waffles with creamed meat or chicken bits in gravy; creamed dried beef; any à la king mixture; spaghetti sauce and tiny meat balls in gravy; or with Welsh rabbit. And are these something!

Fruit-Topped Waffles: Top with crushed, sweetened fruit, defrosted quick-frozen berries, or diced apricots or peaches. Serve with whipped sweet or soured cream sweetened with sugar or honey.

GINGERBREAD WAFFLES

Use prepared gingerbread mix according to directions for making waffles on the package. Serve with a choice of:

Butter and cream cheese
Soured cream and orange marmalade
Butterscotch or chocolate sauce

French Toast

Some people like French toast very soft, as when made with more milk, and less egg; others like it on the crisp side as made with more egg and less milk. But let's not argue about it. The choice depends on your own taste, and the price of eggs.

FRENCH TOAST (SOFT STYLE)
(Serves 2 to 3)

1 *egg*	½ *cup milk*
Few grains salt	4 *full slices white or en-*
Few grains nutmeg	*tire wheat bread*

Butter or margarine

1. Beat the egg. Add the salt, nutmeg and milk.

2. Heat the frying pan, and melt the butter or margarine in it. Do not brown this.

3. Cut the slices of bread in halves. With a fork, dip quickly in and out of the egg batter. Drain a moment.

4. Fry in the butter or margarine on both sides till golden brown. Serve plain, with bacon or panned ham, or with syrup, honey, jelly or jam.

French Toast Crisp Style: Follow the preceding directions with this exception. Use ½ cup milk and two eggs.

Waffle French Toast: Heat the waffle iron. Brush with oil. Prepare the mixture for French toast crisp style; dip the bread in and out. Place a piece in each division, close and bake like waffles.

French Toastwiches: Make thin sandwiches of white bread; put together with minced cooked or devilled ham, or luncheon meat, peanut butter or grated sharp cheese. Dip into French toast batter and fry. Excellent for breakfast, or for lunch or supper with a tossed salad. Even for dinner if it starts with a filling soup.

Biscuits

My conscience would up and slap me down if I did not include directions for tea biscuits in this book. What's a wife without good biscuits? In fact, I'll put in two recipes; and even then you'll probably reach for a package of biscuit mix, or one of ready mixed and cut biscuits, which is all right if you use it right.

MIDGET BAKING POWDER BISCUIT
(Serves 2 to 3)

1 *cup flour*	2 *teaspoons baking powder*
1 *teaspoon granulated*	¼ *teaspoon salt*
sugar	2½ *tablespoons shortening*

6 *tablespoons milk*

1. Sift the dry ingredients together. Chop in the shortening with a pastry blender.

2. Moisten with the milk.

3. Transfer the dough to a board dusted with flour. Roll to ⅓ inch in thickness and shape into rounds with a tiny cutter. Tuck the edges of the dough under as you work so there will be no remnants.

4. Transfer to an oiled baking sheet, and bake in a hot oven (450 degrees, F.), for 12 minutes, or until the biscuits are brown on top. Makes a dozen biscuits.

Cheese Biscuits: Add ⅓ cup grated sharp American cheese to the flour, and finish as directed. Serve very hot. Nice with soup, salads, or hors d'oeuvres.

SOUR CREAM BISCUITS
(Serves 2 to 3)

1 *cup self-rising flour*   ¼ *teaspoon baking soda*
     ½ *cup soured cream*

1. These are extra special. Sift together the flour and soda. Beat into the cream.

2. Transfer to a slightly floured board; pat to ¼ inch in thickness; cut into small rounds, and bake in a hot oven (400–450 degrees, F.) for 12 minutes.

Dropped Sour Cream Biscuits: Are quicker still. Use an extra tablespoon of cream, and drop the dough by small teaspoonfuls an inch apart onto a greased pan. Bake at 400–450 degrees F.

USING BISCUIT MIX

For biscuits with a "bready" texture use according to directions on the package of mix. For rich-textured crisp biscuits, add 1½ tablespoons extra shortening to 1 cup of the mix, and chop it in with a pastry blender.

Scones

Scones are second cousins to biscuits. And by the way, they are pronounced "skuns." There are two schools of scone-makers—those who prefer sweet scones, and the other faction that likes a biscuit-type scone to serve with jam, such as this.

BISCUIT TYPE SCONES
(Serves 2 to 3)

2 *cups all-purpose flour*   ½ *teaspoon salt*
3½ *teaspoons baking pow-*   ¼ *cup shortening*
     der   2 *eggs*
2 *teaspoons sugar*   ½ *cup top milk*

1. Mix and sift the dry ingredients; chop in the shortening.

2. Beat the eggs; add the milk; stir into the first mixture.

3. Divide in two parts. Place on a floured sheet of waxed paper, one at a time. Pat into rounds about ¾ of an inch thick. Cut in triangles. Place on an oiled pan. Brush with any milk and egg left in the bowl. Sprinkle lightly with sugar.

4. Bake in a hot oven (400 degrees, F.), about 15 minutes. Serve hot with butter or jam.

If any are left over, split and toast them. They are delectable.

Muffins

Families of two often go without many homey foods because it seems difficult to make a small enough amount for two. Muffins for instance. But if it is convenient to use the oven, as when baking other foods, tuck in a pan of muffins, either home-made—or, you've guessed it—made from a prepared mix. Muffins add a touch of luxury to any meal. There's quite a choice on the market—plain, corn or bran muffin mix, and they are really good.

HOME-MADE MUFFINS
(Serves 2 to 3)

2½ *tablespoons shortening*	2 *teaspoons baking powder*
1 *tablespoon sugar*	
1 *egg*	¼ *teaspoon salt*
1 *cup all-purpose flour*	½ *cup milk*

1. Cream together the shortening, sugar and the egg, well beaten.

2. Sift together the flour, baking powder and salt.

3. Add alternately with the milk to the creamed mixture.

4. Transfer to small oiled muffin pans; bake 20 minutes in a moderately hot oven (375–400 degrees, F.).

Berry Muffins: Add ½ cup fresh or defrosted quick-frozen blueberries or huckleberries to the flour. Finish as directed.

Nut Muffins: Add ⅓ cup chopped nut meats to the flour; finish as directed.

Cheese Muffins: Omit the sugar. Add ⅓ cup grated sharp American cheese to the flour; finish as directed in home-made muffins.

POPOVERS

Popovers so big and puffy they're worth featuring in newspaper ads. That's how important they are to one of New York's most celebrated hotels. Equally important at home, but a nuisance to make for two in the time-honored way. But a popover mix comes to the rescue. A package makes about 10 big ones. So better make up half, for popovers do not reheat to advantage.

Most popover mixes call for 1 egg. In halving the mixture use ½ egg. To measure this, beat the egg light in a measuring cup, and use half. Utilize the balance in making a sauce, rabbit, an omelet or in scrambling eggs.

When perfect, popovers are high, crispy, crunchy shells, containing a little bit of nothing. Serve very hot with butter, and/or jam or jelly. Or try this next idea for the substantial dish at lunch or dinner:

Meat Filled Popovers: Cut slits in red hot popovers. Fill with any thick creamed meat or fish, or minced meat in thick Spanish or well seasoned tomato sauce. Makes that leftover taste like a million.

Ready Steamed and Loaf Breads

Some of the best foods produced by bakers, or on sale in cans, are the steamed and loaf breads. Nut and date loaf and Boston brown bread are outstanding examples. Either may be served with the meal, or can pinch-hit for dessert. The slices should always be as thin as they can be cut.

Nut and Date Loaf: Is served as a bread; or for service with a fruit salad; or with fruit for dessert, spread with cream cheese mixed with a little butter or soured cream for spreadability.

Nut and Date Loaf Pudding Style: Slice ½ inch thick; place in a double boiler and steam about 15 minutes. Serve with any fruit sauce, rum-flavored butter sauce (page 243), or lemon-honey-cream dressing (page 225).

Boston Brown Bread: Is at its best sliced, spread lightly with butter and heated through in a slow oven, in a double boiler or on top of the radiator. Or place in a grill and heat only until the butter melts.

Boston Brown Bread as Dessert: Is an old New England favorite. Slice, butter and heat as described, and serve with maple syrup.

Boston Brown Bread Tea Slices: Slice the cold bread thin and spread with equal parts of cream cheese and butter. Sprinkle with any kind of chopped salted nuts.

Doughnuts

No sweet bread can be more delicious—nor more distasteful—than doughnuts. This depends to a large extent upon the quality and kind of fat in which they are fried. As it is impractical to make doughnuts for a twosome, better purchase them. Shop around, decide on the best flavor and don't compromise. For any food cooked in fat that has a strong disagreeable taste or smell is not fit to eat. Whenever possible freshen the doughnuts in a slow oven. To do this, put a paper towel in a pan and place the doughnuts on it. Cover with a second pan, and heat. The paper absorbs the excess fat—helpful if the doughnuts are to be dunked. Then sift over powdered sugar mixed with cinnamon. If glazed doughnuts are your fancy, put sugared doughnuts on the grill and slowly heat. The tops will be crunchy and glazed. Or split the doughnuts, toast, and serve with jam or jelly.

Sandwiches

For tea or party service sandwiches should be thin, small, dainty and without crusts. But for luncheon or supper fare, or late evening home snacks, make them substantial, with 2 thin slices of bread, or open style with 1 thicker slice, if reducing is the word. In either case, the filling or the topping can be one and the same mixture. Any kind of bread may be used.

With a family of two it is not economical to use a variety of breads, as much would be wasted. Unless there is a neighbor, also with a family of two, who will exchange a half loaf of her rye, cracked wheat, or raisin bread for a half loaf of your whole wheat or white bread.

SANDWICH FILLINGS OR TOPPINGS

Anything that tastes good with bread and butter may be used as a topping or filling. For instance:

1. Minced tongue, ham, chicken, or veal mixed with plain or horse-radish mayonnaise.

2. Minced ham, or bologna, piccalilli, salad dressing.

3. Minced tuna fish or salmon with salad dressing, minced green pepper and curry powder to season.

4. Chopped, hard-cooked eggs with mayonnaise and chili sauce.

5. Grated, soft American cheese (highly flavored) mixed with mayonnaise and a little chopped pimiento.

6. Cheese-in-Wine (see page 101), with chopped chives.

7. Minced cucumber, well drained, mixed with an equal part of chopped shrimp and mayonnaise.

8. Equal parts of minced chicken and ham with Russian dressing.

9. Lettuce leaves spread with mayonnaise, with or without chopped nuts.

10. Devilled ham and salad dressing topped with thin slices of tomato.

11. Chopped chicken, scallions and nuts mixed with a little chicken gravy or mayonnaise.

12. Minced liverwurst with chopped parsley, mustard and cream cheese.

13. Cottage cheese mixed with chopped scallions and their tender green tops, sliced red radishes, and/or minced cucumber.

OPEN-TOP SANDWICHES

Choose the kind of bread that best harmonizes with the topping. Slice ¼ inch thick. Leave on the crusts. Spread the topping smoothly from crust to crust. Decorate each "sandwich"; to serve, arrange on paper doily-covered plates, trays or platters.

Decorations: Sliced stuffed olives or sweet pickles; tiny sprigs of parsley or cress; grated raw carrot or chopped hard-cooked egg; sliced hard-cooked eggs; rolled anchovies; meras (tiny canned Javanese fish); thin slices of cucumber or small tomatoes; strips of pimientos or green pepper; whole or chopped salted nuts, etc.

SLICED MEAT SANDWICHES

Spread the bread from crust to crust with butter or margarine stirred until creamy. Mustard, curry powder, chutney sauce, chili sauce or horse-radish may be added to the butter. On this fit thin slices of meat or poultry, ham, tongue, meat loaf, butter-panned liverwurst, smoked turkey, etc. Cover with a second slice of buttered bread.

MEAT SALAD SANDWICHES

Add a leaf of lettuce or shredded lettuce, or thin slices of tomato, or cucumber and a little mayonnaise; make as described in the preceding recipe.

SANDWICH PLATES

Sandwich plates are smart, quick and easy for lunch, supper or parties. For instance:

1. Bean 'N'Ham Sandwich Plates: On individual plates arrange baked bean sandwiches, thin slices of ham, each rolled up around a finger-length of cream cheese, sliced tomato and lettuce. Pass Thousand Island Dressing.

2. Chicken Sandwich Plates: On individual salad plates arrange chicken sandwiches, fruits drenched with wine in lettuce nests (page 221), and heated potato chips.

3. Cottage Cheese Sandwich Plates: Pile cottage cheese in ramekins. Pour over soured cream; dust with paprika. Place each in the center of a sandwich plate. On one side put small crab meat or Smithfield ham sandwiches on sliced lettuce; on the other side put sliced tomato and half a stuffed egg in lettuce. Pass French Herbized Dressing (page 223).

BUNWICHES

These are puffy sandwiches made with buns, so thick they are almost impossible to eat, so juicy they generally result in spills and drizzles. Commercially these two difficulties have been overcome and the bunwich emerges in the form of a long soft cylindrical roll, halved to form a hinge, the center removed, and the frankfurter and relish or other filling, slipped snugly into the groove.

For home-made bunwiches use soft round or long buns. Cut almost in halves but do not detach altogether; leave that hinge. Then with a fork, remove the soft interior. This leaves a perfect nest for the filling; but don't make this wet, just nicely moist. Better close up the bunwich without lettuce or tomato. Instead, serve a salad, cole slaw or vegetable nibblers with it. Good for a kitchen, patio or terrace supper party, a picnic or for Sunday nights. And an excellent way to make "oddments" of food into something new.

BUNWICH FILLINGS

1. Minced chicken salad with nuts or olives.

2. Minced hard-cooked egg, scallions, cooked bacon and mayonnaise.

3. Minced tongue, celery, pickle relish and salad dressing.

4. Minced tuna and cucumber with mayonnaise.

5. Very thick creamed dried beef.

6. Butter-panned liverwurst minced with celery, green pepper, and/or chopped hard-cooked egg.

7. Chopped luncheon meat or spiced ham with mustard mayonnaise.

8. Thick cold Welsh Rabbit (page 98), with chopped nuts and pickles.

9. Sausage cakes shaped to fit, with sweet pickle relish.

10. Broiled Vienna sausages with minced vegetable salad and mustard mayonnaise.

TOASTWICHES

These are based on toast instead of bread. And to be really good should be made to order at the table. For toastwiches choose any of the spreads suggested on page 83, or put the toasts together, or top an open toastwich with any of the following combinations.

1. Boston baked beans, mashed with chili sauce.

2. Thin slices of broiled steak, or luncheon meat.

3. Thin slices of broiled bacon, ham, or Canadian bacon.

4. Minced ham or smoked salmon with mayonnaise, and chopped onion and pickle relish.

5. Thin slices Swiss cheese spread with plain horseradish or Bahamian mustard.

6. Bacon and sliced tomatoes.

7. Minced olives mixed with three times as much cream cheese.

8. Scrambled eggs, hot or cold, plain or cooked with minced ham, chicken and fried onions, or cheese.

9. Minced sardines moistened with mayonnaise.

10. Chopped salami and beet relish mixed with mayonnaise.

11. Peanut butter or any kind of jam or jelly.

12. Currant jelly on one slice of toast, minced ham or tongue on the other.

CHOPPED BEEF TOASTS

(2 servings)

¼ *pound chopped raw beef*	1 *tablespoon butter or*
¼ *teaspoon onion salt*	*margarine*
½ *teaspoon meat condiment*	4 *slices white bread*

1. Mix the beef, onion salt and condiment.

2. Spread the bread with half the butter and toast on one side.

3. Spread the untoasted side from crust to crust with

the chopped beef; dot with the remaining butter and grill at moderate heat from 5 to 6 minutes. Serve very hot.

For Gourmet and Gourmette
SPOON BREAD
(Serves 2)

½ cup cornmeal
¾ cup boiling water
½ tablespoon butter or margarine
1 egg

½ teaspoon salt
½ teaspoon baking powder
1½ cups milk

1. Scald the cornmeal with the boiling water; add butter, salt, baking powder and milk. Beat and add the egg.

2. Transfer to two buttered shirred egg dishes, or one small baking-dish. Bake about 20 minutes or until firm in a moderate oven (350–375 degrees, F.).

3. Serve brown and sizzling with crisp bacon, sausages or grilled ham, and lawsy chilluns; you just can't stop eatin'.

For a taste thrill serve spoon bread with pure maple syrup. Good enough for dessert.

CHAPTER VII

Egg and Cheese Dishes

Eggs are ace foods especially useful in families of two. At least three eggs per person a week are needed for good nutrition; better still an egg or even two a day. And eggs taste as good for any meal as for breakfast.

For proof visit the unique Ham-N-Eggs restaurants on New York's Broadway, and you will find crowds enjoying this all-American dish any time of the day or night. The dish is superbly prepared, but any cook can equal it for a twosome. The secret of its appetite-appeal is good ham and good eggs, and the fact that they are not cooked at too high a heat. Eggs are a delicate food, and in whatever way they are prepared they must be cooked at a moderate to slow heat with one exception—boiled eggs.

I Beg to Differ

Contrary to the opinion of many of my colleagues, I maintain that boiled eggs should be *boiled,* not coddled; that is, allowed to stand a certain length of time in boiling water, for you are never sure when they are cooked enough. The standing in hot water method was serviceable in the days before general refrigeration, when eggs were at room temperature when put to coddle. But today with eggs coming from refrigerators at 40 to 50 degrees, F., it is difficult to estimate how long it will take for them to coddle through. And so I boil! As several otherwise successful cooks have told me they cannot boil eggs and be sure of the doneness, here are directions for boiling medium-sized eggs.

BOILED EGGS

Wash the eggs. With a pencil, mark on the shell the length of time they are to boil. You may want 4-minute eggs while John wants eggs à la coq. Gently place the eggs in a deep saucepan. Cover with rapidly boiling water, put on a lid and boil the required time. If the eggs are taken from a refrigerator under 45 degrees, F., add an extra half minute of boiling time. And watch the clock.

Eggs à la Coq (just heated through) . . . 2 minutes
Very soft . . . . 3 minutes
Moderately soft . . . . 4 minutes
Jellied through . . . . 5 minutes
Hard-boiled: Start in cold water, bring to a rapid boil, boil 10 minutes, drain, then cover with cold water, to prevent further cooking and the formation of a green ring around the yolk.

To make it easier to hold hot boiled eggs for opening, run cold water over. Serve them in egg cups if you like; it's fun to decapitate the egg. But I prefer service in small heated glass or china cups, or ramekins that will hold two opened eggs and a generous dab of butter all at once. Or try stirring in crumbled crisp bacon. It makes the best boiled egg taste better.

POACHED EGGS

1. Half fill a deep frying pan with water. Add ½ teaspoon salt and 1 teaspoon vinegar and bring to a rapid boil.

2. To poach the eggs, break each one separately into a

small deep dish and slide it carefully into the boiling water. Do not put the eggs too close together.

3. Reduce the heat, cover and simmer until the eggs are cooked through, about 7 minutes. Remove with a perforated spoon so the eggs will not break or be watery; always serve on buttered toast, fish cakes or some other food. Poached eggs should not be left to skid around a plate. If there is room for an extra gadget in the kitchen, a small egg poacher is helpful. To use, rub with fat, stand it in the pan of water and carefully slide the eggs into the places designated for them. Beautifully round poached eggs are the reward.

All measurements are level
EGGS HOLLANDAISE
(Serves 2)

Simulated or ready-made Hollandaise Sauce	*Broiled or fried sliced tomato*
Leftover string beans, peas, carrots, or other vegetables	*Rounds of toast or toasted English muffins*
	2 large eggs

1. Prepare simulated Hollandaise Sauce (page 173).

2. Heat the vegetables; broil the tomato; toast the bread or English muffins.

3. Poach the eggs.

4. Arrange on a platter as follows: Place the broiled tomato on the toast or split English muffins; top with the poached eggs. Cover with the Hollandaise Sauce; dust with paprika. Surround with the vegetables and decorate with parsley.

For dinner serve with broiled bacon, sausages or panned plain or Smithfield ham.

SCRAMBLED EGGS

1. Allow 1 large or 2 small eggs for each person. Beat thoroughly, add 1 tablespoon milk for each egg used and a few grains of salt and pepper for each egg.

2. Melt ½ tablespoon butter or margarine in a small heavy frying pan; pour in the egg mixture; place over a slow heat to cook. With a tablespoon scrape up the egg as fast as it solidifies. (Don't use a fork. This makes scratched eggs.)

3. Cook only until the mixture is creamy; then serve plain, or on hot toast, which may be topped with broiled or fried tomato, frizzled ham, or creamed dried beef; or top with crisp bacon or small sausages or heated smoked salmon or herring.

Eggs Scrambled with Ham: Add 2 tablespoons minced cooked ham for each person.

Eggs Scrambled with Cheese: Add 2 tablespoons grated cheese for each person.

Eggs Scrambled with Smoked Turkey: Prepare eggs for scrambling, using light cream instead of milk. Add ½ cup chopped smoked turkey to 4 eggs and cook as directed. Too expensive for every day but nice for an evening party snack.

Eggs Scrambled with Tomatoes: Instead of milk use ½ cup canned tomatoes and ¼ teaspoon onion salt to 4 eggs.

Eggs Scrambled with Soured Cream and Chives: Use soured cream instead of milk, and add 1 tablespoon minced chives for each person.

Eggs Scrambled with Salami: For 2 persons dice 4 slices of salami after removing the skin. Fry a moment in a little butter, then add to the scrambled egg mixture.

PLAIN FRIED EGGS

Melt enough butter or bacon fat in the bottom of a small heavy frying pan to almost cover; add ½ tablespoon hot water to prevent too-rapid cooking. Break the eggs into a saucer, 1 at a time, and slide them into the heated fat. Cover and cook very slowly until they are firm throughout. If to be fried on both sides, turn with a pancake turner and cook a moment longer. Dust the eggs sparingly with salt and plentifully with pepper while cooking.

HAM-N-EGGS BROADWAY
(*Individual Service*)

1 *thin slice cooked ham*	*Salt and pepper*
1 *teaspoon butter*	*French fries or heated po-*
2 *eggs*	*tato chips*

1. Cut the ham in halves.
2. Heat an individual-sized round-bottom frying pan. Put in a teaspoon of butter. When it melts put a slice of ham on each side of the pan.
3. In the space between break the eggs. Dust with salt and pepper. Fry slowly 1 minute until the eggs begin to firm.
4. Then slide under a slow broiler heat, and broil until the eggs are done to your liking.
5. Serve in the frying pans, set on thick pottery plates, or on individual round planks. Pass the French fries or potato chips.

FRENCH OMELET
(*Serves Two*)

3 *eggs*	*Few grains pepper*
1/3 *teaspoon salt*	1 *tablespoon hot water*
	1/2 *tablespoon butter*

1. Break the eggs into a bowl; add the salt and pepper; beat until thick and light; add the water.
2. Mix well; melt the butter in a small heavy frying pan; pour in the omelet mixture. Let stand over a low heat

about 2 minutes; then raise the cooked portion gently with a fork to let the liquid portion come in contact with the hot pan.

3. When pale-brown on the bottom and firm throughout, roll ½ the omelet over the other half and serve at once.

Ham Omelet: Sprinkle ⅓ cup minced ham over the omelet when nearly done.

Cheese Omelet: Sprinkle ⅓ cup sharp grated American cheese over the omelet when nearly done.

Omelette aux fines herbes: When nearly done, sprinkle over the omelet 2 tablespoons mixed minced parsley and chives, and ½ teaspoon minced tarragon or basil.

Tomato Omelet: Serve plain or cheese omelet with hot, thick stewed or cubed fried tomatoes in the fold and as a sauce.

Western Omelet: To the mixture for French Omelet, add 2 tablespoons minced cooked ham, and 1 tablespoon each minced onion and green pepper sautéed ½ minute in butter.

Fried Onion Omelet: Cover the omelet with fried onions when nearly done. Serve with additional fried onions and/or grated sharp cheese, crisp bacon, grilled liverwurst or American or Canadian bacon.

CHICKEN AND ONION OMELET
(Serves 2 to 3)

1½ *tablespoons chicken fat or butter*	½ *cup flaked cooked or canned chicken*
¾ *cup sliced onion*	1 *recipe French omelet mixture*

1. Melt the fat in a small frying pan. Add the onion and fry very slowly until soft but not brown. Add the chicken.

2. Prepare the omelet mixture, and stir into the fried chicken and onions. Finish as directed for French omelet.

Smoked Salmon and Onion Omelet: Follow the preceding recipe using smoked salmon instead of chicken.

FRIED POTATO OMELET
(Serves 2)

1½ *cups butter-fried diced*   1 *recipe French omelet*
    potato   *mixture*

1. Sauté the potato in the frying pan to be used for the omelet. Add a little onion if desired.

2. Pour in the omelet mixture and finish as directed for French omelet.

SHIRRED EGGS
(Serves 2)

2 *tablespoons soft bread-*   4 *medium-sized eggs*
   crumbs   *Salt and pepper*
2 *tablespoons top milk or*   ½ *tablespoon butter*
   cream

1. Butter 2 shirred egg dishes. Strew with the crumbs. Add the cream.

2. Break 2 eggs into each dish. Dust with salt and pepper; dot with butter.

3. Bake about 10 minutes in a moderate oven, 350–375 degrees, F., or grill until the eggs are cooked through.

Shirred Eggs with Cheese: Prepare as directed, adding 1 heaping tablespoon grated sharp cheese to each serving before cooking.

Shirred Eggs with Ham: Allow 1 egg per person. Spread 2 tablespoons minced ham over the crumbs and cream; break in the eggs and finish as directed for shirred eggs. A topping of grated cheese may be added.

ESCALLOPED EGGS
(Serves 2)

¼ teaspoon onion salt
1 cup white sauce
4 hard-cooked eggs
¼ cup grated sharp cheese

¼ cup bread crumbs
1 tablespoon melted butter or margarine

1. Rub ramekins with butter. Add the onion salt to the white sauce.

2. Slice the eggs; arrange in layers in the ramekins with the white sauce.

3. Top with the cheese mixed with the crumbs and butter.

4. Bake about 18 minutes or until browned in a moderate oven, 350–375 degrees, F. A few sautéed mushrooms, layered with the eggs makes this a gourmet dish.

Cheese Dishes

A generous cheese dish can pinch-hit for meat at any dinner—if it is combined with plenty of bulky food. For instance, Welsh Rabbit on and with plenty of toast; macaroni au gratin; salad tossed with cheese. Combination with bulk is necessary, because cheese is highly concentrated food; contains no bones like meat or connective tissue; it's sheer nourishment. And because it is made from milk, it is a magnificent source of the plus-calcium most of us need. If not combined or served with something bulky, cheese is eaten too fast; and it takes up so little space in the stomach we are likely to feel there has not been enough to eat, although ample nourishment has been provided.

In cooking we use sharp Cheddar cheese, also known as American, dairy or store cheese, or one of the sharp-flavored processed cheeses. Natural Cheddar cheese should be hand chopped, grated on a coarse grater or put through the food chopper. Processed cheese is smooth and soft, so cut it in very small pieces. It cannot be grated. If the flavor is flat combine with a second processed cheese of high flavor, such as Old English.

Cottage Cheese: Is a fine alternate for meat at lunch, or as a meat supplement for dinner when the main dish is a bit scant. Buy it plain, ready-mixed with chives, or grated carrots or mix it yourself; or add chopped olives, salted nuts or chopped scallions or radishes. For dessert with fruit, serve it plain. Don't try to keep it more than two or three days, and then be sure it is covered and well refrigerated.

All measurements are level
QUICK SPAGHETTI IN CHEESE SAUCE
(*Serves 2 to 3*)

1/4 *pound spaghetti*   1/2 *teaspoon prepared mus-*
1 1/2 *cups white sauce*   *tard*
1 *cup fine-grated sharp American cheese*

1. Break the spaghetti in 1-inch lengths; cook and drain.

2. Meantime make the white sauce (page 171). Add the mustard and cheese; cook slowly, stirring occasionally, until the cheese melts.

3. Combine with the spaghetti. Serve very hot in deep plates or shallow bowls. Dust with plenty of paprika.

Macaroni au Gratin: Follow directions for quick spaghetti but substitute cooked macaroni. Transfer to 2 individual baking dishes, and bake or grill until golden brown and bubbling. Especially good with pickled beets or tomato salad with French dressing.

Macaroni with Ham: Add 1/2 cup minced cooked ham or luncheon meat to the mixture for macaroni au gratin. A good dinner dish.

WELSH RABBIT
(*Serves 2 to 3*)

1 *cup fine-chopped, sharp American cheese*
2 *tablespoons flour*
1 *egg*
⅓ *teaspoon salt*
⅛ *teaspoon pepper*
¼ *teaspoon mustard*
1 *tablespoon butter or margarine*
1⅓ *cups milk*

1. Into a double boiler top put the cheese, flour, egg, salt, pepper, mustard and butter. Stir thoroughly.

2. Place over hot water and gradually add the milk. Cook and beat occasionally with a hand beater until the rabbit is thick and creamy; then beat to insure smoothness.

3. Serve on crisp crackers or toast, or top with crisp bacon or anchovies if desired. If any rabbit is left, it makes a fine sandwich spread.

Almond or Pecan Rabbit: Sprinkle Welsh Rabbit with toasted or salted almonds or pecans.

SAVORY CHEESE PUDDING
(*Serves 2*)

2 *tablespoons butter*
1 *cup bread cut in small cubes*
1 *cup fine-chopped or grated sharp American cheese*
2 *eggs*
¼ *teaspoon baking soda*
⅓ *teaspoon paprika*
½ *teaspoon salt*
⅛ *teaspoon pepper*
1¾ *cups milk*

1. Melt the butter; add the bread and sauté until light brown.

2. Arrange alternate layers of the prepared bread and cheese in ramekins or shirred egg dishes.

3. Beat the eggs slightly; add baking soda, paprika, salt, pepper, and milk. Pour into the dishes and set in a pan of hot water.

4. Bake in a moderate oven, 375 degrees, F., until set and browned, about 25 minutes.

CHEESE SOUFFLE´
(*Serves 2*)

½ *cup scalded milk*
⅔ *cup fine soft white bread crumbs*
¾ *cup grated sharp American cheese*

¼ *teaspoon salt*
⅛ *teaspoon paprika*
¼ *teaspoon baking powder*
2 *eggs*

1. Pour the milk over the crumbs and cheese; add seasonings and baking powder.

2. Separate the eggs; beat the yolks light and creamy; the whites stiff.

3. Combine the yolks with the first mixture; fold in the whites.

4. Transfer to oiled shirred egg dishes; bake 30 minutes in a moderate oven (350–375 degrees, F.). Serve at once with or without tomato sauce.

Cheese and Fruit

Almost any dinner is tops when topped with cheese, fruit and crisp crackers. But it should be the right cheese served at room temperature. The choice lies with the flavor cheeses. As these are the more costly, it stretches the budget a bit to serve them with fruit as well as crackers. For instance:

Sharp American or Cheddar with dates, apples, grapes or pears.

Gorgonzola with apples or pears.

Roquefort or Bleu with apples or pears.

Swiss with apples, prunes, plums.

Gouda with any fruit salad, apples or pears.

Pineapple Cheese to pass with the fruit bowl.

Provolone or Bel-Paese with peaches, apricots, nectarines.

Camembert with figs, dates or dried apricots.

Cream Cheese with strawberries, pineapple, oranges or grapefruit sections, persimmons or stewed fruit. Nice spread on raw apple. Wonderful with any conserve, with guava paste or Bar-le-Duc.

CHEESE, FRUIT AND NUT PLATE
(*For Desserts or Snacks for Two*)

1. Thin-slice 4 rounds of Cheddar from a roll of the processed cheese. Arrange on 2 medium-sized plates; add a cluster of raisins or 2 moist figs to each, a few cracked walnuts or filberts, and some after-dinner mints. Eat the cheese with the nut meats.

2. Serve with coffee or port.

THE CHEESE BOARD

Passing the cheese board is a charming custom, but not practical for the family of two; for a real cheese board display cries out for cheeses of several types, or at least cream cheese, sage cheese, if you can get it; Swiss, Cheddar, Roquefort or bleu, camembert and a gay red Gouda or Edam. If there's a party on, or special company, a cheese board, plus a fruit bowl and plenty of hot coffee topped with whipped cream, is not only a smart dessert, but can also serve as a perfect late evening snack.

Put a paper doily under each kind of cheese to protect the cheese board from fat stains, and arrange on the cheese board, the red Gouda or Edam in the center, the top cut off, the interior scooped out and cut bite-size. Toothpicks for the service. Remove processed cheeses from the wrappers and cut a few slices; leave natural cheeses whole—the guests cut their own. Slice Swiss cheese ¼ inch thick;

take off the wrapping from individual servings of camembert or bleu. Take blocks of cream cheese from the wrappers and place on doilies, with sliced olives or nut meats for the decoration. Pile cheese spreads in flat glass dishes. Arrange thin slices of pumpernickel and crisp crackers around the edge. What, no cheese board? Never mind, use a bread board or a tray, or for a large party, a pastry board.

For Gourmet and Gourmette

EGGS BENEDICT

(Serves 2)

2 *English muffins*	4 *poached eggs*
Hollandaise sauce (simulated)	*Parsley*
	Black or stuffed olives
¼ *pound half slices cooked ham*	

1. Split, toast and butter the muffins.

2. Meantime make the Hollandaise sauce (page 173).

3. While this is cooking, pan-cook the ham (page 151), and poach the eggs (page 90).

4. In assembling—hurry—so the food will be hot. Put the toasted muffins on a heated platter; cover each with a piece of ham and top with a poached egg. Pour over the sauce, garnish each egg with a bit of parsley or black olive, or a slice of stuffed olive.

CHEESE-IN-WINE SPREAD

Cream together 3 tablespoons butter, ⅛ teaspoon mace, ¼ pound grated or mashed soft Stilton or Cheshire cheese and 3 tablespoons dry white wine. Pack in a jar. Delicious as a spread for crisp crackers or canapés. This keeps indefinitely if covered.

CHAPTER VIII

Let's Eat More Fish and Sea Food

FISH, WHOLE, OR IN THE FORM OF FRESH OR QUICK-frozen fillets, and fresh or quick-frozen shellfish are among the best foods suitable for a family of two because they are so quickly cooked, and can be bought in almost any quantity. Just how much fish to buy for two depends on appetite, and whether there is adequate refrigeration for any oddments left after serving. Fish refrigerated at 40 to 50 degrees, F. can be kept safely up to 24 hours. It's better to have a little left over than to serve a skimpy meal. The oddments can be used next morning for breakfast, reheated as is, or creamed, or flaked for fish cakes; or in a luncheon salad, tossed in a first course salad bowl, or made into a fish hors d'oeuvre salad. (For recipes consult the Index.)

Quantities to Buy
Raw and Canned Fish

¾ to 1 pound fillets of any fish
¾ to 1 pound salmon, halibut, swordfish or tilefish steaks
1 large porgy or 2 small ones
1 pound butterfish or any small "pan fish"
2 small mackerel for individual service
1 pound fresh or ocean perch
1 pound smelts

1 (2 lb.) mackerel, weakfish, pike, bass, whiting, white-fish, bluefish, cod, haddock, or any other fish

1 dozen oysters, scallops or clams

1 pound shrimp

½ pound can crab meat, lobster, salmon, fish flakes or tuna fish

Season all fish and seafood with as much monosodium glutamate (Ac'cent) as salt to bring out flavor.

Quick-Frozen Fish

Almost all quick-frozen fish comes in 12-ounce to 1-pound cartons or packages. They include fish fillets of all kinds, frog's legs, frozen crab meat, cooked and raw shrimp, cooked and raw lobster tails, oysters, clams and scallops. If the contents of the carton or package is too much for one meal, cut it in two before defrosting. Rewrap in parchment paper or aluminum foil, and place in the ice chamber or freezer drawer. It may be kept for several days if not allowed to defrost. Once defrosted it must be cooked at once. Fish cannot be refrozen.

How to Cook Whole Fish

Ask the dealer to clean the fish; he will remove scales and fins, the viscera, the vein at the backbone, and also the head of the fish. However, the head is valuable in making fish stock for chowder or gravy (page 109). Before cooking, rinse the fish with 2 cups cold water containing 1 tablespoon salt, but do not let the fish soak, as this draws out flavor and food value. Pat dry with a paper towel.

BROILED FISH

1.   Season with salt, pepper, Ac'cent. Brush with melted butter, margarine or other fat.

2.   Place on an oiled broiler or pan. Put in a preheated broiler 3 inches from the heat; broil until tender; turn once.

3. Allow 8 minutes for fish steaks 1 inch thick; 15 to 20 minutes for whole split fish. Fish is done when it looks flaky. If dry, baste frequently with melted butter or margarine while cooking.

4. If broiling thin fillets do not turn; if the fish is 1 inch thick turn once, using a broad spatula or pancake turner so the fish will not break.

To Broil Quick-Frozen Fish without Defrosting: Follow the preceding directions allowing 2 to 3 minutes longer.

BOILED FISH

1. Thick pieces of fish are usually steamed or boiled. Wrap the fish in a piece of cheese cloth or put in a wire basket.

2. Place in a deep sauce pan; pour in boiling water to ½ the height of the fish, add ½ teaspoon salt and ½ tablespoon lemon juice or plain, herb or tarragon vinegar. Cover closely.

3. Simmer small fish and fish steaks 15 minutes; allow 20 minutes to the pound for fish 2 inches in thickness.

4. Serve with a gravy made from part of the fish stock, or with tomato, Spanish, egg-and-pepper or Hollandaise sauce.

5. Serve with lemon wedges, or maitre d'hotel butter.

To Boil Frozen Fish without Defrosting: Allow 2 to 3 minutes longer. If the fish is very thick cut in 2 pieces before cooking.

POACHED FISH

1. Fresh or quick-frozen small whole fish, fillets, or fish steaks of any kind may be poached. Grease a deep frying pan with butter or vegetable fat. Place the fish in it.

2. Sprinkle with salt, pepper, lemon juice; add a little onion juice if desired.

3. Cover with equal parts of heated milk and water,

or water combined with an equal amount of any dry white wine. Cover the pan, and bake or simmer until tender; allow from 5 to 10 minutes per pound according to size.

4. If to be served hot, use the liquid in which the fish has been cooked as a basis for a gravy (page 109). Otherwise use in making a fish soup or chowder.

BAKED FISH STEAKS, FILLETS OR SMALL FISH

1. Place the fish in an oiled pan; pour over melted butter, margarine or savory fat to moisten.

2. Dust with salt, pepper and crumbs; squeeze over a little onion or lemon juice or sprinkle with tarragon vinegar.

3. Place in a moderate oven (375 degrees, F.); bake until browned. Allow about 15 minutes for fish cut 1 inch thick, 12 minutes for thin fillets, 25 minutes for medium-sized split fish. Baste occasionally with 2 tablespoons butter or margarine melted in ½ cup water, or liquid drained from cooked or canned vegetables.

4. Serve with lemon wedges, catsup, tomato or Spanish sauce, horse-radish sauce or simulated Hollandaise. (See Chapter X.)

Baked Quick-Frozen Fish: Allow 5 minutes extra time.

PAN-FRIED FISH

1. If whole, remove the heads, fins and tails from small fish. Wash, drain, dry and dust the fish with salt and pepper; roll in flour.

2. Melt enough vegetable fat in a heavy frying-pan to barely cover the bottom.

3. When hot, but not smoking, put in the fish and fry slowly until brown, turning once with a pancake turner or broad spatula. If necessary, add a little more fat, putting it in from the side of the pan.

4. Allow about 10 minutes to fry small fish, 8 minutes

for thin fillets, and 12 minutes for thick fillets or fish steaks.

5. Serve with wedges of lemon, catsup, chili sauce, or sauce remoulade (page 177).

BAKE-FRIED FISH
(Whole small fish or fillets)

1. Brush the fish with mayonnaise.
2. Dust with salt and pepper. Roll in fine dry crumbs.
3. Place in a well-oiled pan; bake in a hot oven, 400–425 degrees, F., for 15 minutes, or until brown.
4. Serve with catsup sauce, Chinese mustard or sauce tartare.

Fried Frozen Fish: Defrost before frying, as the thawing liquid prevents that nice crusty coating from forming on the fish.

PLANKED FISH

Use fish steaks, such as halibut, salmon or swordfish, or large fillets, such as whitefish, haddock, split mackerel or boned shad.

1. Oil and heat the plank; place the fish on it flesh side up. Pour over melted butter or margarine; dust with salt, pepper, and Ac'cent.
2. Bake or broil in a preheated broiler until the fish is tender—about 20 minutes.
3. Pipe duchesse potato around the edge, using a pastry bag and tube, or border with spoonfuls of the potato.
4. Brush with beaten egg and brown. Pour a little melted butter over the fish. Surround the fish and garnish the plank with the desired vegetables. Peas, string beans, halved broiled tomatoes, carrots, broccoli or asparagus are suitable. Decorate further with lemon slices.

If you do not own a plank, prepare on a fireproof glass or pottery platter or an aluminum sizzling platter.

Planking Frozen Fish: Defrost before cooking. Allow 4 hours in the refrigerator, 2 hours at room temperature. And don't let it stand out of the refrigerator after defrosting.

All measurements are level

FILLETS OF FLOUNDER, PERCH OR WHITEFISH IN MILK
(Serves 2 to 3)

¾ *pound fillets of fish*	1 *tablespoon flour*
¼ *teaspoon salt*	1 *cup milk*
Few grains pepper	¼ *cup water*
1 *tablespoon butter or margarine*	

1. Dust the fish with salt, pepper and flour.

2. Place on an oiled small baking platter.

3. Pour over the milk and water; dot with the butter; and bake in a moderately hot oven (350–375 degrees, F.), until the fish is flaky and tender or about 25 minutes.

4. Serve in the baking dish. Perfect with baked or whipped parslied white potato.

SMELTS
(Serves 2 to 3)

Buy 1 pound for two people.

Smelts may be broiled, fried, baked, or poached in equal parts of dry sauterne and water. Serve with lemon wedges, cress, or cucumbers in soured cream.

HALIBUT CREOLE
(Serves 2 to 3)

1 *pound halibut sliced thin*	*Paprika*
	Vegetable or bacon fat
Fine crumbs	1 *sweet seeded green pepper minced*
Salt, Ac'cent	
Pepper	1 *medium-sized tomato*

1. Place the fish in an oiled pan; dust with crumbs and seasonings; dot with the fat and sprinkle with the green pepper.

2. Cut the tomato in 4 slices; place on the fish. Dot with butter.

3. Bake 18 minutes or until tender in a moderately hot oven (375–400 degrees, F.). Add 2 tablespoons hot water or tomato juice if the fish cooks too fast on the bottom.

BAKED STUFFED FISH
(Serves 2 to 3)

1 (1½ to 2-pound) fish   *Salt and pepper*
  Any desired stuffing   *Juice ½ lemon (optional)*

1. Dust the fish inside and out with salt and pepper.

2. Place a piece of parchment paper or double waxed paper in a baking pan or dish into which the fish will fit. The edge of the paper should stand up the height of the pan at each end. Or use aluminum foil in the same way.

3. Oil this and lay the fish on it. Fill lightly with the stuffing, making it ½ inch thick, and smooth at the edge. Do not bother to sew it up. Too much to do to waste time in fish embroidery.

4. Dot with butter or margarine, or place narrow strips of bacon or salt pork on top. Place in a moderately hot oven. Bake at 350–375 degrees, F., until the fish begins to turn color. Then baste with liquid from cooked or canned vegetables, or equal parts of dry white wine and water. Bake about 30 minutes in all. Baste 3 times, adding lemon.

5. When done lift out by means of the paper ends; and slide the fish onto a hot platter. Serve with fish gravy. Garnish with cress, parsley, chicory, sliced tomatoes, or tomato-dill pickles.

FISH GRAVY
(*Serves 2*)

1 tablespoon butter or margarine
1½ tablespoons flour
½ cup fish-stock strained

½ cup water
1 teaspoon minced parsley
½ tablespoon minced scallions

1 egg yolk

1.   Melt the butter; add the flour; gradually stir in the fish liquid drained from baking pan, or use the liquid in which fish has been poached or boiled. Add water; boil two minutes. Cook and stir until boiling.

2.   Add remaining ingredients, beating the egg yolk with 1 tablespoon water, or dry white wine.

3.   Stir rapidly into the fish gravy. Serve at once.

FISH STOCK
(*1 quart*)

1 quart water
Head, skin and bones
from 2 pound fresh fish
1 tablespoon minced onion

1 small carrot minced
Bit of bayleaf
1¼ teaspoons salt
¼ teaspoon pepper

2 teaspoons celery salt

1.   Add the water to the fish head, bones and skin, with the onion, carrot and seasonings. Simmer gently until the fish drops from the bones, about 25 minutes. Then strain.

2.   From the residue pick out the bits of fish and return them to the liquid to use if desired as a basis for fish chowder, fish bisque, or a fish and vegetable soup.

STUFFED FISH STEAKS OR FILLETS
(*Serves 2 to 3*)

¾ pound thin halibut or swordfish steak, fillets of flounder or white fish
Tomato stuffing (*page 130*)   Salt and pepper

1.   Cut the fish steak in half, place ½ in a small oiled baking pan and dust with salt and pepper. Spread the stuffing on this.

2.   Put the other piece of fish steak on top of this; dust with salt and pepper and dot with a little butter, bits of salt pork or bacon or fat cut from boiled ham.

3.   Bake 30 minutes in a moderately hot oven (350–375 degrees, F.), basting occasionally with a little boiling water containing 1 tablespoon butter or margarine.

4.   Serve with tomato or Spanish sauce (pages 173, 174).

BROOK AND RAINBOW TROUT
To Fry Trout is "Desecration"

Broil and serve with maitre d'hotel butter (page 170), or poach (page 104).

BROOK TROUT WHITE MOUNTAIN STYLE

1.   Dress the fish but leave on the heads. Dust with salt, pepper and flour mixed.

2.   Place in a well-buttered baking dish. Pour in heated light cream to nearly cover. Dot with a little butter.

3.   Bake tender in a moderate oven (350–375 degrees, F.). Allow 25 to 30 minutes for 1-pound trout.

4.   Serve from the baking dish.

FISH LOAF
(Serves 2 to 3)

1½ cups flaked, cooked halibut, white fish, haddock or cod, or ½ pound canned fish flakes, salmon or tuna fish

½ cup milk
½ cup soft white bread crumbs
⅓ teaspoon salt, Ac'cent
Few grains paprika
Grated rind ⅛ lemon

1 *egg*

1. Remove skin and bones and flake the fish; heat the milk, add the crumbs, and when pasty stir into the fish. Add the seasonings.

2. Separate the egg; add the egg yolk to the mixture; beat the egg white, and fold it in.

3. Transfer to a very small, well-oiled oblong pan. Set this in a larger pan, surround with hot water, and bake 30 to 35 minutes in a moderately hot oven (375–400 degrees, F.).

4. Serve hot or cold with sliced lemon and cole slaw, or cucumbers in soured cream.

FROG'S LEGS SAUTÉ

(Serves two twice)

1 *carton frozen frog's legs*	1 *cup soured cream*
2 *tablespoons dry sherry*	2 *tablespoons flour*
(optional)	*Butter*
Salt and pepper	*Sherry-cream sauce or*
Ac'cent	*Spanish sauce*

1. Defrost the number of pairs of frog's legs to be used. Allow at least 3 pairs per person. Put the carton containing the remainder back into the freezing chamber to use in a day or so, or cook the whole batch, and reheat any left over.

2. Pour over the sherry before defrosting. Turn the frog's legs 2 or 3 times to absorb the flavor. Then drain.

3. Season with salt and pepper, roll in the soured cream, then the flour.

4. Sauté slowly in plenty of butter. Do not let them burn. They should be golden brown in color like fried chicken.

5. Serve plain or with sherry cream sauce or Spanish sauce (pages 172, 174).

PANNED OYSTERS
(Serves 2 to 3)

1½ *tablespoons butter*   *Salt and pepper*
.12 *oysters fresh or quick*   ⅛ *teaspoon mixed herbs*
   frozen   *Buttered toast*

1. Melt the butter in a small frying pan. (Shining stainless steel if you have one.)

2. Add the oysters and seasonings; cook gently until the edges ruffle, about 5 minutes.

3. Serve at the table from the frying pan on toast made at the table. Pour the juice over the toast.

BROILED SCALLOPS
(Serves 2 to 3)

½ *pint scallops*   ⅛ *teaspoon pepper*
 1 *egg*   ½ *cup fine dry bread*
½ *teaspoon salt*   *crumbs*
                    Butter

1. Wash and drain the scallops on absorbent paper.

2. Beat the egg; add the seasonings. Coat the scallops with this.

3. Cover with the crumbs.

4. Place in a well-buttered or margarined pan. Dot with butter or margarine.

5. Put in a preheated broiler; cook at moderate heat 7 minutes if small, 10 minutes if large. Turn once.

6. Serve with Spanish or sauce tartare (pages 174, 176).

Broiled Quick Frozen Scallops: Defrost before cooking.
Broiled Oysters: Cook as directed for broiled scallops.

FRIED OYSTERS
Fresh or Canned

Prepare oysters as directed for preparing scallops for

broiling. Sauté gently in butter. Turn once. Serve on buttered toast, with horse-radish cocktail sauce and a topping of minced raw celery if desired

CLAMS SAUTÉ ON TOAST
(Serves 2)

½ *pint little neck clams* 1 *tablespoon flour*
2 *tablespoons butter* *Dash pepper*
Salt if needed *Butter*
½ *teaspoon Worcestershire* *Buttered toast*
sauce

1. Remove necks from the clams.

2. Wash clams and cut in halves. Add Worcestershire.

3. Roll in the flour, season and fry in the butter about 5 minutes.

4. Serve on toast, with catsup or chili sauce, cole slaw or a tossed green salad.

TO COOK FRESH OR QUICK FROZEN SHRIMP

1. Wash and place shrimp in a kettle; pour in water to the depth of 1 inch. Add ½ teaspoon salt, and 1 teaspoon plain or tarragon vinegar. Use canned clams if desired.

2. Cover, bring to boiling point, and simmer 15 minutes.

3. Drain, cool, peel off the shell and remove the sand vein (the dark line found on the outer edge of the shrimp). Then rinse with cold water.

Save the cooking liquid to use as the basis for a sauce, a soup, or to ice and serve with an equal amount of tomato juice as a cocktail.

SHRIMP FRIED WITH RICE
(Serves 2 to 3)

1 *pound cooked shrimp or*   ¼ *cup chopped celery*
  1 *(5-oz.) can shrimp*   1½ *cups cooked rice (white,*
1 *medium-sized   onion*   *brown or wild)*
  chopped   *Salt and pepper*
1 *green pepper chopped*   *Paprika*
                2 *tablespoons butter*

1.   Combine the shrimp, onion, green pepper, celery and cooked rice.

2.   Add salt, pepper, paprika, and a very little curry if desired.

3.   Melt the butter in a frying pan; slowly fry the shrimp and rice mixture in it, for about 10 minutes. Serve very hot, with or without herb mustard or chutney sauce.

CHINESE FRIED SHRIMP
(Serves 2 to 3)

1 *pound raw fresh or defrosted*   3 *tablespoons flour*
  quick-frozen shrimp   1½ *tablespoons   water*
1 *egg*   ½ *teaspoon   salt*
            Vegetable fat for frying

1.   Peel the shells from the shrimp, but leave on the tails.

2.   Make a slit along the back with a sharp knife, and remove the dark vein. Rinse with cold water and pat dry on paper towels.

3.   Beat the egg slightly with the flour, water and salt, to make a batter.

4.   Put enough fat in a heavy frying pan to barely cover the bottom, and heat. Do not allow it to smoke.

5.   Then, with the tail as a handle, dip each shrimp into the batter. Fry on both sides until golden brown, about 3 minutes.

6. Serve plain, or with heated canned or quick-frozen chop suey, flaky rice and soy sauce.

TO COOK QUICK-FROZEN RAW LOBSTER TAILS

Boiled Lobster Tails: Do not defrost. Place in a deep saucepan with boiling water to the depth of 1 inch. Add ½ tablespoon lemon juice. Cover, and slow boil 15 minutes, or until the shells turn red.

Broiled Lobster Tails: Defrost. Cut out the top shell. Place the tails in a shallow thick-buttered pan. Dot the top of each with 1 tablespoon butter. Place in a preheated broiler. Broil 3 inches from the heat until the shell turns red, and the top is brown and sizzling. Serve with melted butter or maitre d'hotel sauce; accompany by heated potato chips and cress, or a tossed green salad.

SAVORY CANNED SALMON
(Serves 2 to 3)

½ pound can salmon steak
1 onion diced (optional)

1 tablespoon minced parsley, fresh dill or tarragon (optional)

Wedges of lemon

1. The salmon should be well chilled. Add onion. Turn into a deep dish, liquid and all. Sprinkle with the minced herb and garnish with lemon wedges.

2. To get plenty of vitamin D, sop up the liquid with bread or rolls, and chew up the bones for calcium.

CREAMED TUNA FISH
(Serves 2 to 3)

½ pound can tuna fish
1 tablespoon mayonnaise (optional)

1 cup white sauce
1 tablespoon minced parsley

1. Do not mince the tuna fish. Flake it in chunks.

2. Add the mayonnaise to the sauce. Heat the tuna in it. Sprinkle with the parsley. Accompany with whipped or baked potato, or rice.

3. Cook and serve in a pottery utensil. Keeps hot and saves dishwashing.

Creamed Salmon: Follow the recipe for creamed tuna fish substituting canned salmon.

Creamed Crab meat: Follow the recipe for creamed tuna fish using canned or quick-frozen crab meat; add 1 tablespoon sherry and 6 sliced stuffed olives.

TUNA SOUFFLÉ
(Serves 2 to 3)

1 tablespoon butter	¾ cup flaked canned tuna fish
1 tablespoon flour	
⅛ teaspoon dry mustard	3 tablespoons soft bread crumbs
¼ teaspoon salt	
Few grains pepper	½ teaspoon baking powder
⅓ cup milk	1 egg yolk
2 egg whites	

1. Melt the butter; stir in flour and seasonings. Gradually add the milk.

2. Add the tuna, crumbs and baking powder; then the egg yolk. Fold in the egg whites, whipped stiff.

3. Transfer to oiled shirred egg dishes; and bake 15 minutes in a moderate oven (375 degrees, F.).

Salmon Soufflé: Follow the preceding recipe substituting salmon.

Fish Oddments Soufflé: Use oddments of any kind of fish following the recipe for tuna soufflé. Add 1 tablespoon minced parsley or a few drops of tarragon vinegar.

CRAB MEAT AU GRATIN
(*Serves 2 to 3*)

½ *pound can or defrosted*   1 *teaspoon lemon juice*
  frozen crab meat   ¼ *cup fine dry crumbs*
 1 *cup rich white sauce*   ¼ *cup grated mild cheese*

1. Remove the shell, and combine the crab meat, sauce and lemon juice.

2. Transfer to a shallow oiled baking dish, or 2 individual baking dishes.

3. Cover with the crumbs and cheese; bake 20 minutes, or until brown in a moderate oven (375 degrees, F.).

Crab meat in Shells: Make the sauce with cream; add 1 tablespoon of dry sherry and bake individually in shells. This is enough to fill 6 small shells.

LOBSTER AND MACARONI AU GRATIN
(*Serves 3 to 4*)

1 (½ *pound*) *can lobster*   3 *tablespoons fine dry bread*
3 *tablespoons dry sherry*   *crumbs*
1 *can macaroni and cheese*   2 *tablespoons melted butter*

1. Dice the lobster and add the sherry.

2. Arrange in layers with the macaroni in individual baking dishes; make the first and last layers of the macaroni.

3. Cover with the crumbs moistened with the butter; bake about 25 minutes, or until bubbling, in a moderate oven (375 degrees, F.).

SALT CODFISH CAKES
(*Serves 2 to 3*)

½ *cup shredded salt cod-*   ½ *tablespoon milk or*
  fish   *cream*
 1 *cup seasoned hot*   ½ *teaspoon minced parsley*
   mashed potato   *Fine dry bread crumbs*
 1 *egg*

1. Cover the codfish with boiling water; let stand 10 minutes.

2. Drain, and combine with the potato; beat, and add the egg, milk and parsley.

3. Shape into flat cakes containing 2 tablespoonfuls each; roll in the crumbs.

4. Pan fry in vegetable oil or fat, using enough to barely cover the bottom of the frying pan.

5. Drain on paper towels. Serve with catsup; or accompany with creamed eggs or oysters; or with crisp bacon or poached eggs or both.

Codfish Ball Picks: Chill the mixture for codfish cakes and turn onto a piece of waxed paper, sprinkled with 1 tablespoon flour. Dust mixture with a little flour. Pat to ½-inch thickness; cut into rounds with a very small biscuit cutter. Finish as directed.

Salt Codfish Cakes (Quick-frozen or canned): If quick-frozen, defrost before using. Follow the manufacturer's directions. An egg yolk, minced parsley and a dash of onion salt improves the flavor.

KIPPERS
(*Serves 2*)

Buy a pair of kippers (they come 2 to a package). Place in a buttered pan; brush with butter and broil slowly until well heated. Serve with fried onions or lyonnaise potatoes—that is, potatoes fried with onion.

SMOKED SALMON IN CREAM
(*Serves 2*)

¼ *pound sliced smoked salmon*	¾ *cup light cream or top milk*
½ *tablespoon flour*	½ *tablespoon minced parsley*

1. Dust the salmon with the flour. Arrange in a buttered baking dish.

2. Pour in the cream; cover and simmer or bake until the cream bubbles. Sprinkle with parsley.

3. Serve with hot toast, popovers, or toasted rolls. Or with scrambled eggs.

SALT MACKEREL IN MILK
(*Serves 2 to 3*)

1 *small salt mackerel*
2 *tablespoons flour*
¼ *teaspoon pepper*
1¼ *cups heated milk*

1 *tablespoon butter or margarine*
Quick baked white potatoes

1. Cover the mackerel with cold water; soak several hours or overnight to remove excess salt. Rinse with cold water.

2. Place mackerel in a buttered baking dish. Dust with the flour and pepper; add the milk. Dot with the butter.

3. Bake until the fish flakes, 25 to 30 minutes, in a moderate oven (375 degrees, F.). Serve with the baked potatoes.

Finan Haddie in Milk: Substitute ¾ pound finan haddie for the mackerel in the preceding recipe, but soak the fish only 1 hour. Complete as directed.

PANNED SARDINES
(*Serves 2 to 3*)

1 *small can sardines*
Half slices of lemon
Strips of toast

1. Heat the sardines in the oil from the can.

2. Arrange each one on a strip of toast; garnish with lemon.

For Gourmet and Gourmette

FILET OF SOLE SAUTÉ

¾ *pound filet of sole*   *Salt and pepper*
½ *cup soured cream*   ½ *cup minced hazel nuts*
                Tarragon Butter Balls

1.   Brush the sole with the soured cream. Dust with salt and pepper; roll in the hazel nuts.
2.   Sauté slowly in butter.
3.   Serve with balls of tarragon butter, and braised celery or finnochio.

For Tarragon Butter Balls: Cream 2 tablespoons butter with 1 teaspoon minced, crushed fresh, or scalded, drained and dried tarragon leaves. Chill and form into balls with butter paddles.

CHAPTER IX

Meat, Poultry and Game

THE QUANTITY OF MEAT TO BUY FOR TWO DIFFERS WITH the various kinds and the way it is to be cooked. The amount needed by the average person is a minimum of ¼ of a pound to a meal. This means all meat, not part bone and waste.

Here is a guide in buying meats and poultry for two persons for one meal:

Quantities of Meats for Two

½ to ¾ pound chopped meat—beef, pork, veal or lamb.
¾ to 1 pound sirloin, round, flank or chuck steak.
2 filets mignons, cut 1 inch thick.
½ to ¾ pound veal cutlet.
½ to ¾ pound fresh pork steak.
½ to ¾ pound lamb steak.
4 loin or rib lamb chops, or 2 English mutton chops.
½ to ¾ pound liver.
1 lamb or calf's heart.
6 turkey hearts.
1 pair sweet breads.
6 lamb kidneys.
2 veal kidneys.
2 small lamb's tongues or 1 large one.

1 (1½ to 2 pound) broiling or frying chicken.
1 duckling.
  For two meals buy—
1½ pounds beef, lamb or veal for stew.
1½ to 2 pounds chuck or round steak for pot roast.
2 pounds rack of lamb (for a roast).
2 pounds fresh loin of pork (for a roast).
1 to 1½ pounds thick sirloin steak (for a roast).
1 fryer rabbit.
1 (3 pound) roasting chicken.
1 (3 pound) duck.
½ pound bacon—enough for two breakfasts, or for 4
   breakfasts if served with eggs, French toast, etc.
½ pound cooked ham.
¾ to 1 pound sliced raw ham.
1 pound sausages—one meal and a little over.
1 pound sausage meat—two meals.
1 can luncheon meat.

Selecting Meat

Beef: Should feel elastic to the touch, with the lean
portion quite a bright red with traceries of fat. The sections of fat should be firm and white.

Lamb and Mutton: Should have fat that is hard and
white, with flesh of a dark red color.

Veal: Should be firm to the touch, the fat white and
the lean rather pink.

Pork: The lean is slightly pink, the fat white and softer
than that of beef or lamb.

Poultry: Should be firm and plump, quite free from pin
feathers and with a clean fresh smell.

Better find a reliable meat man, and if you do not know
how to choose meat, be frank and tell him so. Ask his ad-
vice. He will tell you why the cut is good, and soon you
will learn from him how to select meat.

Ways of Cooking Meat

There are 10 fundamental ways to cook meat which may be defined as follows:

Broiling: Cooking by direct heat, over a bed of glowing coals, wood embers or charcoal, or by exposure to direct gas or electric heat in the preheated broiling compartment of a range, or in an electric broiler. Used for meat, fish and certain vegetables.

Pan Broiling: Cooking thin tender slightly fat cuts of meat in a preheated heavy frying pan. Do not add any fat.

Roasting: Cooking meat by dry indirect heat in the oven. The oven of any type range may be used, or use a portable oven or electric roaster.

Pot Roasting: Simmering prebrowned meat, in a heavy covered utensil with a small amount of liquid; enough to cover the bottom of the pan to the depth of one inch.

Braising: Simmering meat on a bed of vegetables in a little meatstock for a long time in a covered ceramic or other thick utensil or Dutch oven.

Boiling: Cooking meat in water or stock to half or nearly cover, starting with a galloping boil; put on the lid and reduce the heat to simmering point for the required length of time.

Stewing: Simmering meat cut into serving portions or bite-size pieces, with or without vegetables, in liquid to cover, to be served with the meat.

Fricasseeing: A combination of boiling and stewing.

Frying: Cooking by exposure to hot fat.

Pressure Cooking: Cooking in live steam in a pressure cooker. See the book, PRESSURE COOKING, by Ida Bailey Allen.

Preparing Meat for Cooking

Season all meat with as much monosodium glutamate (Ac'cent) as salt for finer flavor.

Trim off excess fat. Wipe the meat all over with a damp paper towel or small clean cloth. Season with salt and pepper either before or after cooking.

If the meat is to be first browned or seared, vegetable fat or savory fat may be used.

Savory Fat: This is the fat drained from bacon, sausage or ham while cooking. It should not be burned.

Basting Liquid: Use hot water, liquid drained from cooking vegetables, tomato or fruit juice, or wine as designated, heated with 1 tablespoon butter or margarine to ¼ cup.

Broiling: Suited to tender meats such as porterhouse and sirloin steaks, lamb chops, thin loin veal chops, young poultry, and ham, sliced thin. The broiler should be preheated, then rubbed with fat, the meat put in, and seared or browned at once. Turn immediately before the juices on the under side begin to drip out. If turned every 2 or 3 minutes the juices will run back and forth in the meat instead of being wasted. Use cooking tongs to do this, as a fork pierces the meat and causes juices to be lost. If a gas or electric range is used, a pan containing a very little hot water should be put under the broiling meat to catch the drippings which can be used for pan gravy.

Broiling time: This depends upon the thickness of the meat.

Chops or steaks cut 1 inch thick .   *7 to 8 minutes*
Chicken .   .   .   .   *20 to 30 minutes*
Fresh or smoked ham—cut ½ inch
   thick .   .   .   .   *15 minutes*

Pan broiling: Adopted when a kerosene stove is used, or when a regular broiler is not available. To pan broil, heat a heavy frying pan smoking hot, but do not add any fat. Put in the meat; turn at once to sear the other side; continue to turn occasionally with cooking tongs until done, allowing the same time as for broiling. Salt when done.

Frying: There are two methods of frying meats—pan frying and deep fat frying. The latter is too complicated to use often in cooking for two. (See French Fried Potatoes, page 198).

To pan fry: Used for plain tender meat, as steaks and chops; heat a little fat in a heavy frying pan and slowly fry the seasoned meat in it. Turn as soon as the meat begins to brown. Then fry, first on one side, then on the other. Allow 10 minutes for meat cut from ½ to an inch thick.

To pan fry breaded meat such as pork chops or veal chops: Dust the meat with salt and pepper, then with flour. Dip in a slightly beaten egg diluted with ¼ cup milk; cover with fine dried bread crumbs. Put enough vegetable oil in a heavy frying pan to cover the bottom. Heat and put in the meat. Fry brown, first on one side then on the other. Allow about 10 minutes for meat cut a scant ½ inch thick. Add more fat if the meat begins to stick to the pan.

Sautéing: Same as pan frying. Also used with a little more fat in frying fish and vegetables.

Roasting

There are two methods of cooking a roast—known as the Quick Searing method, and the Constant Temperature method. If you like a well-browned crisp surface and wish to save time, choose Quick Searing. I prefer and recommend this method. If you do not care for a crisp surface, but prefer a roast uniformly done throughout, and time is of no consequence, choose the Constant Temperature method.

Quick Searing Roasting: Place a wire rack or trivet in the roasting pan and put the meat on it fat side up. Start with a very hot oven, 450 degrees, F., for the first

15 minutes to sear the meat. Then reduce the heat to 350 degrees, F. Instead of drying up and becoming tough and unsavory, the meat cooks gradually and will be tender. No matter what kind of roast is being prepared, it should be dusted with salt, pepper and flour after placing in the pan. Some of the flour should be allowed to fall upon the bottom of the pan so it will blend with the drippings and later help to thicken the gravy. While roasting, baste the meat occasionally with ¼ cup hot water or other specified liquid in which a tablespoon of fat has been melted.

The time allowed for quick searing roasting depends upon the meat being prepared.

Beef (rare)	*20 minutes to the pound.*
Beef (medium) . . .	*25 minutes to the pound.*
Beef (well done) . . .	*30 minutes to the pound.*
Lamb	*25 minutes to the pound.*
Veal	*25 minutes to the pound.*
Pork	*30 minutes to the pound.*
Chicken, Duck and	
Turkey	*25 minutes to the pound.*

"Constant Temperature Roasting"

The exact length of time to be allowed for constant temperature roasting, depends on the weight of the cut, and whether or not it is solid meat, or contains bone. With heavy cuts the timing per pound becomes shorter. And it takes a little less time to roast meats containing bone, which is a conductor of heat. The following procedures and timings cover solid, or boned and rolled meats, up to 4 pounds, as well as poultry.

Place a wire rack or trivet in the roasting pan, and put the meat on it fat side up, so the fat will automatically baste the meat. Brush the meat with a good liquid gravy seasoning to improve flavor and color. Dust with salt and pepper. Preheat the oven to 350 degrees, F. and keep it at that temperature. Put in the meat and roast as follows:

Beef (rare) . . . . *38 minutes to the pound.*
Beef (medium) . . . *45 minutes to the pound.*
Beef (well done) . . . *50 minutes to the pound.*
Lamb (average) . . . *40 minutes to the pound.*
Veal (average) . . . *40 minutes to the pound.*
Pork (average) . . . *45 minutes to the pound.*
Chicken and Duck
   (small) . . . . . *30 minutes to the pound.*
   for a four pound bird . *36 minutes to the pound.*
Turkey—(7 to 10 pounds) *30 minutes to the pound.*
Larger birds . . . . *20 minutes to the pound.*

If the cut of meat or the bird being roasted is large, the exact degree of doneness may be tested with a meat thermometer. However, this is not practical for small cuts. If not sure use the time-honored method—cut off a small piece and find out.

Using a Meat Thermometer

A meat thermometer is inserted before the meat is put in the oven to roast and left there until it is cooked. Stick in a sharp pointed skewer to make an incision and in this carefully insert the thermometer. The black pointed end should be in the center of the meat. Do not let it contact bone or gristle. When the black liquid in the thermometer tube reaches the desired temperature the meat or poultry will be done.

Boiling Meat: The water should half or barely cover the meat, and should be boiling hard when the meat is plunged in. Put on the lid and place over a low heat so the water will merely simmer; that is, bubble only around the edges of the utensil. Salt when half done. Do not use salt in boiling smoked meats.

The time of cookery depends upon the kind of meat. A 2-pound piece of round of beef, breast of mutton, smoked pork tenderloin, or a small chicken should cook tender in 1½ to 2 hours, or less. Vegetables for the meal may be boiled with the meat.

The liquid from the meat should be used in a soup. Remove the fat from the top of the liquid after it cools, and use for frying.

All measurements are level
Good Gravy

Good gravy is never lumpy or greasy; is pleasantly flavored and has a distinct meaty taste. Brown gravy should be dark golden brown in color; if not, add a little bottled gravy seasoning, according to the manufacturer's directions. There are 2 kinds of gravy, unthickened pan gravy, and thickened gravy, which resembles brown sauce.

Pan gravy: Make from drippings remaining in the pan after meats have been roasted, broiled or pan broiled. To make, add 1 tablespoon butter or margarine and 2 or 3 tablespoons boiling water to 2 tablespoons drippings.

Thickened gravy: Use the drippings of broiled, pan-broiled or roasted meat. To make this for two, pour off all but 1 tablespoon drippings; scrape up all the brown particles and put the measured drippings in a small sauce pan. Blend in 1½ tablespoons flour; stir in 1 cup boiling water or use soup stock or liquid from canned or cooked vegetables. Season with salt and pepper and a little meat condiment sauce or gravy seasoning. Cook and stir constantly until the gravy boils over. If desired, a larger quantity of gravy may be made. It will keep several days in the refrigerator.

Substitute gravy: If all the gravy has been used the first time the meat is served, and you wish to reheat the oddments of meat in gravy, make a sauce by blending a scant tablespoon butter and 1½ tablespoons flour; stir into this 1¼ cups boiling stock of any kind; or use boiling water and 1 teaspoon beef extract. Cook and stir for 3 minutes. Add ½ teaspoon gravy seasoning.

Tomato gravy: Pour from the pan all but 2 tablespoons of the drippings and transfer them to a small sauce pan. Sprinkle in 1½ tablespoons flour; stir until slightly browned. Stir in ½ cup water and 1 cup sifted canned tomato or tomato juice. Simmer 3 minutes; season highly with salt and pepper and a little thyme.

Giblet gravy: Make thickened chicken or turkey gravy and add the cooked giblets chopped fine.

Stuffings

Stuffings are just as good and as useful for the family of 2 as for a houseful of people. But how can they be used with small quantities of meat? Try them in roast halved broilers, ducklings or in squab; stuffed into slit thick lamb or pork chops, or slit calves' or turkey hearts. Or you don't even have to bother to stuff the meat; instead spoon the stuffing into a baking dish, pop it into the oven with the meat, and for flavor pour over some of the meat drippings as it bakes. Or you can pat the stuffing into one corner of the roasting pan, which saves oven room and washing a dish.

I'm all for using good packaged stuffings for 2, unless there is an accumulation of bread to use up. But if a commercial stuffing is used, do something to individualize it. Add some fried onion, chopped mushrooms, green pepper, celery, or chopped nuts. Or moisten it with tomato juice or a bouillon cube dissolved in water. And be a bit extravagant by adding 2 or 3 tablespoons of butter or margarine.

SAVORY BREAD STUFFING
(Serves 2 to 3)

1½ *cups soft bread crumbs*   ½ *teaspoon poultry season-*
½ *teaspoon salt*   *ing*
¼ *teaspoon pepper*   1 *tablespoon melted*
1 *teaspoon minced onion*   *butter or margarine*
     ½ *cup hot water, stock or vegetable liquid to moisten*

Combine the ingredients in the order given. Fry the stuffing a few minutes in 1 tablespoon fat.

Herb Stuffing: Omit poultry seasoning; add 1 teaspoon ready-mixed dried herbs.

Sausage Stuffing: Add 2 ounces broken up slightly fried sausage meat to the ingredients for bread stuffing.

Stuffing for Roast Chicken or Duck: Double the recipe for Savory Bread Stuffing.

Stuffing for a Small Turkey: Use 4 times the recipe for Savory Bread Stuffing.

Beef for Two

All measurements are level

ROAST BEEF
(Serves 2 to 3)

1 *to* 1½ *pounds thick sir-*   *Flour*
   loin steak   *Salt and pepper*
1 *small slice salt pork*

1.   Place the steak in an oiled baking pan just large enough to hold it. Dust with salt, pepper and flour; lay thin strips of the salt pork over the top.

2.   Bake about 30 minutes in a moderate oven (375 degrees F.). Small halved white potatoes may be baked in the same pan. Baste occasionally with 2 tablespoons hot water in which 1 tablespoon butter has been melted.

3. Remove the meat and make pan gravy or thickened gravy (page 128).

4. To serve, slice thin crosswise; arrange overlapping on the platter, the potatoes on each end. If pan gravy is made, pour it over, but pass brown gravy.

Instead of potatoes serve with crisp waffles for a change.

POT ROAST OF BEEF WITH VEGETABLES
(Serves 2 to 3)

1 tablespoon savory fat	⅓ teaspoon thyme
1 small onion sliced	Flour
1 pound chuck or rump of beef, sliced 1 inch thick	6 small peeled carrots
	2 small peeled white turnips
Salt and pepper	

4 small peeled white potatoes

1. Melt the fat in a small heavy utensil and fry the onion in this.

2. Dust the meat with salt, pepper, thyme and flour; brown all over in the fat.

3. Add water to a little more than cover the bottom of the utensil; cover closely, simmer 45 minutes; turn the meat over once. Add the vegetables and simmer 30 minutes longer. Make gravy.

4. To serve cut meat in thin strips. Arrange in the center of a heated platter; pour over thickened gravy and surround with the vegetables. Garnish with parsley.

MINUTE STEAK
(Serves 2)

½ pound porterhouse, sirloin or tenderloin steak sliced thin, or use cubed steak	Butter or margarine
	Salt and pepper

1.   Slash the fat edge of the steak in 2 or 3 places so it will lie flat. Place the steak in a preheated broiler, and broil about 3 inches from the heat.

2.   Allow 5 minutes for rare steak, 7 minutes for well-done. Turn once as soon as browned.

3.   When done, dust with salt and pepper, place on a platter, dot with butter and keep warm until it melts.

4.   Serve the vegetables for the meal on the same platter.

Steak with Mushrooms: While the steak is broiling, open and drain a 4-ounce can of mushrooms. Sauté in butter, with a few grains nutmeg for seasoning. Spoon over and around the steak. Garnish with parsley.

STEAK CREOLE
(*Serves 2 to 3*)

½ *tablespoon savory fat*	1 *tablespoon flour*
¾ *pound round steak cut*	1 *small onion minced*
in half-inch strips	½ *seeded green pepper*
⅓ *teaspoon salt*	*shredded*
Few grains pepper	¾ *cup canned tomato*

Flaky boiled rice

1.   Melt the fat. Dust the steak with the salt, pepper, flour and brown in the fat with the onion.

2.   Add the green pepper and tomato; simmer 20 to 25 minutes.

3.   To serve, pile the rice in the center of a hot platter. Arrange the meat and gravy around this. Garnish with parsley. Pass grated cheese.

FILET MIGNON
(*Serves 2*)

2 *filets mignons 1 inch thick*	4 *buttered toast points*
1 *tablespoon butter*	*Maitre d'hotel butter*
Salt and pepper	*Parsley or cress*

1. Pan fry the *filets* for 7 minutes in the butter (page 125). Season with salt and pepper.

2. Spread with maitre d'hotel butter (page 170).

Serve garnished with buttered toast points, parsley and sautéed broiled mushrooms if desired.

Planked Filets Mignons: Arrange the pan-fried *filets mignons* on an oiled heated plank, or use individual planks. Edge the plank with fluffy spoonfuls of duchesse potatoes (page 197). Brush with beaten egg yolk and lightly brown in the grill. Top the *filets mignons* with maitre d'hotel butter. Arrange heated asparagus, or grilled halved tomatoes in the empty spaces. And tuck in a few sautéed mushrooms for that luxury touch.

Ways with Chopped Beef

You will notice this section is not headed ways with "hamburger." This is because hamburger as sold in many stores, is ground of a nondescript mixture of meats, not always fresh meats, and is loaded with fat—and sometimes water. In other words, hamburger is not a good buy. It is wasteful and often unsafe to eat. So get a thrifty cut of beef steak instead—flank, chuck or round—and watch the butcher put it through his chopping machine. For specially smooth texture for meat balls, ask him to put it through the chopper twice.

BEEF BURGERS
(Serves 2 to 3)

¾ *pound ground beef*	½ *teaspoon salt*
1 *teaspoon onion juice*	⅛ *teaspoon pepper*

1. Mix the seasonings with the beef; form into 4 or 5 thin, rather large round patties.

2. Sauté quickly on each side in fat; then cook more slowly for 7 minutes.

3. Put a little butter or margarine on each patty and let stand a moment to melt.

4. Serve on toast; toasted halved English muffins; or with fried onions, French fries or heated potato chips; or with grilled tomatoes and lyonnaise potatoes.

Wined Beef Burgers: Prepare beef burgers. Half sauté; then add 3 tablespoons dry red wine and finish cooking. Nice atop crisp waffles.

Planked Beef Burgers: Don't think for a moment that a fine steak or *filet mignon* is the only meat you can plank. Try planking wined beef burgers—by the same recipe too (page 133).

CHILI CON CARNE
(Enough for two meals)

1 *tablespoon savory fat*	½ *teaspoon salt*
½ *small peeled onion minced*	½ *teaspoon pepper*
	¾ *cup boiling water and a bouillon cube*
1 *section garlic*	
½ *pound chopped round steak*	1 *(No. 2) can kidney beans*
½ *tablespoon chili powder*	

1. Melt the fat in a frying pan; add the onion and garlic. Fry until beginning to turn yellow.

2. Add the meat, cook until browned. Add the seasonings and bouillon cube dissolved in the water.

3. Cover with a lid; simmer for 30 minutes; add the beans and simmer 15 minutes longer.

4. Serve in Mexican bowls lined with boiled rice. Or for a change, use piping hot canned chow mein noodles. Excellent.

INDIVIDUAL MEAT LOAVES
(Serves 2 to 3)

¼ *pound ground raw beef* ½ *teaspoon salt*
¼ *pound ground raw veal* ⅛ *teaspoon pepper*
¼ *pound ground raw pork* 1 *teaspoon scraped onion*
¼ *cup soft crumbs* ½ *tablespoon table mus-*
¼ *cup milk* *tard*
1 *egg*

1. Combine ingredients and pack into oiled muffin pans. Bake in a moderate oven (375 degrees, F.) for 25 minutes.

2. Unmold on toast.

3. Serve with mushroom or Spanish sauce.

To vary the flavor add any one of the following:

2 *teaspoons minced basil*
1 *teaspoon minced sage*
¼ *cup minced celery*
½ *minced seeded green pepper*

Or use half tomato catsup and half tomato juice instead of milk.

Lamb for Two

There are many ways to prepare lamb for two. Just one secret for deliciousness—cut off all excess fat before cooking.

STUFFED LAMB CHOPS
(Serves 2)

2 *boned loin lamb chops* 2 *long strips bacon*
4 *good-sized mushrooms* *Salt and pepper*
½ *tablespoon butter* *Duchesse or whipped po-*
2 *tablespoons soft bread* *tato*
  crumbs

1.   Split the chops on the side to form pockets.

2.   Peel and chop the mushrooms, cook 1 minute in the butter, add the crumbs and a little salt and pepper.

3.   Fill the pockets in the chops with this, then roll up tight; fit a strip of bacon around each, and fasten with toothpicks.

4.   Place in a baking pan; dust with salt and pepper, grill, or bake 15 minutes in a hot oven (400 degrees, F.).

5.   Cover the tops with duchesse or whipped potato, and continue to cook until this browns, about 5 minutes longer.

6.   Remove toothpicks. Serve the chops on a small hot platter, with buttered peas, asparagus, mixed vegetable or baked tomato halves. Mint jelly is good with this.

ROAST RACK OF LAMB
(*Two meals for 2*)

2 *pounds rack of lamb* (*bones cracked*)	1 *small peeled onion*
1 *teaspoon salt*	1½ *tablespoons flour*
⅛ *teaspoon pepper*	4 *medium-sized white or sweet potatoes*

1.   Cut off excess fat and place the lamb in a small roasting pan. Dust with salt and pepper. Slice the onion over the meat. Dust with the flour. Peel the potatoes and arrange around the lamb.

2.   Brown in a hot oven (425 degrees, F.) about 15 minutes.

3.   Reduce the heat to 350 degrees, F. Baste with 2 tablespoons hot water and roast until well done, about 40 minutes, basting again with 2 or 3 tablespoons of hot water. Turn the potatoes once, to brown both sides.

4.   Remove the lamb from the pan; pour off the excess fat, and make a thickened gravy (page 128). Or serve with mint sauce (page 176).

5. Serve the lamb and potatoes together on a platter. Pass the gravy or sauce.

CHOPPED LAMB STEAK
(Serves 2)

½ *pound minced raw lamb*
2 *tablespoons soft bread crumbs*
½ *teaspoon dried mint*

1 *tablespoon milk*
⅓ *teaspoon salt*
Few grains pepper
Few drops onion juice

1. Combine the ingredients in the order given and form into thin flat cakes.

2. Place on an oiled preheated broiler and broil 7 minutes, turning once. Dot with butter and reheat.

3. Serve on a platter with creamed potatoes; or with noodles in tomato sauce. Scallions for a nice garnish.

LAMB CHOP GRILL
(Serves 2)

2 *loin lamb chops*
2 *slices tomato*
2 *large mushroom caps*

Salt
Pepper
Butter or margarine

1. Order the chops cut 2 inches thick, boned and rolled, with a small sausage placed in the center of each and a piece of bacon wrapped around the outside.

2. Place in a preheated broiler and cook at moderate heat about 25 minutes; turn frequently so they will cook evenly.

3. About 5 minutes before the chops will be done, place a slice of tomato and a mushroom cap on top of each. Dust with salt and pepper, dot with butter or margarine and finish broiling.

4. Serve smartly arranged with sautéed potato or

whipped parslied potato on a small heated platter or individual planks.

BARBECUED LAMB RIBLETS
(*Serves 2*)

1 *pound lamb riblets*
  Barbecue sauce (*page*
  174)

1 *tablespoon butter or margarine*
  Barbecue sauce (*page* 0)

1. Ask the butcher to separate the riblets. Pour over the sauce and let stand a few hours to season.

2. Put in a baking pan; dot with butter or margarine; place in a hot oven (400 degrees, F.) for 15 minutes, then bake at 350 degrees, F. 20 minutes longer. Baste with barbecue sauce.

3. Serve with moist vegetables, such as whipped white or sweet potato, mixed vegetables or stewed tomato.

Veal for Variety

Plan to serve veal once a week. It's always appetizing and even thrifty. Cuts for two will cook tender quickly without drying up. Just two secrets—season well and use plenty of fat, as veal is very lean.

BRAISED VEAL CHOPS
(*Serves 2*)

½ *tablespoon butter or*
  bacon fat
1 *tablespoon minced*
  onion
2 *good-sized veal chops*
  Salt

Pepper
1 *tablespoon flour*
  Boiling water
½ *teaspoon beef extract*
½ *cup soured cream*

1. Melt the fat; add the onion and cook until softened.

2. Dust the chops with salt, pepper and flour; brown in the fat.

3. Add beef extract to enough boiling water to cover the bottom of the pan to the depth of about ¼ inch; put on the lid and simmer 30 minutes.

4. Add the soured cream and let stand until very hot.

5. Serve with flaky boiled potatoes rolled in melted butter and minced parsley or chives.

BAKED VEAL CUTLET
(Serves 2)

¾ *pound veal cutlet sliced*   ⅛ *teaspoon granulated*
    thin   *sugar*
    Salt and pepper   *Fine dry bread crumbs*

1 *egg*

1. Cut the veal in individual portions; dust with salt, pepper and the sugar; then roll the cutlets in crumbs.

2. Beat the egg slightly; add 1 tablespoon of water. Dip the veal in this; then roll in crumbs again.

3. Place in a pan well rubbed with vegetable fat; dot plentifully with more fat; bake 25 minutes in a hot oven (400 degrees, F.) or until tender and brown.

4. Accompany with chili sauce or tomato sauce. Or arrange on a heated platter with creamed potatoes or noodles, or spaghetti in tomato sauce with grated cheese.

Veal Cutlet Holstein: Top each portion of veal cutlet with a poached or fried egg; dust with minced parsley.

ITALIAN VEAL BALLS
(Serves 2 to 3)

½ *pound chopped raw veal*   ¼ *cup milk*
¼ *cup minced parsley*   *Butter, margarine or*
 1 *teaspoon garlic salt*   *olive oil*
⅛ *teaspoon pepper*   2 *tablespoons flour*
 1 *egg yolk*   1 *cup hot water*
½ *cup   fine   soft   bread*   ½ *teaspoon meat extract*
    crumbs

Spaghetti or noodles Italienne

1.　Thoroughly mix the veal, parsley, seasonings, egg yolk, crumbs and milk; let stand 15 minutes. Form into flattened balls, containing 1 tablespoonful each.

2.　Dust with flour; brown in the fat. Add water and meat extract; cover and simmer 25 minutes.

3.　Mix any remaining gravy with the spaghetti or noodles. Put in the center of a heated deep platter. Surround with the veal balls. Pass grated cheese, Parmesan preferred.

Fresh Pork for Two

Fresh pork is due for a meal or two each week. It is especially rich in B Complex vitamins. Just one caution: It must be thoroughly cooked. Slow and sure is the rule.

ROAST LOIN OF PORK PORTUGUESE
(Enough for two or more meals)

2 *pounds loin of pork*	1 *teaspoon cumin seed*
(bones cracked)	2 *sections garlic peeled and*
1½ *teaspoons salt*	*sliced*
⅛ *teaspoon pepper*	1 *cup dry red wine*

1.　Place the pork in a bowl; sprinkle with the seasonings, garlic and wine. Cover closely and refrigerate a few hours.

2.　To roast, drain and transfer to a pan; sprinkle with 1 tablespoon flour, and place in a hot oven (450 degrees, F.) for 15 minutes. Reduce the heat to 350 degrees, F. and bake until the pork is tender, about 1 hour longer. Baste with the drained wine.

3.　Serve with fluffy mashed potatoes, and a green vegetable arranged on the same platter. Make a gravy from the drippings.

ROAST SPARERIBS FOR TWO

1 *strip spareribs (cracked)*   1 *can hominy*
½ *teaspoon salt*   ½ *tablespoon minced on-*
½ *teaspoon dry sage*   *ion*
⅛ *teaspoon pepper*

1. Cut the spareribs in halves crosswise; dust with the salt, sage and pepper.

2. Season the hominy with the onion and a little salt and pepper. Pile it in an oiled baking dish, stand the spareribs up over this, one piece on each side; dust with flour.

3. Roast in a hot oven (450 degrees, F.). When the meat starts to brown, reduce the heat to 350 degrees, F. and bake 50 minutes.

4. Serve from the baking dish. Garnish with radishes or any crisp green.

BAKED PORK CHOPS

2 *large pork chops*   ¼ *teaspoon sage*
  Salt and pepper   1 *tablespoon flour*
    ½ *onion sliced thin*

1. Place the chops in a baking dish. Dust with the salt, pepper, sage and flour; lay the onion on top.

2. Place in a hot oven (450 degrees, F.) for 10 minutes. Cook at 350 degrees, F. 25 minutes longer. Baste with 3 tablespoons hot water or dry wine.

3. Small potatoes may be baked with the meat; if large, cut in halves or quarters.

4. Serve in the baking dish.

PORK STEAKS IN MILK
(Serves 2)

1 *teaspoon table mustard*   1 *tablespoon flour*
2 *small pork steaks*   1 *cup milk*
Salt and pepper   1 *teaspoon margarine*

1.   Spread the mustard on the steaks. Dust with the salt, pepper and flour.

2.   Put in a baking dish. Pour in the milk. Dot with the margarine; bake 35 minutes at 375 degrees, F.

Stews, Goulashes, Curries, and Meat Pies

Every country serves stewed meat in some form. There's Irish stew, Hungarian goulash, French ragout, English meat pie, Indian curry. And all of these are suited to the family of two.

The following recipes make enough for two meals; just refrigerate part to serve day after next. Cool before covering and storing in the refrigerator.

IRISH STEW
(Serves 2 twice)

1 *tablespoon butter*	1 *cup sliced carrots*
1 *peeled onion sliced*	8 *small peeled white pota-*
2 *pounds boned breast of*	*toes*
lamb	2 *tablespoons flour*
1 *teaspoon salt*	1 *cup canned or cooked*
⅛ *teaspoon pepper*	*peas (optional)*

Drop puffy dumplings (page 143)

1.   Melt the butter and brown the onion in it.

2.   Cut the meat bite-size; add to the butter and brown lightly. Barely cover with boiling water, using about 4 cupfuls. Add the salt and pepper; simmer until the meat is almost tender, about 1 hour. Then add the carrots, and the potatoes cut in quarters; cover and boil slowly 15 minutes longer. If much water has evaporated from the stew add a little more.

3.   Blend the flour with 2 tablespoons cold water, and add; stir until boiling hard. Then add the peas.

4. Drop dumplings by small teaspoonfuls into the stew. Cover closely and simmer 12 minutes. Serve in deep plates.

Veal Stew: Substitute breast of veal for lamb in the preceding recipe.

Beef Stew: Substitute 1 pound chuck of beef for the lamb in Irish stew. Add 4 small halved peeled onions with the vegetables.

CHICKEN STEW
(*Serves 2 to 3*)

1 (1½ pound) broiling chicken	½ cup diced celery
	1½ cups boiling water
⅓ teaspoon salt	½ cup peas
Few grains pepper	½ cup light cream
2 tablespoons flour	Herb-flavored dump-
2 tablespoons butter	lings (page 144)

Cook in a ceramic ware, pottery or aluminum utensil that can go to table.

1. Order the chicken dressed. Clean and disjoint it, dust with salt and pepper and roll in the flour. Fry lightly in the butter.

2. Add the celery and boiling water; cover and simmer until tender, about 1 hour. Then add the peas and cream.

3. Have the dumpling mixture ready. Drop by teaspoonfuls onto the stew. Cook as directed below.

4. Serve steaming hot in the same utensil.

DROP PUFFY DUMPLINGS
(*Serves 2 to 3*)

¾ cup all-purpose flour	¼ teaspoon salt
1 teaspoon baking pow-	½ tablespoon shortening
der	¼ cup cold water

1. Sift together the dry ingredients; chop in the shortening with a pastry blender.

2. When flaky stir in the water. Drop by small teaspoonfuls onto the stew. Cover and simmer 12 minutes longer.

Dumplings with Biscuit Mix: Mix according to directions on the package.

Herb-flavored Dumplings: Add ¼ teaspoon mixed dried herbs to the flour in puffy dumplings.

MEAT OR CHICKEN PIE
(*Serves 2 to 3*)

This can be made of any meat or chicken stew mixture. Even with canned stew if a little extra seasoning is added. Heat the stew. Transfer to one baking dish or two good-sized shallow baking dishes. Cover with piecrust, bringing it down well over the edge. Slash the top in three places with a sharp knife to let the steam escape. Brush lightly with milk and bake golden brown in a hot oven (400–425 degrees, F.). Frozen meat pies make a good light entrée.

INDIAN CURRY

The perfect way to prepare curry is to start with raw ingredients, and simmer a long time until the flavors completely blend. But this is not practical for a family of two. Instead make the curry sauce; add it to slightly browned bite-sized pieces of raw or cooked meat, cover and simmer to season. Allow an hour to cook raw meat curry, 20 minutes if the meat is already cooked.

Delicious curries for two can be made from the following:

Beef Curry: 1 pound diced chuck steak browned in butter, or use 1½ cups diced cooked beef.

Lamb Curry: 1 pound breast of lamb, boned, cut bite-size and browned in butter, or 1½ cups diced cooked lamb.

Veal Curry: 1 pound breast of veal, boned, cut bite-size and browned in butter, or 1½ cups diced cooked veal.

Chicken Curry: 1 small cleaned, disjointed broiling chicken, disjointed frozen chicken, or 1¼ cups diced cooked or canned chicken meat.

Lobster Curry: 2 diced cooked lobster tails, heated in the curry sauce.

Shrimp Curry: 1 pound cooked fresh or frozen shrimp, whole or halved and heated in the curry sauce.

INDIAN CURRY SAUCE
(*Serves 2 to 3*)

1 *tablespoon butter*	1 *tablespoon flour*
½ *medium-sized onion sliced*	¾ *cup canned tomatoes*
½ *medium-sized carrot sliced*	¾ *cup boiling water and a bouillon cube*
½ *tablespoon curry powder*	½ *small apple chopped*
	½ *tablespoon pickle relish*

1. Melt the butter; fry the onion and carrot in it till yellowed. Add the curry and fry a few seconds. Stir in the flour, then the tomatoes and water.

2. Add remaining ingredients and simmer 5 minutes.

If possible add 2 tablespoons grated raw or defrosted frozen coconut to this sauce—a touch de luxe.

Goulash

A goulash is the Hungarian counterpart of our familiar stew. Make it of beef, veal or chicken as you like. Hot it up with paprika. Serve it with flaky potatoes. A dish for high days and holidays, or to serve when the food money is low.

HUNGARIAN GOULASH
(*Enough for two meals*)

4 *medium-sized onions sliced*	1 *teaspoon salt*
	⅛ *teaspoon pepper*
¼ *cup butter, margarine or drippings*	1 *teaspoon paprika*
	1 *4-oz. can tomato purée*
1 *pound round or chuck steak in inch cubes*	*Boiling water*
	Paprika potatoes

1. Cook the onions slowly until yellowed in the fat. Then remove, and brown the meat in it.

2. Put back the onions; add the salt and pepper, paprika, tomato purée and an equal amount of boiling water; cover, and simmer until the meat is tender, about 2 hours.

3. Serve on a deep platter, with flaky boiled potatoes rolled in melted butter and dusted with paprika.

The "Innards"

Some of the most appetizing and epicurean of meat dishes for two may be made from liver, hearts, kidneys, etc. In other words, those "innards." They are thrifty—for they are all meat—and they cost comparatively little, but they are vitamin rich.

BAKED STUFFED HEART
(*Serves 2*)

1 *calf or lamb heart*	½ *teaspoon salt*
Herb stuffing	½ *teaspoon pepper*
3 *tablespoons cooking fat*	½ *cup boiling water or stock*
2 *tablespoons flour*	

1. Plunge the heart in and out of boiling water; drain and remove the connective tissue.

2. Make a deep gash and spread it open. Pack and heap with the stuffing.

3. Rub over with savory fat, sprinkle with the flour, dust with salt and pepper; put into a casserole.

4. Add the boiling water, cover, and bake in a moderate oven (350 degrees, F.) until tender—about 1 hour.

5. Serve with halved Idaho potatoes baked in the same oven, and a tossed bowl salad.

Braised Turkey Hearts: Allow 3 hearts per person. Prepare as described for baked heart with this exception: bake in tomato or Spanish sauce instead of water. Add 2 tablespoons of dry red wine. Serve on buttered toast.

How to Prepare Liver

Five kinds of liver may be purchased: calves', beef, lamb, pork or veal. All are equally nutritious if properly prepared. In any case, order it sliced thin.

Since liver lacks fat, it may be sautéed. If broiled, melted butter should be poured over before serving, unless the liver is served with bacon.

Calves' liver may be cooked without any preliminary treatment, as it is very tender.

To Prepare Beef, Pork or Lamb Liver: These come from mature animals, have a thick outer skin and tough tubes which should be removed. However, treated as follows, any of these livers will prove tender and appetizing.

Dip the sliced liver in and out of a bowl filled with boiling water. Then pull off the tough outside skin, and cut away the tubes with scissors. The boiling water removes any strong flavor, and loosens the outside skin so it can be peeled off.

Liver Saute: Slowly pan-fry the liver on both sides in melted butter or fat from previously cooked bacon. Allow

5 minutes. Dust with salt and pepper. Serve with steam-fried onions, grilled tomatoes or bacon.

Broiled Liver: Use calves' liver as is, or beef, pork or lamb liver prepared as directed. Brush the liver with melted butter or savory fat, season with salt and pepper, place on a preheated broiler, and broil 3 inches from the heat, first on one side, then the other. Allow 5 to 6 minutes for thin slices. Serve with melted butter containing minced parsley poured over, or with bacon or steam-fried onions (page 192).

BROILED LIVER PLATTER
(Serves 2)

½ *pound any kind liver,* ½ *cup sliced canned or*
   sliced thin   *fresh mushrooms*
   Salt   ½ *cup drained canned to-*
   Pepper   *matoes*
   Melted butter or bacon   2 *tablespoons bits of bacon*
   fat

1. Prepare the liver for cooking as directed.

2. Dust with salt and pepper; place on a preheated broiler. Pour over a little melted butter and broil 5 minutes; keep about 6 inches from the heat. Turn once so both sides will be cooked.

3. Cover with the mushrooms and tomatoes, making a thin layer. Dust with salt and pepper; place the bacon on top, and broil about 6 minutes longer.

4. Serve with parslied or whipped potato.

CHICKEN LIVERS ON TOAST
(Serves 2)

½ *pound chicken livers*   4 *slices bacon*
 1 *tablespoon flour*   2 *scallions cut up*
       Buttered toast

1.   Cut off any green edge; this is from the gall bladder and has a bitter taste. Rinse, drain and separate the livers. Cut in 2 pieces each and roll in the flour.

2.   Fry the bacon until crisp; pour off half the fat.

3.   Add the chicken livers and fry slowly until well-browned, about 4 minutes. Just before they are done add the scallions and cook 1 minute more.

4.   Serve on the toast. Garnish with the bacon.

GIBLETS

Giblets consist of the heart, gizzard and liver of poultry. To cook, remove the tubes from the heart, and the tough inside lining of the gizzard. Wash the giblets. Simmer the heart and gizzard in salted water to cover about 40 minutes. Then add the liver (which needs less cooking) and simmer 20 minutes. Chop and use in gravy, stuffing, scrambled or shirred eggs, or add to consommé with a little cooked rice, to make giblet soup.

SWEETBREADS

However cooked for final serving, sweetbreads need the following preliminary preparation to make them firm and appetizing:

Soak 30 minutes in cold water. Drain, cover with 1 quart boiling water, add ½ teaspoon salt and 1 tablespoon vinegar, and simmer 15 minutes. Drain, plunge into cold water, and when cool enough to handle, trim off the tubes and membranes and cut as indicated in the recipe.

Broiled Sweetbreads: Prepare as directed. Split lengthwise, brush with melted butter or margarine, dust with salt and pepper, place in a preheated broiler and broil 6 minutes. Serve on toast with melted butter containing minced parsley poured over. Or pour over mushroom sauce.

BRAINS

Precook the same as sweetbreads. Then broil, cut in dice and heat in tomato or à la king sauce, or scramble with eggs.

KIDNEYS EN BROCHETTE
(*Serves 2*)

6 *lamb kidneys*   2 *thick slices bacon cut in inch squares*

1. Remove all fat and soak the kidneys 15 minutes in cold salted water to remove the strong flavor. Cut out the white eyes. Split the kidneys lengthwise.

2. Slip a square of bacon on a long metal brochette or skewer. Then slip on half a kidney and a second square of bacon. Continue in this way until filled.

3. Dust with a little salt and pepper; place in a pan and broil at moderate heat, about 7 minutes. Serve on the brochettes.

But what if you have no brochettes? Use wires from the tops of cream bottles. Cut the kidneys in quarters, and slip them on alternately with bacon squares; fasten to form a circle; then grill. Looks cute, and is very easy to serve.

BROILED TRIPE
(*Serves 2*)

½ *pound pickled honey-comb tripe*

Fine cracker or dry bread crumbs
¼ *cup melted margarine*
Salt and pepper

1. Cut the tripe in individual servings; simmer 30 minutes in boiling water to cover. Drain. This can be done in advance.

2. Dip in crumbs, then in the margarine, and in

crumbs again. Place on an oiled preheated broiler and cook
5 minutes altogether; start smooth side up, for 3 minutes;
finish with the rough side.

3.   Place on a hot platter rough side up. Season with
salt and pepper, dot with butter and place in the oven to
become very hot.

4.   Good with chili sauce, hot mashed potato and cole
slaw.

Smoked Meats and Sausages

Tenderized ham, smoked pork tenderloin, Canadian and
American bacon, dried beef and sausages of all kinds, are
well adapted to cooking for two. And there's the added
advantage that they can be bought a few days in advance
and kept in the refrigerator until needed. Smoked tongue
can be cooked at a convenient time, rolled in waxed paper,
and kept in the refrigerator for a week.

Cervelat or Salami: Buy a pound or two at a time.
Slice it as needed and add to an hors d'oeuvre plate. Or
scramble with eggs.

Polish Sausage: Cut in thin slices and add to canned
baked beans, split pea soup, or use in shirring eggs.

BROILED SMOKED PORK TENDERLOIN
(*Serves 3*)

1 *small smoked pork ten-*   *Butter*
   derloin   *Minced parsley*
Pepper

1.   Cut the tenderloin in scant ½-inch slices and scald
it with boiling water.

2.   Drain, dust with pepper and place on a preheated
broiler about 3 inches from the heat. Broil about 10 minutes; turn once.

3.   Dot with butter; sprinkle with the parsley and heat for a minute.

4.   Serve with string beans, or sauerkraut seasoned with caraway seed.

HAM AND FRUIT PLATTER
(*Serves 2 to 3*)

1 *pound   tenderized smoked ham steak 1 inch thick*
½ *teaspoon dry mustard*
2 *tablespoons brown sugar*
3 *tablespoons cooking fat*

6 *whole cloves*
2 *tablespoons butter*
4 *slices canned pineapple*
4 *whole peeled bananas*
4 *prunes*
  Water cress or lettuce

1.   Sprinkle the ham with the dry mustard; cover both sides with the sugar.

2.   Melt the fat in a heavy frying pan; place the ham in it, and stick the surface with cloves. Brown quickly in a frying pan until the sugar melts.

3.   Reduce the heat; half cover with boiling water and simmer until tender—about 30 minutes.

4.   Meanwhile, melt the butter in a second frying pan; add the pineapple and sauté until slightly glazed. Put a prune in the center of each piece. Add the peeled bananas cut lengthwise and again in halves; sauté lightly until golden brown.

5.   Arrange the ham in the center of a platter with the fruit as a garnish. Serve with grilled sweet potatoes.

PANNED HAM
(*Serves 2*)

½ *teaspoon sugar*
1 *teaspoon butter or margarine*

½ *pound cooked ham sliced thin*

1. Melt the sugar in a frying pan. Add the margarine or butter and the ham.

2. Cook not more than a minute turning once. The ham should be heated through but not browned.

CANADIAN BACON

Heat the frying pan. Put in the desired quantity of bacon; heat through on one side; then turn and heat through the other side. Cook until the fat around the edges is lightly browned. The bacon should be moist and tender when done.

AMERICAN BACON

Fried Bacon: Fry slowly in a thick frying pan until the fat runs freely, then pour it off. Turn and continue to fry until of the desired doneness. Drain on crumpled absorbent paper.

Time-Saving Prefried Bacon: Half fry a whole pound of bacon. Drain on absorbent paper, and store in a covered jar in the refrigerator. Finish frying as needed.

BACON FAT

Do not allow the fat to smoke and burn when cooking bacon. Turn into a jar, cover, store in the refrigerator and use for frying potatoes, eggs, omelets, meat, or for seasoning cabbage or "greens."

SAUSAGE LINKS

To bake: Place in a baking pan; prick each link 3 or 4 times with a sharp-tined fork. Add 2 tablespoons water. Bake in a hot oven until golden brown, 15 to 20 minutes, according to the size of the sausage. Drain on crumpled paper towels.

To fry: Place the sausage links in a frying pan; prick each link 2 or 3 times with a sharp-tined fork. Fry slowly, allowing about 10 minutes. Pour off the fat when half fried. Turn occasionally. Drain on crumpled paper towels before serving.

Sausage Cakes: Shape sausage meat into small, flat cakes, or slice roll-sausage ½ inch thick. (Be sure to remove the cellophane covering.) Fry or broil slowly until well-browned. Serve with browned corn meal mush, glazed apple slices, with creamed potatoes, waffles or pancakes.

Sausage Links with Hot Stuffed Apples: Bake or fry the sausage links; serve on lengths of toast with hot stuffed apples.

HOT STUFFED APPLES

1.   Cut red apples in halves crosswise; scoop out the centers to form cups.

2.   Cook 7 minutes in enough boiling water to almost cover. Then drain. Fill with either of the mixtures given below.

3.   Place in a baking pan; dot with butter; add water or cider to barely cover bottom of pan; bake in a hot oven until the apples are tender, about 18 minutes.

FILLINGS FOR STUFFED APPLES

1.   Fill the apple cups with mashed sweet potato mixed with grated orange rind and chopped raisins.

2.   Fill with any desired mixture of fresh or canned fruits, mixed with a little butter and a very little sugar.

FRANKFURTERS BROILED WITH BACON

Select thick, skinless frankfurters. Wrap a slice of bacon around each one, and fasten in place with toothpicks. Broil about 6 inches from the heat until the bacon is done, about 7 minutes. Nice for dinner with baked beans or flaky boiled potatoes in rich white sauce, and sprinkled with minced parsley.

PANNED FRANKFURTERS
(Serves 2 to 3)

1½ tablespoons butter or   1½ tablespoons prepared
   margarine   mustard
                          6 skinless frankfurters

Melt the butter or margarine in a frying pan. Add the mustard; when very hot add frankfurters. Cook gently until slightly browned. Serve with potato salad, mixed vegetable salad, or with creamed potatoes.

BARBECUED FRANKFURTER ROLLS

Dip frankfurters in barbecue sauce. Grill until browned. Serve in hot, split buttered frankfurter rolls.

CHEESED FRANKFURTER ROLLS

Cover the open edge of the frankfurter-filled rolls with thin slices of sharp American cheese, or Old English spread; grill until the cheese melts.

CREAMED DRIED BEEF
(Serves 2)

2 ounces dried beef   2 tablespoons flour
2 tablespoons butter   1½ cups milk
Toast

1. Pull the dried beef into medium-sized pieces with the fingers. Brown lightly in the butter.

2. Add the flour; gradually stir in the milk; cook and stir until thick and boiling. Season to taste with salt and pepper; serve on toast or with baked white potatoes.

BOILED SMOKED BEEF TONGUE
(For 2 or 3 meals)

1 (3 to 4 pound) smoked   ½ teaspoon mixed pickle
  beef tongue   spice

1. Put the tongue in a small kettle; cover with cold water, bring to boiling point; boil 5 minutes, then drain. This removes excess salt.

2. Cover with boiling water; add the spice, put on a lid, and simmer until tender, about 4 hours.

3. Peel off the skin; remove the untidy root ends; slice and serve with mustard or horse-radish sauce.

Bake for the next serving; to do this spread the remainder with 1 tablespoon honey and 2 tablespoons sweet pickle vinegar, mixed with ½ cup fine dry bread crumbs and 1 tablespoon melted butter; slow-bake until brown. Serve with a moist vegetable such as tomatoes or potatoes escalloped in the same oven.

Use the remainder in hash, salad, sandwiches, scrambled eggs or in creamed noodles or potatoes.

POULTRY AND GAME

To Prepare Poultry for Cooking

1. Order bird cleaned by butcher.

2. Singe off hairs by holding the bird over a gas flame, or by means of a lighted candle.

3. Remove pin feathers by means of tweezers. Cut out oil sac which is the protuberance at the tip of the tail.

4. Scrub with a brush in water containing mild soap to remove surface soil and extra oil. Rinse twice. Drain, and pat dry with paper towels.

5. For extra fine flavor rub the bird all over with the cut surface of a lemon. Or rub a little powdered ginger inside.

To Truss Poultry

If to be stuffed, lightly spoon the stuffing into the cavity. Put a spoonful under the skin at the neck. Fasten the neck skin over onto the back with crisscrossed toothpicks or use poultry lacing pins. Fasten up the cavity with criss-crossed toothpicks or lacing pins, and lace them together with white string. Then press the legs close to the body; pull the wings back and tie snugly together, anchoring the twine at the tip of the tail. Before serving, remove the twine, toothpicks or lacing pins.

BROILED CHICKEN
(*Serves 2*)

1 (1½ to 2 pounds) broil-ing chicken	*Butter or margarine*
	Salt
1 *slice lemon*	*Pepper*

1. Order the chicken split for broiling. Save the heart and giblets for gravy (page 128). Prepare for cooking as directed. Rub with the lemon.

2. Roll in melted butter or margarine. Dust with salt and pepper. Place on an oiled broiler, flesh side up, and broil until light brown. Turn; pour over a little more melted butter or margarine, and broil until the chicken is almost tender, about 15 minutes more.

3. Transfer to a small baking pan; dot with a little more butter or margarine; pour 2 tablespoons water into the pan to keep the chicken moist. Cover close and bake about 15 minutes at 350 degrees, F.

4. Serve plain or with giblet gravy based on the drippings in the pan.

Chicken Platter: Pile broiled chicken in the center of a heated platter or plank. Surround with asparagus tips, corn fritters or overlapping slices of grilled sweet potatoes. Garnish with parsley.

Broiled Sherried Chicken: Broil as directed; baste while in the oven with ¼ cup dry sherry.

Broiled Guinea Chicken: Follow the recipe for broiled

sherried chicken. Serve with a sauce made from the drippings in the pan. Garnish with currant jelly in lettuce nests.

FRIED CHICKEN
(Serves 2)

1 (1½ to 2 pound) broil-   ½ teaspoon salt
  ing chicken   Few grains pepper
½ cup flour   Vegetable fat for frying
            One small onion

1. Prepare chicken as directed on page 156, and quarter.

2. Mix the flour, salt and pepper in a paper bag. Put in the chicken and shake until well-covered with the flour.

3. Heat enough vegetable fat in a good-sized frying pan to cover the bottom generously. Add a small peeled onion. Put in the chicken; fry slowly; turn occasionally until golden brown all over. This should take about 20 minutes. Discard the onion.

4. Drain on absorbent paper; serve plain, or with cream gravy.

Chicken Maryland: Accompany the fried chicken with cream sauce and corn fritters.

CHICKEN DE BRESSE
(Serves 2)

1 (1½ to 2 pound) broil-   4 tablespoons   butter   or
  ing chicken   margarine

1. Order the chicken split and dressed. Prepare for cooking as directed (page 156).

2. Rub a casserole with a thick coating of butter or margarine. Put in the chicken skin side up. Dust with salt and pepper. Dot with the remaining fat; cover closely, and bake in a hot oven (425–450 degrees, F.) 30 to 35 minutes. Do not add any water, and do not open while cooking.

3. Serve from the casserole.

ROAST STUFFED BROILER HALVES
(*Serves 2*)

1 (1½ to 2 *pound*) *broil-*   2 *tablespoons flour*
  ing chicken   *Salt and pepper*
4 *tablespoons melted butter*   *Herb stuffing*
  or margarine

1. Singe, split, wash and dry the chicken. Brush with melted butter; dust with the flour, salt and pepper. Spoon the stuffing into the chicken.

2. Place in an oiled pan, stuffing side up. Dust with a little flour; pour over the melted butter; bake in a moderately hot oven (375–400 degrees, F.) for 20 minutes. Then turn to cook brown, about 15 minutes more. Baste twice with melted butter or margarine.

3. Serve with gravy or mushroom sauce.

ROAST CHICKEN
(*For 2 to 3 meals*)

1 (3 to 4 *pound*) *chicken*   3 *tablespoons butter or*
  Any stuffing desired   *margarine*
3 *tablespoons flour*   ½ *cup water*
            Salt and pepper

1. Prepare the chicken as directed on page 156. Cut off the long neck and tips of wings.

2. Stuff and truss as directed on page 156. Lay the chicken breast down in a small roasting pan. Rub all over with the flour and butter or margarine creamed together.

3. Place in an oven at 450 degrees, F. Roast for 15 minutes; then lower the heat to 350 degrees, F. and finish cooking, allowing about 1½ hours longer. Baste 3 times, using in all ½ cup water heated with 3 tablespoons butter or margarine.

4. Turn the chicken on its back when half done. Meanwhile, simmer the giblets, neck and tips of wings in 2½ cups water for 1 hour. Save the broth; chop the giblets fine. Return to the broth to use for gravy. There should be 2 cups.

5. When roasted, remove the toothpicks or poultry lacing pins and twine, and keep the chicken hot while making the gravy. To do this add 3 tablespoons flour to the fat in the pan and cook and stir until smooth and brown; slowly add the giblet broth; stir constantly until boiling. Simmer 2 minutes; add salt and pepper to taste.

Roast Turkey: Prepare as for roast chicken. Fill with bread stuffing to which small halved oysters may be added. For roasting, allow 20 minutes to the pound after the preliminary browning; be sure to reckon the weight of the stuffing.

Roast Stuffed Half Turkey: Prepare as for roast stuffed broiler (page 159), using 3 times the recipe for herb stuffing. Rub over the surface of the turkey with equal parts of flour and butter or margarine creamed together. Then follow the recipe for roasting chicken, allowing 20 minutes to the pound.

Roast Pheasant: Dry pick, eviscerate and clean thoroughly. Be sure all shot are removed. Prepare and cook as for roast chicken, basting with ½ cup hot orange juice containing 2 tablespoons butter.

CHICKEN FRICASSEE
(Serves 2 to 3)

1 (1½ to 2 pound) broiling chicken

2 tablespoons butter or diced salt pork

2 tablespoons chopped celery

1 tablespoon chopped onion

2 cups boiling water

½ teaspoon salt

Few grains pepper

2 tablespoons flour

½ cup sweet or soured cream

Buttered toast or split biscuit

1. Prepare the chicken as directed on page 156; disjoint and separate into 10 pieces.

2. Melt the butter or fry the salt pork in a heavy saucepan until fat begins to run. Add the celery and onion and cook 1 minute.

3. Put in the chicken; add the boiling water and seasonings. Cover and simmer until the chicken is tender, about 35 minutes. Add the flour and cream stirred together to make gravy. Boil 2 minutes.

4. Serve with chicken and gravy on toast or biscuit, or in a ring of flaky rice or whipped potato.

Turkey Sections

Turkey is now available not only in halves but quarters. Ask the meat man to dissect the quarter. Use the smaller pieces for fricassee (see preceding recipe); prepare the drumstick as follows:

STUFFED TURKEY DRUMSTICK
(*Serves 2*)

1. Remove the leg bone with a sharp knife. Put a skewer under each of the 5 white tendons and draw them out.

2. Fill with 1 recipe savory bread stuffing (page 130). Fasten together with toothpicks or poultry lacing pins. Put 2 small pieces of fat bacon on top.

3. Place in a well-buttered casserole. Cover and bake 1½ hours at 350–375 degrees, F., or until fork tender. Serve with mushroom sauce.

ROAST DUCKLING
(Serves 2 to 3)

1 *duckling （about 2½ pounds)*　　　1½ *tablespoons butter or margarine*
Salt and pepper　　　　　　1½ *tablespoons flour*
Plain or herb stuffing

1. Singe, tweeze out the pinfeathers, clean and wash the duck; rub inside and out with salt. Stuff and truss as described (page 156).

2. Rub the duck with the butter and flour creamed together. Place breast down in a small baking pan; start to roast in a hot oven (450 degrees, F.). When the duck begins to turn golden, reduce the heat and roast slowly, at 350 degrees, F., basting occasionally with 2 tablespoons hot water.

3. After 30 minutes, turn the bird on its back and finish roasting, allowing about 1 hour altogether.

4. Serve with gravy, franconia white or sweet potatoes cooked in the same pan; a green vegetable, apple sauce or hot stuffed apples (page 154).

BROILED SQUAB
(Serves 2)

2 *large squab*　　　　　¼ *teaspoon mixed herbs*
Salt and pepper　　　　1½ *tablespoons butter*
2 slices buttered toast

1. Order the squab dressed and split for broiling.

2. Singe, tweeze out the pinfeathers, wash and pat dry on paper towels.

3. Rub with salt, pepper and the herbs blended with the butter.

4. Place (flesh side up) in a pan; cook at moderate

heat in a preheated broiler for 7 minutes. Then turn to brown the skin.

5. Serve on toast, with a garnish of parsley, cress, and/or a baked stuffed tomato, asparagus tips or broccoli.

Cold Meat Platters

1. Arrange cold sliced roast beef or individual meat loaves in the center of a platter. On one end arrange potato and cucumber salad made with French dressing and mayonnaise. On the other arrange cold broccoli, allowed to stand in a remoulade sauce or French dressing at least ½ hour. Decorate with parsley, cress or lettuce.

2. Arrange alternating slices of cold meat or chicken loaf and baked ham on one side of a platter. On the other arrange nut and grape salad in lettuce nests. Decorate with clusters of grapes.

3. Place slices of cold tongue and Swiss cheese overlapping in the center of a platter. At either end heap cole slaw containing minced green peppers. On the sides put halves of tomatoes stuffed with macaroni salad.

4. In the center of a large round platter or tray arrange a cluster of tomatoes stuffed with celery and nut salad. Surround with cold sliced turkey, veal or lamb. Encircle with small carrot sticks and radish roses; border with crisp potato chips.

Oddments of Meat and Poultry

Most people do not like the word "leftover," especially men. It connotes something that is a has-been, something undesirable. And yet leftovers are just as valuable as the original food. Let's avoid controversy and call them "oddments." In families of two, the use of controlled oddments is a great help. By "controlled" I mean deliberately cooking enough food for two meals, with the planned purpose of using the oddments 24 or 48 hours later. This is possible, however, only with safe refrigeration, and when the food is closely covered when stored. Otherwise, unless there is a very cold pantry or a covered box or cupboard on a porch, leftover food must be eaten at the next meal. If the weather is very warm, leftover fish or custard mixtures should be thrown out.

Chicken or Poultry Patties: Cream oddments of cooked chicken or poultry or heat in gravy. Serve in reheated tart shells.

Minced Meat or Poultry on Toast: Melt 1 tablespoon butter or margarine. Add 1 teaspoon minced onion and cook a moment; add 1 teaspoon flour; stir in ¾ to 1 cup minced cooked beef, lamb, veal or poultry. Add ⅓ cup water or gravy; bring to a boil, season with salt, pepper and meat condiment. Serve on hot buttered toast.

Meat or Poultry Toast Cakes: Heat cut-up cooked meat or poultry in plenty of gravy, rich cream sauce or commercial meatless spaghetti sauce. Add oddments of cooked corn, celery, onions, carrots or peas if you like. Serve between and on top of 2 slices of buttered toast.

Potato Meat or Poultry Pie: In 2 shirred egg dishes combine 1¼ cups fine-chopped cooked meat or poultry with ½ cup well-seasoned gravy; top with whipped potato mixed with an egg yolk. Heat and brown in a hot oven (400 degrees, F.).

Creamed Ham or Tongue with Potatoes: To 2½ cups diced creamed potatoes add ½ cup diced cooked ham or tongue. Season with onion salt.

Browned Beef Hash: Combine ¾ cup cooked fine-chopped beef with 1½ cups chopped cooked white potato, ½ tablespoon scraped onion, ⅛ teaspoon pepper and ½ teaspoon salt. Add enough gravy or milk to hold the mixture together. Heat ½ tablespoon butter or bacon fat in an 8-inch frying pan, and slowly fry the hash in this. When golden brown on the bottom, fold over like an omelet and slide onto a hot platter. Nice with scrambled eggs, pan-fried sliced tomatoes or both.

Browned Lamb or Chicken Hash: Make as beef hash; ¼ cup minced green pepper adds fine flavor.

Croquettes

Traditional croquettes are fried in deep fat. But for the average family of two, deep frying is not practical. It is often smelly, which is not so good in cramped quarters, and there is little space to keep the can of fat between fryings. Better not attempt it without a real kitchen. However, baked croquettes are a good substitute. So that is the method given in this book.

BAKED CROQUETTES
(Serves 2 to 3)

1 *cup minced cooked or canned meat, chicken or fish*	⅛ *teaspoon pepper*
	⅛ *teaspoon marjoram*
	1 *egg yolk*
⅓ *cup cracker dust*	1 *teaspoon minced parsley*
⅓ *cup milk*	*Fine dry bread crumbs*
½ *teaspoon salt*	

Melted butter, margarine or fat

1.   Combine the meat, chicken or fish with the cracker dust, milk, seasonings, egg yolk and parsley.

2.   Form into flattened balls containing one tablespoonful of the mixture each. Cover with fine dry bread crumbs mixed with ¼ the quantity of melted butter, margarine or vegetable fat. Place in a heavily greased pan; bake golden brown in a very hot oven (450 degrees, F.) about 10 minutes.

3.   Serve with a creamed vegetable, or with tomato or Spanish sauce (page 174).

Canned Meats and Poultry

These include beef, Irish and lamb stew, tongue, corned beef or roast beef hash; chili con carne, tamales, hamburgers, ham patties, Vienna sausage, chicken and turkey breasts, chicken and noodle dinner, ravioli dinner and spaghetti dinner with meat balls.

These are all time-savers, and contribute real food value. With additional seasonings and a little butter or margarine for richness, they become individualized and appetizing. For instance:

Canned Stew: Serve with dumplings or made into meat pies.

Canned Tongue: Slice and sauté in butter and table mustard.

Canned Hash: Pep up with minced fried onion, and serve with bacon. Or chill, cut open both ends of the can and slide the hash onto a board; cut in $\frac{1}{2}$ inch slices, brown and serve topped with fried tomato, poached eggs, or creamed or curried hard-cooked eggs.

Canned Corned Beef: Escallope with a can of macaroni and cheese; or heat on top of boiling potatoes, carrots and cabbage, and serve as a boiled dinner, dressed with plenty of melted butter.

Canned Scrapple: Chill, open at both ends, slide out and cut in $\frac{1}{2}$-inch slices. Cover with fine, dry crumbs or dust with flour; pan fry in butter or bacon fat. Serve with scrambled eggs, or topped with poached eggs. Or use with bacon or pan broiled ham. This is an excellent combination. Makes the meat go twice as far.

Canned Chicken: Prepare à la king, or as savory turnovers.

Canned Turkey Breasts: Heat, and serve in a nest of flaky rice with à la king or Newburg sauce and a garnish of ripe olives.

Canned Chicken Noodle Dinner: Sauté a sliced onion or sweet green pepper or both in butter, and add to this dinner. Heat and serve sprinkled with fried croutons. Nice with canned peas or asparagus.

SAVORY LUNCHEON MEAT STEW
(Serves 2 to 4)

1 *peeled sliced onion*	1 *cup canned tomatoes*
1 *peeled sliced section garlic*	1½ *cups water*
	1 *bouillon cube*
2 *tablespoons butter or margarine*	1 *cup diced celery with leaves*
1 *(12-oz.) can luncheon meat*	½ *cup shredded green beans*
2 *tablespoons flour*	½ *cup sliced carrots*

Cooked rice (any kind)

1. Sauté the onion and garlic in the butter until softened. Dice the luncheon meat, roll in the flour, add to the sautéing vegetables and lightly brown.

2. Add the remaining ingredients except rice. Cover, and simmer for 30 minutes.

3. Serve over the rice.

CHILI FROM LUNCHEON MEAT
(Serves 4)

4 *peeled onions sliced*	1 *(No. 2) can tomatoes*
2 *peeled sections garlic sliced*	½ *teaspoon Worcestershire*
	¼ *teaspoon mustard*
2 *tablespoons butter or margarine*	½ *tablespoon chili powder*
	1 *small can kidney beans*
1 *(12-oz.) can luncheon meat*	*Cooked rice*

1. Sauté the onions and garlic in the butter or margarine.

2. Add the luncheon meat, tomatoes and seasonings. Cover, and simmer 30 minutes.

3. Add the kidney beans; simmer 20 minutes longer and serve on rice.

Cold Cuts Made Hot

With the exception of salami, these are likely to lack individuality. But they can be quickly made appetizing.

Liverwurst: Sauté lightly in butter or margarine. Serve with or without bacon or scrambled eggs, or steam-fried onions (page 192).

Veal Loaf: Put two slices together with table mustard. Sauté in butter or margarine and serve with creamed potatoes or noodles.

French Toastwiches: Use sliced tongue, ham or veal loaf, as a filling (page 77).

Grilled Cheesed Cold Cuts Toasts: Toast slices of bread on one side. Then on the untoasted side fit a slice of spiced ham, veal loaf, tongue or cooked ham, spread with table mustard or drained pickle relish; top with sliced sharp American cheese, and grill until the cheese bubbles. Serve with coleslaw or a tossed salad.

Bologna Slices: Quickly sauté bologna. Top with scrambled eggs, plain or cooked with chopped scallions.

CHICKEN NEWBURG
(*Serves* 2)

2 *raw chicken breasts*	*Newburg sauce*
½ *pound slice Smithfield ham*	*Black olives*

1. Casserole the chicken breasts de Bresse style (p. 158).

2. Trim the ham in 2 oval-shaped pieces and broil.

3. Make the Newburg sauce (page 172).

4. To serve, put the ham on a small platter. Top with chicken breasts; pour over sauce, garnish with olives.

Spectacular! Chicken Baked in Foil

Can be prepared and refrigerated ready to bake when desired. It needs no watching. If dinner is delayed, it can stand in a 325° F. oven up to an hour without drying out.

Prepare 1 sectioned fresh broiler for frying (p. 156), or use thawed frozen chicken already prepared for frying. In either case pan-fry until half browned. Then add 2 peeled white onions, 2 mushroom caps and 4 slices peeled carrot for each serving. Cut as many 12-x-14-inch squares of heavy-duty aluminum foil as needed. In the center of each arrange 2 or 3 pieces of chicken, and the vegetables, mushrooms on top. Dust with salt, Ac'cent, paprika and minced parsley. Bring up the foil to form a box. Add 2 tablespoons light cream to each; fold over the foil, then double fold it to form a "packet." Place on a shallow pan. Bake 1 hour in a hot oven, 425° F. To serve, place on dinner plates; snip the top foil with scissors to form a large crisscross, then fold back to make a glamorous frame for an enticing food picture!

More Ways with Foil

One way to foil at least part of the clean-up-after-meals problem is to use plenty of heavy-duty aluminum foil!

Line frying pans smoothly with foil ½ inch up the sides.

Wrap seasoned vegetables prepared for cooking snugly in foil, and boil two or three kinds in one pot.

Place a square of aluminum foil on the oven-rack under a frozen-fruit pie while thaw-baking. It won't boil over into the oven, but onto the foil which you throw away.

If a cake, brown-n'serve rolls, or what-not is getting too brown in the oven, on with a piece of foil!

Line pans with heavy-duty aluminum foil before roasting chicken, turkey, duck, or baking fish.

Cover the bottom of the broiler pan with aluminum foil.

CHAPTER X

Glamorize with a Sauce

A GOOD SAUCE IS TO FOOD WHAT GOOD ACCESSORIES ARE to a woman's costume. Sauces can be easy or difficult to make; they can call for a few ingredients or a pantry full. The sauces I have selected for this book are quick and easy to make with few ingredients. Yet they have the chic that glamorizes a dull dish.

They serve 2 to 3 or more. If any sauce is left, use at a subsequent meal with oddments of meat, fish, or vegetables or mixed with the filling for sandwiches, for hors d'oeuvres or for canapés. It can be safely refrigerated in covered jars up to 3 or 4 days. Be sure to keep up-to-date with new frozen and canned sauces. Many are excellent.

All measurements are level

MAITRE D'HOTEL BUTTER
(*Serves 2*)

2 *tablespoons butter*	1 *heaping teaspoon minced*
¼ *teaspoon salt*	*parsley*
Few grains pepper	½ *tablespoon lemon juice*

Cream the first 4 ingredients until blended. Then cream in the lemon juice. Use with steak or fish.

BROWN BUTTER

Melt the desired amount of butter in a small thick frying pan and let it turn golden brown. Use for seasoning vegetables, or to pour over broiled fish.

White Sauce

In itself, white sauce is bland and dull. But as it is the background for so many dishes, it should be perfectly prepared. It will not be pasty or lumpy if carefully made. In making creamed dishes use almost ½ as much white sauce as food to be creamed.

WHITE OR CREAM SAUCE
(Serves 2 to 3)

2 tablespoons butter or   ¼ teaspoon salt
  margarine   Few grains pepper
2 tablespoons flour   1 cup whole milk

1. Melt the butter in a saucepan, or use a double boiler; remove from the heat; stir in the flour and seasonings.

2. Return to the heat; stir in the cold milk a little at a time. Allow the sauce to thicken with each addition of liquid before adding more; this prevents lumps.

3. When boiling point is reached, add the food to be creamed. Place over hot water and heat for 10 minutes.

If a richer looking and tasting sauce is required, stir in 1 egg yolk beaten with 1 tablespoon cream.

Cheese Sauce: Prepare white sauce. Add ¼ teaspoon dry mustard, ⅛ teaspoon garlic salt, and ¾ cup diced sharp processed cheese. Stir until velvety smooth. If plain cheddar cheese is used, it should be coarse-grated.

Anchovy Sauce: Add 1 teaspoon anchovy paste and

½ tablespoon minced parsley to one recipe for white sauce. Serve with broiled fish, chunks of heated tuna or salmon, or poured over quartered hard-cooked eggs on toast.

Sherry Cream Sauce: Make white sauce with light cream. When done, stir into an egg yolk beaten with 1 tablespoon dry sherry wine. Return to the heat and cook and stir a few seconds. Serve with broiled chicken, croquettes, use in creaming diced chicken, veal, ham, shell fish or sliced eggs.

BROWN SAUCE
(Serves 2 to 3)

2 *tablespoons butter*	⅛ *teaspoon pepper*
2 *tablespoons flour*	¼ *teaspoon mixed herbs*
¼ *teaspoon salt*	1 *cup soup stock or bouillon*

Melt and slightly brown the butter. Add the flour and seasonings and cook and stir until golden brown. Slowly stir in the soup stock and cook until boiling rapidly. Use with meat of any kind.

Mushroom Sauce: Follow the preceding recipe, first sautéing in the butter 2 tablespoons minced, sliced fresh or canned mushrooms. Season with a few grains nutmeg; or add 2 tablespoons dry Madeira or sherry wine.

NEWBURG SAUCE
(Serves 2 to 3)

3 *tablespoons butter*	¾ *cup light cream*
¼ *teaspoon salt*	3 *egg yolks*
¼ *teaspoon paprika*	3 *tablespoons dry sherry*
½ *scant tablespoon flour*	

1. Melt the butter; stir in the seasonings and flour.

2. When smooth gradually stir in the cream. Simmer 1 minute.

3. Beat the egg yolks light, mix with the sherry.

4. Remove the thickened cream from the heat. Stir in the egg and sherry.

5. Return to the heat and stir constantly until the sauce almost boils. Use at once with crab flakes, diced lobster, broiled fish or with flaked chicken.

HOLLANDAISE SAUCE—SIMULATED
(*Serves 2 to 3*)

¼ cup butter	⅛ teaspoon pepper
2 egg yolks	1 tablespoon herb or cider
1 tablespoon flour	vinegar
¼ teaspoon salt	1 tablespoon lemon juice

½ cup boiling water

1. Melt the butter in a double boiler top. Beat the egg yolks and add the flour, salt and pepper.

2. Stir in the vinegar and lemon juice. Add to the melted butter, stirring constantly; then slowly stir in the boiling water; cook and stir until thick. Do not have more than 1 inch of hot water in the double boiler bottom, otherwise the sauce cooks too rapidly and may separate or look curdled.

TOMATO SAUCES

Use canned tomato sauce (8 oz. can) as a base. Vary as follows:

Tomato Onion Sauce: Sauté 4 tablespoons minced onion until yellowed in 1½ tablespoons butter or margarine. Add 1 can tomato sauce, and bring to boiling point. Serve with boiled, baked, or poached fish; tongue; veal cutlet; meat loaf or hash.

Tomato Herb Sauce: Add 1 teaspoon butter and ¼ teaspoon mixed herbs to 1 can tomato sauce. Heat and use with fish, curried rice, meat burgers, sautéed liver or chicken livers, pork or lamb steak, or fried chicken.

Spanish Sauce: Sauté 2 tablespoons each diced green pepper and onion in 1½ tablespoons butter or margarine. Add ¼ teaspoon oregano (Mexican sage) if convenient, and ¼ cup sliced canned mushrooms. Add 1 can tomato sauce, and bring to a rapid boil. Then, if convenient, add 3 sliced stuffed olives. Use with white, brown or wild rice; boiled or poached fish; meat or fish loaf or croquettes; liver in any form; with hard-cooked or poached eggs on toast; or in the fold and as a garnish to Spanish omelet.

HORSE-RADISH SAUCE (HOT)
(Serves 2 to 3)

½ tablespoon butter	⅓ teaspoon sugar
½ tablespoon flour	Few grains pepper
½ cup soup stock or ½ a bouillon cube dissolved in ½ cup hot water	1 tablespoon grated horse-radish
	1 teaspoon wine vinegar

1. Melt the butter; add the flour; and then slowly add the soup stock.

2. Stir in the seasonings, horse-radish and vinegar. Bring to boiling point and serve with boiled beef, smoked tongue or smoked pork tenderloin.

BARBECUE SAUCE
(Serves 3 to 4)

1 tablespoon minced onion	½ tablespoon cider or herb vinegar
½ tablespoon butter or margarine	½ teaspoon chili powder
½ cup tomato catsup	¼ teaspoon salt
½ tablespoon Worcestershire sauce	½ cup water

Sauté the onion in the butter. Add the remaining ingredients; simmer 5 minutes and use as indicated.

A dash of "liquid smoke" (on sale in specialty food

stores) will give the flavor of charcoal cooking; good with broiled fish.

Wine Barbecue Sauce: Make as directed, using ¼ cup dry red wine and ¼ cup water.

CURRY SAUCE
(Serves 2 to 3)

See page 145. Plenty of curries there, too.

Wine Sauces

MADEIRA SAUCE
(Serves 4)

1 *tablespoon butter*	¼ *teaspoon paprika*
1½ *tablespoons flour*	1½ *tablespoons minced*
1 *cup well-seasoned*	*celery*
brown soup stock or 2	3 *tablespoons Madeira*
bouillon cubes in 1 cup	*wine*
water	

1.   Melt the butter and slightly brown it. Stir in the flour; cook until yellowed, stirring frequently.

2.   Gradually add the soup stock, paprika and celery; simmer 10 minutes and sieve.

3.   Just before serving, stir in the Madeira. Use with ham, game, beef or veal.

SAUTERNE SAUCE
(Serves 2)

2 *tablespoons butter*	*Few grains pepper*
2 *tablespoons dry Sauterne wine*	

Combine the ingredients; cook 2 minutes. Serve over broiled ham or fish, or cooked carrots, cabbage, Brussels sprouts or sliced beets.

Cold Sauces

CUCUMBER SAUCE
(Serves 2)

½ cup coarse-grated crisp   ¼ teaspoon paprika
  cucumber   Few grains salt
⅓ cup soured cream   Few grains sugar
                 Lettuce

Combine the first 4 ingredients in the order given. Put
the sauce in nests of lettuce; serve very cold with fish,
shrimp, lobster, or canned salmon or tuna in chunks.

SAUCE TARTARE
(Serves 4)

½ cup mayonnaise   1 tablespoon minced green
½ tablespoon chowchow   pepper
½ teaspoon scraped raw   ½ teaspoon minced pars-
  onion   ley

Combine the ingredients in the order given. Serve with
fish, tongue, or with meat or fish loaves.

MINT SAUCE
(Serves 2 to 4)

⅓ cup wine vinegar   1 tablespoon sugar
         ¾ tablespoon crumbled dried mint or
           1½ tablespoons minced fresh mint

Heat the vinegar and sugar. Pour over the mint. Steep,
(that is let stand) an hour before serving. This keeps indefinitely. Use with lamb, mutton or ham.

SAUCE REMOULADE
(Serves 2 to 3)

1½ *teaspoons minced pars-*
ley
1½ *teaspoons minced*
chives
½ *teaspoon dry mustard*
1 *section garlic, peeled*
and crushed

3 *tablespoons salad oil*
1½ *tablespoons wine vine-*
gar
⅓ *teaspoon salt*
Few grains cayenne

1. Combine the herbs, mustard and garlic.

2. Gradually add 1 tablespoon of the oil. Then add the remaining oil alternately with the vinegar. Season and serve at once. If to stand, the sauce should be thoroughly stirred before using.

A teaspoonful of anchovy paste may be added.

Use with fish cocktails; cold canned tuna fish; vegetable, meat or fish salads; cold sliced tongue or ham; or fish or meat loaves.

Fish Cocktail Sauce: Prepare sauce remoulade, and add 2 tablespoons chili sauce, also ½ tablespoon grated horseradish if you like.

For Gourmet and Gourmette

ALMOND-BUTTER SAUCE

To pour over broiled fillets of whitefish, sole, or flounder: Melt 2 tablespoons butter in a small round-bottomed frying pan. When bubbling, add 2 tablespoons sliced blanched almond meats. Turn down the heat. Stir until they begin to turn color; then add 2 tablespoons any dry white wine. Bring quickly to a boil and pour over the fish.

CHAPTER XI

Vegetables and Cereals

WHEN IT COMES TO VEGETABLES, FOUR DIFFICULTIES confront the family of two: Monotony, insufficiency, waste and extravagance. Sounds rather grim, doesn't it? But this is merely because we are accustomed to thinking of cooking vegetables in large amounts, while really there is no food better adapted to small quantity cooking. And certainly there is none more necessary to well-being—or, shall we say, being well.

Selecting Vegetables

Greens and Salad Plants: Should be fresh and crisp.

Root Vegetables: Should be clean and of even size. When possible select beets and turnips with fresh-looking tops to use as "greens."

String and Snap Beans: Should be plump and literally snap with a clean break when broken.

Green Peas: Should look fresh and green, not yellowed and shrivelled. Pods should be plump, but not full.

Fresh Lima Beans: Pods should look fresh and full.

Summer Squash, Cymlings and Zucchini: Should look plump and fresh, have thin skins and should not be bruised.

Green Corn: Pull down the husks to peek. The kernels should look full but not crowded or large. Watch out for worms!

Cauliflower: Should be creamy white, not rusty looking.

Green and Red Cabbage: Should be fresh and crisp, even the outside leaves.

Brussels Sprouts: Should look fresh and green, no yellow outer leaves.

Broccoli: Should be green, no yellowed tops.

Tomatoes: Should be fully ripe for immediate eating, and nearly ripe all over if to be kept a day or so. For frying or grilling, select partly ripened tomatoes, as they keep their shape when cooked.

White Potatoes: Select even-sized clean potatoes. Why pay for dirt?

Radishes: Buy only those with crisp green tops, and use these in mixed greens.

Celery: Should have fresh, crisp tops. If possible buy pascal celery. This is practically stringless, slightly green, rich in vitamins and good to the last bite. For hors d'oeuvres service buy celery hearts.

Asparagus: Select crisp, medium-thick stalks. Watch out for sand.

How Much to Buy

The following list suggests the major kinds of vegetables; what quantity to buy for two, ways they best can be prepared, and suggestions for using them.

French Artichokes: Purchase a medium-sized artichoke for each person. Serve plain boiled, or halved and broiled with plenty of butter or sauce remoulade. Serve with poultry, beef, veal or lamb.

Asparagus: Purchase ½ pound for 2 persons. Serve plain cooked with melted butter, as an accompaniment to poultry, beef, veal, lamb or tongue.

Lima Beans, Fresh: Purchase 1 pound unshelled, or ¾ pound shelled, for 2 persons. Serve plain cooked with a seasoning of butter or margarine, with any meat of pronounced flavor, as ham, smoked tongue, beef or lamb.

String Beans: Purchase ½ pound for 2 persons. Serve plain cooked and seasoned with butter or margarine or bacon fat, with any fish, meat or poultry.

Beets: Allow 6 small beets for 2 persons. Use plain cooked and seasoned with butter or lemon juice with any meat or fish.

Broccoli: Purchase ¾ pound for 2 persons. Serve plain cooked and seasoned with butter, with poultry, beef, lamb, or fish. Or serve hot with real or simulated Hollandaise sauce in place of salad.

Brussels Sprouts: Purchase ½ pound for 2 persons. Plain cook, season with butter or margarine, and serve with any meat, poultry or fish.

Cabbage: Purchase a small head, about 1 pound for 2 persons. Chop, boil 7 minutes, season with butter or margarine, and serve with any kind of meat; especially good with smoked or salted meat.

Carrots: Use 1 bunch of young carrots or 3 good-sized mature carrots for 2 persons. Serve plain cooked and seasoned with butter, with beef, ham, lamb, veal or tongue.

Cauliflower: Select 1 small cauliflower for 2 persons. Serve buttered, margarined or creamed with any plain or smoked meat or fish.

Celery: Buy 1 small head for 2 persons. Serve plain cooked, braised, or creamed, with poultry, lamb or beef.

Corn, Green: Select 1 large or 2 small ears for each person. Serve with any kind of meat, poultry or fish.

Cucumbers: Select 1 medium-sized cucumber for 2 persons. Dice, plain cook, season with butter or margarine and pepper; serve with fish, lamb or beef.

Eggplant: Use 1 small eggplant for 2 persons. Serve fried; plain cooked and mashed; or diced and seasoned with butter or margarine, with any kind of fish, poultry or veal.

Onions: Use 2 or 3 medium-sized onions for each person. Serve plain cooked, buttered or creamed, with any kind of meat or fish.

Parsnips: Use 1 or 2 good-sized parsnips for each person. Serve plain cooked, mashed or fried, with any kind of smoked meat.

Potatoes, White: Use 1 medium-sized or 2 small potatoes for each person. Serve plain boiled, mashed, parslied, fried or baked, with any kind of meat, poultry or fish.

Potatoes, Sweet or Yams: Use 1 or 2 medium-sized sweet potatoes or yams for each person. Serve plain boiled, baked, or fried with any kind of meat or fish. Serve glacéed with poultry or ham.

Spinach, Greens or Swiss Chard: Allow 1 pound for 2 persons. Plain cook, season, and serve with any kind of meat or fish.

Squash, Summer: Use 1 medium-sized squash for 2 persons. Serve mashed or diced and seasoned with butter or margarine, with any kind of meat, poultry or fish.

Squash, Winter, or Pumpkin: Use ½ pound for each person. Serve plain cooked, seasoned with butter or mace, then mashed or diced; or else bake; serve with poultry or ham.

Turnips: Use ¾ pound for 2 persons. Serve boiled and diced, seasoned with butter or margarine, with beef or any salt or smoked meat.

Green Peas: Purchase 2 pounds; plain cook, season with butter or margarine, and serve with any delicately flavored meat or fish.

How to Cook Vegetables

The method of cooking the vegetable depends somewhat upon the way the other foods in the meal are being prepared. If boiled meat is to be served, for instance, the potatoes, onions or cabbage may be boiled with it. If a roast is being cooked, the same oven heat will cook the potatoes or any other vegetable. If chops are being broiled, vegetables that can also be broiled should be selected. But however vegetables are to be cooked, certain rules must be followed to insure full flavor and food values.

1. Do not allow vegetables to stand in cold water before cooking as they lose food value and become water-soaked.

2. Vegetables should be covered while cooking. No exceptions.

3. Vegetables should not be overcooked or overseasoned.

4. Thoroughly wash all green vegetables such as greens and salad plants, as well as cabbage, Brussels sprouts, broccoli and cauliflower to remove dirt and insects. Let cauliflower and Brussels sprouts stand 5 minutes in well-salted water to draw out insects.

5. Remove roots from spinach and all greens; then wash the leaves twice in cold water and once in warm water to remove grit. A spray is helpful for the last washing.

6. Cook whole with the skins on if possible.

7. To quick-cook vegetables, peel, slice, shred, julienne, or dice according to variety. Small pieces of vegetable cook tender in ⅔ less time than when whole.

8. Use as soon as cooked to prevent oxidation due to exposure to the air, which impairs vitamin efficiency.

9. In boiling or steam-boiling, always add ½ teaspoon salt and also ½ teaspoon Ac'cent for each pint (2 cups) of boiling water used. The Ac'cent makes up in flavor for the natural sugars cooked out by boiling.

10. Season each half pint of diced, mashed, shredded or sliced vegetable with a little pepper and ½ tablespoon of butter or fortified margarine. Keep warm until absorbed.

11. Vegetables to be baked should be rubbed with fat to keep the skins soft.

12. Do not use baking soda in cooking vegetables; it lowers the potency of the vitamins.

13. Cook vegetables until they are tender, but not mushy. Present them "al dente"—with a little "bite" to the teeth.

Preparing Vegetables to Boil

For boiling prepare vegetables as follows:

Root vegetables (including potatoes, parsnips, carrots, turnips and the like): Scrape or peel. Leave the skins on potatoes when possible and always on beets.

Brussels Sprouts: Wash and slash at stem ends.

String Beans: Remove the strings.

Broccoli: Thoroughly wash and cut into 4-inch strips. Peel and slash the stems.

Cabbage: Cut out the core; slice or shred cabbage and wash.

Cauliflower: Remove the tough outer leaves, but leave on the tender green ones; wash the cauliflower thoroughly. Cut out the core.

Lima Beans and Peas: Open pods and remove contents.

Onions: Peel. Do this under water if the eyes are sensitive.

Squash: Peel and slice unless otherwise indicated.

To Boil Vegetables

Add one inch boiling water, and $\frac{1}{4}$ teaspoon each salt and Ac'cent to the prepared vegetables. Cover tight and boil until barely tender. Season as desired.

Using Vegetable Water

Use the vegetable water in making soups and gravy; or if almost boiled away, as a sauce with the vegetable. It adds flavor, and conserves those valuable vitamins and minerals.

Steam-Boiling Vegetables (Waterless Cooking)

Prepare the vegetable as directed. Place in a heavy kettle, pour in ½ inch boiling water; add ½ tablespoon butter or margarine; dust with salt, and a trace of sugar, cover closely and steam-boil until the vegetable is tender.

Boiling Vegetables in the Oven

Dice, slice or shred the vegetable; place in a glass or metal casserole rubbed with butter or margarine. Add ⅓ the quantity of boiling water. Add ¼ teaspoon each salt, Ac'cent, and sugar to a cup of water. Cover and place in the oven with roasting meat, baking cake or whatever food is being cooked. Allow ⅓ longer than when boiled on top of the stove.

Mashed, Puréed or Whipped Vegetables

White or sweet potatoes, turnips, oyster plant, parsnips and carrots may be mashed, puréed, or whipped, all of which mean the same thing.

Method: Boil or steam boil the vegetable until tender. Drain, and press the vegetable through a potato ricer or food mill. Measure, and to each cupful add ½ teaspoon butter, a few grains of salt and pepper and 2 tablespoons hot milk. Beat until very fluffy by hand or with an electric mixer.

Broiling Vegetables

Vegetables to be broiled include peeled, sliced white or sweet potatoes; egg plant; unpeeled ripe or green tomatoes; peeled sliced onions. Cut vegetables ¼ inch thick.

Method: Rub a fine-meshed broiler with butter or margarine; or if you do not have such a broiler, rub a shallow pan with butter or margarine. Put in a layer of vegetables, dust with salt, pepper and a trace of sugar. Dot with additional butter or margarine. Place under a preheated broiler, about 3 inches from the heat; broil about 12 minutes, turning once. Dust with a little Ac'cent.

Baking Vegetables

Vegetables to be baked include white or sweet potatoes; large carrots; beets; hubbard or acorn squash; pumpkin; parsnips.

Method: Scrub the vegetables thoroughly. Remove all imperfections with a sharp knife; rub with any good cooking fat. Place in a pan with water to barely cover the bottom. Bake until the vegetable is tender—from 30 to 45 minutes according to the size. Squash or pumpkin may be baked in the shell. In this case, cut in suitable sections, scrape out the seeds and strings, dot the squash with butter or margarine, season with salt, pepper and Ac'cent and bake. Serve in the shell, or scrape out and put through a potato ricer or food mill.

Vegetables in Fancy Shapes

Cutters to shred, slice and dice vegetables cost little and are worth the money. Vegetables for garnishing, such as pimientoes, green peppers, etc. may be cut into diamonds, hearts, clubs and spades by means of tiny vegetable cutters; whipped potato and rice may be quickly shaped into balls with an ice cream scoop. Cut white potatoes into balls before cooking by means of a French potato cutter.

Pressure Cooking Vegetables

This is the best of all ways to cook vegetables, as it saves time, nutritive values and flavor. For full instructions consult PRESSURE COOKING, by your friend and advisor Ida Bailey Allen.

Vegetable Cooking Chart

Note: To steam vegetables, allow ⅓ more time than for boiling. Bake whole vegetables at 375–400 degrees, F., 35 to 45 minutes. To boil or steam-boil vegetables in ⅓ to ½ less time, peel, dice, shred or chop them.

Vegetable	Boiling	Broiling
Artichokes (Globe, Whole)	30–40 min.	20 min. (Halved)
Artichokes (Jerusalem)	20 min.	
Asparagus	20–30 min.	
Beans, Broad	1 hour	
Beans, Fresh Lima	20–30 min.	
Beans, Shredded String	15 min.	
Beans, String (Whole)	25–30 min.	
Beets, New	30–40 min.	
Beets, Old	2 hrs.	
Broccoli	20–30 min.	
Brussels Sprouts	20–30 min.	
Cabbage, Shredded or Chopped	7–10 min.	
Cabbage, Sliced	12–15 min.	
Carrots, Diced	12–20 min.	
Carrots, Whole Medium	25–35 min.	15–20 min. (Sliced)
Cauliflower Fleurettes	15–20 min.	
Cauliflower (Whole)	25–30 min.	
Corn, Green	7–10 min.	
Cucumbers, Diced	5–8 min.	8–10 min. (Sliced)
Eggplant, Cubed	10–12 min.	8–10 min. (Sliced)
Kale, Spinach and Greens	10–20 min.	
Mushrooms, Sliced	8–10 min.	10 min. (Whole)
Okra, Sliced	10–15 min.	
Onions, Small, Whole	25–35 min.	10–15 min. (Sliced)
Parsnips, Diced	15–20 min.	20–30 min. (Sliced)
Peas (Green)	15–20 min.	
Potatoes (White or Sweet) Whole	30–40 min.	
Potatoes (White or Sweet) Sliced	15 min.	12–15 min. (Sliced)
Potatoes, medium-sized (White or Sweet) Whole Baked	35–45 min.	
Squash, Summer (Sliced)	10–12 min.	
Squash, Winter (Sliced)	20–25 min.	
Swiss Chard	20 min.	
Tomatoes, Fresh Stewed	15–20 min.	5–8 min. (Sliced)
Turnips, Diced	20–35 min.	

Canned Vegetables

Almost all vegetables are sold in canned form. This means that they are ready-cooked and merely need to be heated before serving.

Use the liquid from the can as a sauce with the vegetable, add it to a soup, or use in making gravy. It contains valuable food elements. Canned onions are useful.

Season canned vegetables as you would cooked fresh vegetables, using any of the suggestions and methods given in this book. Canned white and sweet potatoes are time savers.

Quick-Frozen Vegetables

Follow directions given on the package exactly. Do not overcook. When done, season with butter or fortified margarine and pepper; serve with cooking liquid as a sauce. All quick-frozen vegetables must be cooked, as they are frozen in the raw state. A wide variety is available.

TO SEASON VEGETABLES FOR TWO

All measurements are level

Buttered Vegetables: Use ¼ teaspoon salt and a few grains pepper to each cup of cooked vegetable. Or grind over a little black pepper in a pepper grinder. If vegetables are not garden-fresh, add a scant ¼ teaspoon Ac'cent; allow ½ tablespoon butter or fortified margarine to each cup of cooked vegetable, and keep hot to melt and blend.

Buttered Vegetables with Lime Juice: Prepare as directed for buttered vegetables, adding as much lime juice as butter to each cup of prepared vegetable. Use with naturally sweet vegetables, or with cauliflower, Brussels sprouts, broccoli or asparagus.

Sweet-Sour Vegetables: Use ½ tablespoon melted butter or margarine, ½ tablespoon lemon juice or mild vinegar, and ½ tablespoon sugar heated together. Good with cooked red or white cabbage, carrots, string beans, parsnips or turnips. Enough for 1 cup prepared vegetable.

Parslied Vegetables: Add butter or margarine as directed, with ½ tablespoon minced parsley. Suited to potatoes or any root vegetable.

Vegetables Vinaigrette: Add vinaigrette or remoulade sauce (page 177), and serve hot or cold. Suitable for cooked or canned string beans, asparagus, broccoli, cauliflower, sliced beets, or turnips, cooked wedges of cabbage, fleurettes of cauliflower or quartered carrots.

Vegetables Mayonnaise: Add ½ tablespoon top milk and 1 teaspoon lemon juice to 2 tablespoons mayonnaise for each cup of cooked vegetable. Season with paprika.

Vegetables with Soured Cream: Add 2 tablespoons soured cream, and 1 teaspoon lemon juice to each cup of cooked vegetable (any kind); or use with whole potatoes or carrots. Add paprika. Or heat with 2 tablespoons soured cream and 2 tablespoons sliced stuffed olives to the cup of cooked vegetable.

Butter-Relish Vegetables: To each cup of prepared vegetable add ½ tablespoon butter or margarine and ½ tablespoon pickle relish. Heat; serve with smoked or salt meats, or a pot roast. Suited to cooked beets, carrots, parsnips, green or red cabbage, cauliflower, Brussels sprouts or string beans.

Herbed Vegetables: Melt one tablespoon butter or fortified margarine for each cup of cooked vegetable. Add a scant ¼ teaspoon dried mint, thyme, basil, tarragon or herb mix, and let stand a few minutes to steep out the flavor. Then stir into or over the vegetable. Suitable for potatoes, peas, red cabbage, artichokes, quartered parsnips or mushrooms.

Herb-Vinegared Vegetables: Melt 1 tablespoon butter or margarine. Add 1 teaspoon any herb vinegar desired—

garlic, tarragon, basil or mixed herb vinegar. Stir into or pour over 1 cup of the prepared vegetable. Suitable for string beans, sliced beets, caulifleurettes, cabbage, Brussels sprouts, broccoli, quartered carrots, sliced turnips, celery or grilled tomatoes.

Curried Vegetables: Melt 1 tablespoon butter or margarine for each cup of prepared vegetable. Add ½ teaspoon curry powder; fry a moment, and stir through the vegetable. Suited to any kind of vegetable, cooked fresh or canned; or for dried beans, peas, or lentils.

Mixed Vegetables

Vegetable medleys or macedoines may be made from a mixture of fresh-cooked or oddments of vegetables combined with white sauce, melted butter, or tomato sauce.

Suitable combinations are: string beans, carrots, and cauliflower in white sauce.

String beans, carrots, and cabbage in white sauce.

Asparagus, carrots, and celery in white sauce or butter.

Peas and cauliflower with diced tomatoes barely heated through in melted butter.

ASPARAGUS ITALIAN
(Serves 2)

Arrange ½ pound cooked, fresh or frozen asparagus, or ½ can heated asparagus on toast. Dot with 1 tablespoon butter. Cover with 3 tablespoons grated cheese, and grill until it melts.

BROCCOLI OR CAULIFLOWER WITH CHEESE
(Serves 2)

½ pound cooked broccoli or 1¼ cups cooked cauliflower broken into fleurettes

Slices buttered toast
Cheese sauce (one recipe)

Heap the broccoli or cauliflower on buttered toast; pour over Cheese Sauce; (page 97).

BROCCOLI OR ASPARAGUS REMOULADE

Thoroughly moisten hot broccoli or asparagus with remoulade sauce. Heat a moment and serve as a hot salad vegetable; or chill and serve as a salad.

GREEN CORN FRITTERS
(*Serves 2*)

1 *tablespoon shortening*	½ *teaspoon salt*
¾ *cup corn cut from the cob*	2 *teaspoons baking powder*
1 *cup all-purpose flour*	½ *cup milk*

Vegetable fat for frying

1. Melt the shortening; add the corn and remaining ingredients except fat, in the order given.

2. Drop by small tablespoonfuls onto a well-oiled frying pan or griddle; fry slowly, turning once. Allow 3 minutes. Very good with Canadian or crisp bacon for breakfast.

Canned Corn Fritters: If using canned corn add only ¼ cup milk.

FRIED EGGPLANT
(*Serves 2*)

1 *small tender eggplant*	*Flour*
Salt	1 *egg*
Pepper	*Vegetable fat*

1. Wash the eggplant; do not peel; slice ¼ inch thick. Dust with salt, pepper and flour.

2. Beat the egg; add ¼ cup water, and dip the eggplant in it.

3. Dust with flour again; fry until golden on both sides in sufficient vegetable fat to prevent sticking.

4. Serve plain as a vegetable, or with bacon, or spaghetti sauce and grated cheese as a main dish.

SAUTÉED MUSHROOMS
(*Serves 2*)

¼ *pound fresh mush-*   1½ *tablespoons butter*
  rooms   *Salt and pepper*
Few grains nutmeg

1. Wash the mushrooms; do not peel; remove and cut the stems crosswise but leave the tops whole.

2. Melt the butter. Add the mushrooms; sauté slowly about 8 minutes, or until tender. Season with salt, pepper and a trace of nutmeg.

BROILED MUSHROOMS
(*Serves 2*)

8 *large mushrooms*   *Pepper*
  Salt   2 *tablespoons butter*

1. Wash. Remove stems and set aside for soup or seasoning. Place the mushrooms, caps down, on a slightly oiled pan. Sprinkle each with salt and pepper and put a little butter in each one.

2. Place under a slow heat in a preheated broiler and cook until the mushrooms are tender, about 10 minutes.

BROILED MUSHROOMS—CANADIAN
(*Serves 2*)

Prepare broiled mushrooms. After 6 minutes cooking, place 4 slices Canadian bacon on the broiler. Cook about 4 minutes longer; serve 2 mushrooms on each piece of bacon.

STEWED GREEN ONIONS
(*Serves 2*)

10 *young onions*   ⅓ *teaspoon sugar*
⅓ *teaspoon salt*   2 *tablespoons melted*
                                        butter

1. Cut the green tops from the onions to within 3 inches of the roots. Half cover the onions with boiling water; add the salt and sugar; boil until barely tender, about 15 minutes.

2. Drain; pour over the melted butter, dust with pepper and serve as is or arrange on buttered toast.

STEAM-FRIED ONIONS
(*Serves 2*)

6 *medium-sized mild*   ½ *teaspoon salt*
 onions   ⅛ *teaspoon pepper*
¼ *teaspoon sugar*   1 *tablespoon boiling water*
2½ *tablespoons butter or*
 margarine

1. Peel and slice the onions ¼ inch thick.

2. Melt the sugar in a small, heavy frying pan and add the butter or margarine; then put in the onions; season with the salt and pepper.

3. Add the water, cover closely and fry very slowly. Turn only once, using a pancake turner. Cook 15 to 20 minutes.

SPINACH ITALIAN
(*Serves 2*)

1 *pound tender spinach*   2 *tablespoons olive oil*
1 *teaspoon salt*   ⅛ *teaspoon pepper*
1 *section garlic peeled and*
 sliced

1. Remove any yellowed leaves and the root ends from the spinach. Wash thoroughly 3 times. Drain and place in a kettle with the salt. Do not add any water. Cover and cook until barely tender, from 10 to 15 minutes.

2. Meanwhile slice the garlic and heat with the oil; add the pepper.

3. Drain the spinach, add the oil and garlic and serve with or without a sprinkling of coarse bread crumbs fried in a little of the oil.

ESCALLOPED SUMMER SQUASH OR ZUCCHINI
(Serves 2)

1½ cups sliced peeled summer squash or zucchini

½ tablespoon flour
½ teaspoon salt
⅛ teaspoon pepper

½ cup hot milk
½ cup fine dry bread crumbs

1½ tablespoons melted butter

¼ cup grated cheese

1. Slice the squash or zucchini in rings. Peel and remove the squash seeds, unless very young and tender.

2. Place in layers in a shallow baking dish (or use 2 shirred egg dishes), sprinkling with the flour, salt and pepper. Pour in the milk. Cover with the crumbs, mixed with the melted butter, and then with the cheese.

3. Bake 25 minutes in a moderately hot oven, 375 degrees, F.

4. Serve as a luncheon dish, or with a vegetable meal.

SAUERKRAUT WITH APPLE
(Serves 2)

1½ cups sauerkraut
½ tablespoon butter

1 small chopped apple
1 teaspoon lemon juice

1. Rinse the sauerkraut with cold water. Melt the butter in a saucepan; add the apple and cook 1 minute.

2. Then add the sauerkraut, and slowly heat, allowing at least 20 minutes. Stir in the lemon juice and serve.

Season further with ¼ teaspoon caraway seed if desired.

BAKED ACORN SQUASH
(Serves 2)

1 *acorn squash*	⅛ *teaspoon pepper*
¼ *teaspoon salt*	1 *teaspoon sugar*

1 *tablespoon butter*

1. Cut the squash in halves lengthwise; scrape out the seeds. Place in a baking pan. Dust with salt, pepper and sugar. Dot with the butter.

2. Pour in a very little hot water to keep the squash from sticking, and bake until tender, 35 to 40 minutes in a moderate oven (375 degrees, F.).

GRILLED TOMATOES
(Serves 2)

2 *medium-sized firm ripe or half ripe tomatoes*	1 *teaspoon sugar*
Salt	2 *tablespoons buttered crumbs*
Pepper	

1. Cut the tomatoes crosswise in thirds. Place in a well-buttered or margarined pan. Sprinkle with the salt, pepper and sugar.

2. Cover the tops with the crumbs. Broil under a moderate heat until the tomatoes are soft, but hold their shape, and the crumbs are browned, about 5 minutes.

INDIVIDUAL VEGETABLE PIES
(Serves 2)

Tart shells	1¼ *cups creamed vegetables*

1. Bake the tart shells (page 266); keep hot. Fill with the creamed vegetables and serve at luncheon or dinner with the meat course. Or sprinkle with grated cheese and serve as the main course at lunch or supper.

2. Suitable creamed vegetables that may be used are: Creamed asparagus; creamed carrots with peas; creamed string beans; or a medley of vegetables, such as asparagus, corn, and string beans in cream sauce.

DANDELIONS WITH POTATOES
(Serves 2 to 3)

2 small slices fat salt pork 4 small white potatoes
½ teaspoon salt   peeled
            ½ pound dandelion greens

1. Dice the salt pork and fry. When crisp, add the salt, potatoes and boiling water to cover. Boil 15 minutes.

2. Add the dandelion greens and cook 20 minutes longer, or until both vegetables are tender.

3. Drain and season with a little pepper.

FLAKY BOILED POTATOES
(Serves 2)

1. Peel white potatoes; barely cover with boiling water; add ½ teaspoon salt. Cover, and boil slowly and steadily about 35 minutes, or until the potatoes are tender when a sharp fork is stuck in.

2. Drain off the liquid, and use in diluting condensed soup or making gravy.

3. Gently shake the utensil containing the potatoes over a low heat until they look flaky. Serve at once.

Potatoes in the jackets: Do not peel. Scrub well; remove blemishes, and cook as for flaky boiled potatoes. They are darker in color than when flaky boiled, but the vitamins and minerals are conserved.

FRANCONIA POTATOES
(*Serves 2*)

Peel medium-sized or sweet potatoes. Place in the pan with roasting meat, and bake 45 minutes. Turn once to brown evenly.

BAKED WHITE OR SWEET POTATOES
(*Serves 2*)

Scrub potatoes. Remove any blemishes. Rub with any good fat. Place on a rack in a hot oven at 425 degrees, F. and bake until tender when pressed hard with the fingers —35 to 40 minutes for medium-sized potatoes, 50 minutes for Idahos. Serve at once, plain, or with the tops slashed, the potato pulp "popped" or pressed up, and topped with a square of butter or margarine.

MASHED OR WHIPPED WHITE POTATOES
(*Serves 2*)

4 *medium-sized white pota-* *toes*	1 *tablespoon butter*
	⅓ *teaspoon salt*
2 *tablespoons milk*	⅛ *teaspoon pepper*

1. Peel the potatoes and slice them thin. Add water to half cover, put in 1 teaspoon salt, and boil rapidly until tender, about 12 minutes.

2. Measure the milk, butter and seasonings into a medium-sized saucepan and heat. Put the potatoes through a potato ricer into this and beat until fluffy with a wire whisk or electric mixer.

Variations: Add 1 tablespoon chopped parsley, 2 tablespoons grated raw carrot, ¼ cup fried minced onion.

Mashed or Whipped Sweet Potatoes: Follow the preceding recipe, for white potatoes, using sweet potatoes.

Variations: Beat in ⅓ cup chopped toasted nuts of any

kind; or use raisins and nuts. Or add a grated raw apple, or ¼ cup grated canned pineapple.

POTATO OMELET
(Serves 2)

2 eggs

1 cup hot mashed potatoes

Frying fat

¼ cup minced parsley

1. Beat the eggs; add to the mashed potatoes.

2. Melt enough fat in a large frying pan to barely cover the bottom. Drop in the potato mixture by large table-spoonfuls; flatten with a spoon to ⅓ inch in thickness.

3. Fry slowly until browned. Cover with the parsley and fold over to form individual omelets.

4. Serve plain, or with ham, bacon or sausage.

DUCHESSE POTATOES
(Serves 2 to 3)

3 good-sized white po-
    tatoes

½ teaspoon salt

Few grains pepper

2 tablespoons top milk

1 egg yolk, beaten

1. Peel the potatoes; cut in small pieces and boil until tender. Drain.

2. Put through a potato ricer and add the remaining ingredients. Beat until fluffy, then use as directed.

POTATO PANCAKES
(Serves 2 to 3)

3 medium-sized raw white
    potatoes

1 egg

1 tablespoon flour

¾ teaspoon salt

1. Wash, peel and fine-grate the potatoes.

2. Add the egg yolk, flour and salt; fold in the egg white, whipped stiff.

3. Drop by tablespoonfuls onto a hot, well-oiled griddle or frying pan; fry until brown, first on one side, then on the other. For a meaty flavor, use bacon, sausage or ham fat.

BUTTER-FRIED POTATOES
(Serves 2),

1½ *cups freshly cooked*   *Butter*
  white potatoes sliced
  small

1. The potatoes should be sliced in bits—really chipped on a coarse grater. Melt sufficient butter in a frying pan to barely cover the bottom. Do not let it brown.

2. Put in the potatoes in a thin layer. Dust with a little salt and pepper and brown on 1 side. Fold over omelet fashion and serve very hot.

LYONNAISE POTATOES
(Serves 2)

3 *tablespoons butter or.*   ½ *teaspoon minced pars-*
  savory fat   *ley (optional)*
1 *small onion minced*   *Salt and pepper to*
1½ *cups sliced cooked po-*   *taste*
  tatoes

1. Melt the fat. Add the onion and cook until it begins to turn yellow; add the potatoes; fry slowly, turning occasionally so they will not burn.

2. Sprinkle with salt, pepper and parsley just before serving.

FRENCH FRIED POTATOES
(Serves 2 to 3)

1 *pound white potatoes*   *Vegetable fat for deep*
        Salt   *frying*

1.   Peel potatoes, wash, cut in fingerlength strips and rinse.

2.   Drain, and dry on paper towels.

3.   Half fill a deep heavy saucepan with vegetable fat or oil; heat to 325 degrees F. by a fat thermometer, or until a 1 inch cube of bread browns in 1½ minutes.

4.   Cover the bottom of a frying basket or large strainer with the potatoes; lower into the hot fat. When the potatoes rise to the top and are golden brown, lift out the frying basket. Drain a moment, tip out the potatoes onto paper towels to absorb the fat and sprinkle with salt.

The Legumes—Dried Peas, Beans and Lentils

When it comes to legumes for the family of two, better turn to canned foods, as it is a waste of time to cook dried legumes. A generous choice is available.

Season and serve with imagination and you will produce foods that will stand service as a main dish once or twice a week. For instance:

Canned Dried Limas: Heat in spiced tomato sauce; serve strewn with fried croutons.

Canned Garbanza Beans: Heat with butter, and a touch of cumin seed if you like; serve with bacon, sausage links, grilled salami or bologna.

Canned Lentils: Heat with a little sliced Polish sausage and onion sautéed in butter.

Canned Split Pea Purée: Use condensed split pea soup. Do not add water. Season with butter or bits of fried bacon, heat and serve with a vegetable plate.

BEANS AND BACON ON TOAST

Add ½ tablespoon butter to a can of baked beans. Heat. Serve heaped on hot buttered toast. Garnish with crisp bacon or sausage links. Excellent for breakfast.

BEANS WITH ONIONS
(*Serves 2 to 3*)

1 *can baked beans*　　1 *tablespoon butter, bacon*
4 *small cooked onions*　　　*fat or sausage fat*

1. Place the beans in an oiled dish with the onions in the middle.

2. Pour in the melted fat; let it trickle through; bake about 20 minutes in a moderate oven (350–375 degrees, F.).

BOSTON BAKED BEANS SHERRIED
(*Serves 2 to 3*)

2 *tablespoons minced*　　¼ *cup drained canned to-*
　onion　　　　　　　　　*matoes*
1 *tablespoon bacon or*　　¼ *teaspoon mustard*
　sausage fat　　　　　1 *tablespoon dry sherry*
1 *can baked beans*　　　*Cooked-bacon garnish*

1. Fry the onion until yellowed in the fat.

2. Combine ingredients in a shallow casserole; bake 25 minutes in a moderate oven, 375 degrees, F. Serve garnished with bacon.

KIDNEY BEANS WITH HAM AND ONION
(*Serves 2*)

½ *medium-sized onion*　　⅓ *cup cooked ham, minced*
　chopped　　　　　　　*or diced*
1 *tablespoon butter or*　　1 *small can kidney beans*
　meat drippings　　　　*Buttered toast*

1. Fry the onion in the butter until softened. Add ham and beans.

2. Heat and serve heaped on the toast.

Concerning Cereals

Young or old, we all need cereals. Whole grain cereals provide those B Complex vitamins in natural form; fortified cereals contain them in synthetic form. Both types are nutritionally sound. And to make sure plenty of B Complex is provided, any serving of cereal, dry or cooked, may be sprinkled with a tablespoonful of wheat germ.

I sincerely recommend cereal for breakfast. If it is a "dry" ready-prepared cereal, recrisp by heating in the oven or broiler and serve with cold milk. If cooked, serve with heated milk. Or use the top of the bottle for cream, and save the remainder of the bottle for cooking. If a cooked cereal is to be the main breakfast dish, better cook it with milk to add protein. In this case, use equal parts of water and canned evaporated milk (not sweetened). Whole cereals can be served in place of potatoes at dinner, and they can form the basis of many substantial dishes.

All measurements are level

To Cook Whole Cereals
(*Serves 2*)

Follow the directions on the package using ½ the amount of cereal and water. Or better, cook the full quantity, enough to serve twice. Transfer the unused portion to a refrigerator dish. Cover while warm to prevent the formation of crust on top and refrigerate.

To reheat cooked cereal: Put in a double boiler. Pour over 2 tablespoons water; cover and steam about 15 minutes. Stir occasionally with a fork to hurry the heating.

Fried cereal slices: Turn cold cereal out of the refrigerator dish onto waxed paper dusted with fine dry bread crumbs or flour. Cut in ½-inch slices. Coat with the crumbs or flour. Fry slowly on both sides in bacon fat, butter or margarine. Serve with buttered syrup, honey or jelly.

FLAKY RICE
(Serves 2 to 3)

¾ cup white rice   ½ teaspoon salt
1½ cups cold water

1. Combine the ingredients. Cover closely and cook over a moderate heat until the water is nearly absorbed.

2. Reduce the heat and finish cooking, allowing 20 to 25 minutes altogether, until dry; do not drain or rinse.

BROWN RICE
(Serves 2 to 3)

1. Bring 2 cups water to a rapid boil. Add ½ teaspoon salt and ¾ cup brown rice. Slow boil 45 minutes to 1 hour until the rice is tender.

2. During the last 10 minutes uncover, and put an asbestos mat under the rice. It should be dry enough to serve without draining. Add 1 tablespoon butter if desired.

Wild Rice: Pick over and wash rice; cook as above.

CURRIED RICE

Add 1 tablespoon butter melted with ½ teaspoon curry powder for each cup of cooked rice—any kind.

SPANISH RICE
(Serves 2 to 3)

¾ cup uncooked rice   1¾ cups canned tomatoes
1 tablespoon oil or savory   1 tablespoon minced on-
  drippings   ion
2 tablespoons diced green   ½ teaspoon sugar
  peppers   ½ teaspoon salt
     ½ cup sharp grated cheese

1. Lightly brown the uncooked rice in the oil; add the peppers, tomatoes, onion, and seasonings; simmer till the rice is tender, about 25 minutes.

2. Serve with the cheese.

Spanish Rice with Sausage or Ham: Add ½ cup diced cervelat, Polish sausage or cooked ham to Spanish rice while cooking.

Savory Rice with Crab Meat, Lobster or Oysters: Prepare Spanish rice. Ten minutes before it will be done add ½ cup canned crab meat, diced lobster meat or 6 halved oysters.

SPAGHETTI al DENTE
(*Serves 2*)

Bring about 2 quarts of water to a rapid boil. Add 1 teaspoon salt, or 2 or 3 bouillon cubes. Hold ¼ pound sticks of spaghetti by the ends. Lower into the boiling liquid, and as the spaghetti softens, press it down under the water. Boil rapidly about 10 minutes, when it should be al dente, which means tender, but not soft to the teeth. Do not rinse with cold water.

ITALIAN NOODLES
(*Serves 2*)

¼ *pound noodles*
2 *teaspoons olive oil*
½ *peeled section garlic crushed*
1 *seeded minced green pepper*

1 *4-ounce can tomato purée*
½ *teaspoon salt*
Few grains paprika
½ *cup diced cooked ham*
½ *cup grated Parmesan or American cheese*

1. Boil the noodles tender in salted water to cover for 10 minutes.

2. Heat the oil with the garlic; add the green pepper,

tomato purée and equal amount of water, and the seasonings. Simmer until reduced ¼.

3. Then add the ham and ½ the cheese. Stir in the noodles; reheat and serve in a deep hot dish; sprinkle with the remaining cheese.

For Gourmet and Gourmette

EGGPLANT ITALIAN
(Serves 2)

1 *small eggplant*
2 *tablespoons flour*
¼ *teaspoon salt*
⅛ *teaspoon pepper*

3 *tablespoons olive oil*
1 *cup tomato sauce*
Grated cheese preferably Parmesan

1. Wash the eggplant; slice crosswise a scant ½ inch thick.

2. Mix together the flour, salt and pepper; dip the eggplant in this. Then brown in the oil on both sides until almost tender.

3. Place in a baking dish in alternating layers with the tomato sauce, with a little grated cheese between.

4. Top with grated cheese; bake about 20 minutes in a moderate oven, 375 degrees, F.

CHAPTER XII

The Salad's the Thing!

SALAD MAKING IS FUN, WHETHER FOR TWO OR TWENTY—
the greatest chance in all cookery for imagination to run
riot. But it should be tempered with good taste. Marsh-
mallows for instance do not belong in salads; nor does
onion harmonize with orange, or baked apples with mayonnaise. A number of far-fetched food combinations have
been perpetrated as salads on the long-suffering public. So
be sure the ingredients you combine in a salad are foods
that would harmonize if served separately in the same
course.

How to Crisp-Keep Salad Ingredients

Start by buying fresh, crisp salad greens. If there is good
automatic or ice refrigeration, they will keep crisp and
free from rust in the hydrator that comes with the refrigerator; or lacking that, in a small covered enamelware roasting pan; or use polyethelene bags.

Wash thoroughly and trim all salad ingredients as soon
as purchased. Then drain well (a wire dish drainer is good
for this) and pack into the hydrator or container. Small
vegetables such as radishes, trimmed scallions or cress,
should be wrapped in waxed paper. Well chilled and
properly refrigerated salad vegetables will keep a week.
And herein lies the answer to the variety problem. Instead

of buying one head of lettuce and using it for 2 meals, get 3 kinds of salad greens and a few odd vegetables, such as tomatoes, cucumbers, scallions and carrots. They will last a week and provide various combinations for the salad bowl. Add a few olives, an occasional chopped hard-cooked egg, a handful of chopped toasted nuts, or oddments of cooked vegetables, and you will achieve such a variety that salads will never become a bore.

What—No Refrigerator?

In this case, keep the salad greens in a covered old-fashioned crock set in a cool place. If a breath of fresh air blows on the crock so much the better. Or if you are in the country vacationing, and the weather is warm, line a pail or enamelware cooking utensil with waxed paper; put in the washed salad ingredients; cover closely, and put right on the cellar floor, or on the cool ground under the house or trailer. The contents will keep crisp for 24 hours. Really!

And if you're on a houseboat, you know what to do. Put the green salads in a pail; seal the cover on with adhesive tape, tie a string to the handle, and lower it into the water (select the shady side).

Types of Salads

In the interest of more intelligent menu planning, I am classifying salads in 5 groups as follows:

I. **First Course Salads:**   Individual tossed salad bowls, served as the first course, California Style.

Hors d'Oeuvres: Served salad style, as anchovy fillets on lettuce, cress or slaw.

Saladettes: That is small portions of chicken, lobster, crab, salmon, herring, egg or some other made salad, attractively arranged on sliced tomatoes, Chinese cabbage or a salad green, and served as a first course. A nice way to utilize oddments, and add interest, food value and chic to lunch or dinner.

II. Tossed Bowl Salads: When made with plain salad greens and French dressing, these are dinner salads. A big serving of tossed salad can be the second vegetable served for dinner. When a little Roquefort, Bleu or other cheese is added, they are still suitable dinner salads, because cheese—traditionally served with salad in the grand manner—is served in it instead.

When tossed salads are fortified with plenty of chopped nuts, flaked fish, juliennes of cheddar cheese, sausage or canned luncheon meat, flakes of cooked chicken or other poultry, or with diced meat of any kind, they are really Main Dish Salads.

III. Main Dish Salads: These include the reinforced tossed salads just described, and all made salads based on protein foods—meat, poultry, fish, shell fish, eggs, cottage or cheddar cheese, cooked dried beans or lentils, or dried or green soy beans. They also include "made" vegetable or nut salads. By "made" I mean the salad ingredients are cut up and combined with a heavy dressing, as mayonnaise, Russian, or cream cheese dressing. In this same group we have molded or jellied salads made from any of the proteins, correctly based on a savory aspic.

IV. The Slaw Family: Coleslaw is known to everyone in some form or other. Traditionally it is simply made of white or red cabbage, dressed with French dressing, and served at dinner, luncheon or supper, or with sandwich snacks. However, lettuce, celtuce, green savoy cabbage and Chinese cabbage are also shredded to make slaw. When put together with mayonnaise, Russian, cooked salad dressing, or soured cream dressing, the slaw should be served only at lunch or supper. It is too substantial for dinner.

V. Fruit Salads: These are in a class by themselves,

and can be the most delectable of foods, or positively horrific, according to the way they are made and the dressing served with them. We will assume that you will use only the good kind, such as, well, er—of course I mean the ones described in this book. In this case they may be the main dish of a summer luncheon or supper, or dessert with cream cheese and crisp wafers.

To give directions for making all kinds of salads would take a book in itself. So I am including typical and popular salads suited for 2 in each classification. With these recipes as a basis, you will enjoy working out your own salad spécialités.

Arranging and Serving Salads

No matter what the salad, keep it dainty and appetizing. Use chilled plates or individual salad bowls, and do not fill them too full. (I like deep plates or shallow bowls. Easier to fork up the salad.) By the way, both knives and forks are correct to use in eating salads. Cut that sliced lettuce as boldly as you would a steak. Eat up every last vitamin. Go easy with the salad dressing; put a little extra on the table, rather than drown the salad with it. And be sure to add an attractive garnish. For instance:

Bread and butter pickles	*Radishes*
Olives, ripe, green and stuffed	*Strips of pimiento*
Little melon pickles	*Rings of green pepper*
Carrot sticks	*Cress*
Scallions	*Parsley*
Capers	*Nut meats*
Anchovy fillets	*Diced cheese*
Meras	*Small cheese balls (rolled or cut*
Slices of cream cheese	*with a potato scoop)*

However, remember that an attractive looking salad is casual in arrangement. Never, never, should it look like a mountain glaciered with mayonnaise, fenced with green pepper strips, polka dotted with capers, and surmounted with a tree of parsley—landscape salads are definitely "out."

Hors d'Oeuvres Salad Combinations

There are as many possible combinations as there are hors d'oeuvres. For instance:

1. Crab meat with sauce remoulade (page 177), on lettuce. Garnish with sliced red radishes.

2. Liver pâté mixed with chopped hard-cooked egg, and chopped olives or scallions; serve with lettuce and/or cress. Garnish with sliced stuffed olives.

3. Sardines, tomato wedges, slaw and romaine. Place each sardine in a large romaine leaf, partly filled with chopped slaw. Season with lemon juice.

4. Overlapping slices smoked salmon; balls of cottage cheese and chives; lettuce or shredded center leaves of spinach and French dressing. Garnish with ripe olives.

5. Chilled cooked or canned dried lima, green or soy beans, cubes of fresh tomato, French garlic dressing, lettuce and black olives.

All measurements are level
ANCHOVY SALAD HORS D'OEUVRE
(Serves 2)

2 quarters of a head of lettuce	4 slices pickled beets
2 pimientoes quartered	2 cleaned radishes
4 anchovies	2 cleaned scallions
2 quarters hard-cooked egg	2 hearts of celery or celery curls
2 slices salami	Olives

1. Arrange individually. Place the lettuce in the center of the salad plate. On this arrange 2 pieces of pimiento. Cross 2 anchovies on top.

2. Around this center arrange the remaining ingredients. Add the olives for finish and garnish. Pass oil and wine vinegar.

Tossed Salad Bowls

Salad bowls are made of crisp lettuce or any group of crisp or green vegetables, and are easily dressed at the table with salad oil, vinegar and seasonings. Use a good sized salad bowl to allow plenty of room for mixing with a wooden salad fork and spoon. For dinner service only simpler salad bowls should be chosen, such as a lettuce or mixed greens salad bowl with oil and vinegar or lemon juice dressing. For lunch or supper a more elaborate salad bowl may be used, as a crab meat salad bowl, fruit and nut salad bowl, or the Chef's Salad Bowl, given in this book. In any case, the oil and seasonings are first sprinkled over the salad and thoroughly mixed in before the vinegar (or lemon juice) is added; for if the vinegar is put on first, the oil slides off the leaves and cannot be thoroughly blended in. Use wine vinegar, herb-flavored garlic or tarragon vinegar for a change.

Or the salad may be tossed with prepared French dressing if it is not "sweet."

CHEF'S SALAD BOWL
(*Serves 2 to 3*)

1 *section garlic*	½ *tomato diced*
¼ *small head lettuce shredded*	1 *scallion diced*
¼ *cucumber sliced*	¼ *cup celery, shredded*
¼ *cup sliced radishes*	¼ *cup shredded carrot*
	¼ *cup French dressing*
1 *tablespoon chili sauce if desired*	

Rub the salad bowl with a cut section of garlic. Combine all the ingredients in it. Toss and serve.

Chef's Salad Bowl with Meat: Add ½ cup diced or julienned cooked lamb, beef, tongue, ham, chicken or turkey. Finish as directed.

Chef's Salad Bowl with Fish: Use crab meat, lobster, tuna or flaked salmon, instead of meat; garnish with anchovy fillets.

Chef's Salad Bowl with Cheese: Make Chef's Salad Bowl as described, using diced or julienned sharp cheddar or Old English cheese. Add 2 tablespoons chopped salted peanuts or toasted Brazil nuts if desired.

SALADETTES

These can look like a million and cost little, as they can be made with oddments or canned foods.

1. Chicken-Nut Saladettes: Mix chopped chicken with chopped salted nut meats and sauce tartare. Chill and serve in romaine leaf boats, or on sliced tomato.

2. Salmon-Olive Saladettes: Mix flaked salmon with chopped celery, stuffed olives, mayonnaise and a squeeze of lemon juice. Serve in lettuce nests, or on sliced cucumbers. Garnish with olives.

3. Ham-N-Egg Saladettes: Mix minced ham, hard-cooked egg and a little sweet pickle relish, with a little table mustard and salad dressing. Serve on sliced lettuce or tomato, or on crisp hot toast with parsley or cress. Garnish with red radishes.

4. Tongue Horse-Radish Saladettes: Mix minced tongue with minced green pepper, celery, horse-radish and mayonnaise. Serve on sliced tomato or cucumber, or on a split slice of canned pineapple, with chicory tossed in French dressing.

Coleslaw and Its Variations

PLAIN COLESLAW
(*Serves 2*)

1. Remove the core of a crisp white, green or savoy cabbage; shred fine with a cabbage shredder, or put the section of cabbage on a vegetable board and shred down the desired quantity with a sharp knife. Do not chop. Allow 1½ cups for 2 servings.

2. Place the cabbage in a sieve; rinse with cold water; refrigerate a few minutes to crisp. Toss with the French dressing of your choice. Serve with or without lettuce, a thin slice or two of tomato, or big cubes of tomato aspic.

Varying Coleslaw: Add a choice of the following:

½ *tablespoon minced parsley*

2 *tablespoons diced green pepper*

2 *tablespoons squares of pimiento*

4 *sliced stuffed olives*

4 *sliced red radishes*

¼ *cup julienned celery*

¼ *cup julienned raw carrot*

¼ *cup diced scallions*

¼ *cup coarse-cut cress*

¼ *cup diced red-skinned apple*

2 *tablespoons coarse-chopped salted or toasted nuts*

COLESLAW WITH SOURED CREAM
(*Serves 2*)

1½ *cups finely shredded crisp white, green or savoy cabbage*

¼ *seeded green pepper minced*

1 *small carrot peeled and coarse-grated*

⅓ *cup chilled thick soured cream*

¼ *teaspoon salt*

1 *tablespoon vinegar*

½ *teaspoon sugar*

Few grains white pepper

¼ *teaspoon paprika*

1. Combine the cabbage, green pepper and carrot.
2. Make an uncooked soured cream dressing by combining the cream, salt, vinegar, sugar, pepper and paprika. Mix thoroughly and stir into the cabbage mixture.
3. Serve on lettuce. Garnish with ripe olives, sliced stuffed olives or radishes, or sliced carrot.

Main Dish Salads

All saladettes may be served in larger portions as main dish salads. For best results dice or flake the ingredients; do not mince or put through the chopper. Let the main ingredients marinate, that is stand with French dressing, for at least 15 minutes in the refrigerator to chill and season. Then add avocado, Russian dressing, mayonnaise, cooked salad dressing, or cheese or cream dressing of your selection. Mix, arrange on the salad green and garnish. Such salads will stand 30 minutes before serving, if refrigerated or in a cold pantry. Here are several recipes calling for various types of substantial ingredients.

All measurements are level

SALMON SALAD MOLDS
(Serves 2)

½ *pound can salmon*	1 *hard-cooked egg*
¼ *cup fine-diced celery or firm portion cucumber*	2 *tablespoons French dressing*
½ *tablespoon minced parsley*	*Mayonnaise or salad dressing*

Lettuce or chicory

1. Drain oil from salmon. Remove skin and bones and flake the fish. Add the celery or cucumber and parsley; chop and add the hard-cooked egg.

2. Toss with French dressing; add mayonnaise or salad dressing to blend.

3. Pack into custard cups and chill 15 minutes.

4. Unmold on the lettuce; garnish with extra dressing, sliced tomato or cucumber, pickles, or green peas.

Tuna Salad Molds: Follow the preceding recipe using tuna fish.

Lobster Salad Molds: Make as salmon salad, using fresh, canned or quick-frozen lobster. Garnish with slices of avocado.

Fish-Oddments Molds: Make as salmon salad, using flaked oddments of any fish, bones removed, of course. (Use tweezers for de-boning.) Excellent with halibut, cod, ocean perch or swordfish.

CHICKEN SALAD
(*Serves 2*)

1 *cup diced cold cooked chicken*
2 *tablespoons French dressing made with oil or chicken fat*
1 *teaspoon scraped onion*
⅓ *cup diced celery*

2 *tablespoons coarse-chopped toasted nuts, (optional)*
Mayonnaise to blend
Lettuce
Parsley, olives or slices of avocado

1. Do not use the chicken skin. Combine the chicken, French dressing and scraped onion. Refrigerate 15 minutes to season and chill.

2. Add the celery, nuts and mayonnaise. Serve in lettuce nests, or on chilled, split slices of canned pineapple. Garnish with parsley, olives or slices of avocado.

Duck or Turkey Salad: Follow the recipe for chicken salad. Serve on sliced tomato, or with tomato aspic.

SWEDISH EGG SALAD
(*Serves 2*)

2 *hard-cooked eggs*   *Mayonnaise*
Herring, sardine, or an-   *Mixed vegetable salad*
chovy paste   *Lettuce or romaine*

1. Cut eggs in halves lengthwise. Remove yolks and mix with a little of the fish paste and mayonnaise.

2. Heap the mixture back into the egg whites; top each with a sprig of parsley, fresh dill, a caper, or bit of green pepper.

3. Chill and serve in nests of lettuce, with a spoonful of diced cooked vegetables in mayonnaise on the side.

MISSISSIPPI SALAD PLATE
(*Serves 2*)

Shredded crisp lettuce   2 *slices crisp bacon*
2 *slices pineapple*   12 *cooked shrimp*
½ *a cream cheese*   4 *tablespoons fish cocktail*
1 *large tomato*   *sauce or French dres-*
                        sing

1. Bed the lettuce on large salad plates. Top with the pineapple, and top this with the cheese which should be cut in two pieces.

2. Slice the tomato thin. Place on one side of the plate. Top with the bacon.

3. Arrange the shrimp on the opposite side.

4. Pour over the French dressing.

5. Serve with hot toasted corn muffins or rolls.

POTATO SALAD
(Serves 2)

2 *cups diced warm cooked potato*

½ *onion grated*

1 *tablespoon vinegar*

½ *teaspoon salt*

¼ *teaspoon sugar*

⅛ *teaspoon pepper*

3 *tablespoons salad oil*

½ *tablespoon minced parsley*

1 *hard-cooked egg chopped*

Mayonnaise, salad dressing or soured cream dressing, cooked or uncooked

Lettuce

1. Combine the potato with the onion, vinegar, seasonings, oil, and parsley.

2. Add the chopped hard-cooked egg and mayonnaise to blend.

3. Chill and serve in nests of lettuce.

For a special touch add ½ teaspoon cumin seed to the salad mixture. Or stir in 3 tablespoons chopped toasted nut meats, and garnish with nuts.

Stuffed Vegetable Salads

Tomato, Patty Pan Squash, Green Peppers or Cucumbers: All these are fine containers for a salad stuffing. As to their preparation, life is too short to stop to peel the tomatoes, so leave on the skin and keep the food values. Wash and hollow out to form cups. If very large, cut in halves. Don't peel the squash. Just boil until tender, then hollow out. Cut the tops from the peppers; remove the seeds and let the peppers stand 1 minute in boiling water to take out the excess "bite"; then chill. Cut the cucumbers lengthwise into "boats," and spoon out the seeds. Don't peel unless they are old and the skin is tough.

Season inside with salt, pepper and a dash of any herb

vinegar you like. Or use lemon juice. Then fill with a salad stuffing.

Fillings for Stuffed Vegetable Salads

1. Any of the mixtures suggested for saladettes (page 211), or main dish salads (page 213).

2. Chopped tongue or luncheon meat salad.

3. Raw or cooked vegetable salad mixed with the dressing of your choice. (I like mayonnaise.)

4. Cheddar cheese salad, or chived or nutted cottage cheese.

5. Pimiento cheese, chopped celery and nuts.

When stuffed, chill, garnish, and serve on sliced lettuce or Chinese cabbage, or with tossed salad greens. Hot butter-fried croutons are a tasty accompaniment.

NUT SALADS
(*Serves 2*)

1 *small head lettuce*	½ *teaspoon lemon juice*
12 *walnut meats*	2 *tablespoons salad oil*
1 *tablespoon orange juice*	*Few grains salt*
Few grains paprika	

Shred the lettuce and arrange in nests. Combine the remaining ingredients and sprinkle over. Serve with cold meat or chicken.

Nut and Grape Salad: Follow the preceding recipe, adding ½ cup seedless green or halved seeded malaga grapes.

CHEDDAR CHEESE SALAD
(*Serves 2*)

1 *cup diced cheddar cheese*	8 *sliced stuffed olives or*
½ *cup diced celery*	2 *tablespoons broken pecan meats*
	French garlic dressing
Lettuce	

1.   Combine the cheese, celery, and olives or nuts with dressing to moisten; chill.

2.   Serve in lettuce nests, with tomato wedges, rings of green pepper and/or paper thin slices of cucumber. Dark bread with this.

Jellied Salads

"Molded in aspic" or "jellied" salads mean one and the same thing to most people. But in reality they are different. When molded in aspic the salad should be savory in flavor, as fish, chicken, or egg salad, and the aspic base should have a tart or meaty taste. (Prepared packaged aspic is excellent and time-saving.) Or a savory tart tomato aspic may be used. In this case the foundation is available in packaged form, or it may be easily made with unflavored granulated gelatin and tomato juice. But jellied salads are too often made with a *dessert* gelatin, such as lemon or lime, with vinegar or lemon juice added to neutralize the sweet taste. But it never does. We do not even get a real sweet-sour flavor. Consequently many persons, especially men, do not like jellied salads. And persons with discriminating taste do not like salads molded by means of cornstarch. But real aspic salads are another proposition; appetizing, easy to make, thrifty and so important looking.

CONSOMMÉ ASPIC SALADS
(*Serves 2 twice*)

1.   Purchase a can of concentrated consommé (or chicken broth), and heat as is.

2.   Combine 2 tablespoons cold water, 1 envelope unflavored granulated gelatin, and melt over hot water. Stir into the consommé.

3. Add ½ tablespoon lemon juice, and 1 teaspoon of any herb-flavored vinegar if you like.

4. Stir in the mixture or food to be jellied.

5. Rinse custard cups with cold water and fill with the aspic-mixture. Chill until firm—at least 4 hours in a really cold refrigerator. Better still, make ready the day before.

6. Serve with lettuce or sliced tomatoes or any salad green; pass Russian dressing or mayonnaise.

Aspic Salad Mixtures

1. Meat-in-Aspic Salad: 1½ cups fine-diced chicken, duck, turkey; or mix ham or tongue with the poultry; add ½ cup fine-diced celery, cucumber or green peppers, a few peas, diced cooked carrots or diced string beans.

2. Fish-in-Aspic Salad: Use any flaked, boiled or poached fish, canned fish flakes, salmon, tuna fish, shrimp, lobster or crab meat plus the vegetables enumerated.

TOMATO ASPIC SALAD
(Serves 2 twice)

1 *envelope plain unflavored gelatin*	1 *pint canned tomato juice*
2 *tablespoons cold water* Juice ½ *lemon or* ½' *tablespoon mild vinegar*	½ *teaspoon Worcestershire sauce*
	½ *teaspoon onion juice*
	⅓ *teaspoon salt*

Few grains pepper

1. Add the gelatin to the water. Then dissolve over boiling water. Add the lemon juice and stir until well mixed.

2. Combine all the ingredients and transfer to individual molds. Refrigerate until firm, at least 6 hours. Unmold and use as desired.

Tomato Aspic Salad Mixtures: Use any of the Aspic Salad mixtures suggested.

Fruit Salads

Just what is fruit salad? A fruit cocktail or cup, or a served-on-lettuce salad? To answer, the name is rightly given only to a salad served with lettuce; the dressing should harmonize with the fruit. A lemon or lime-juice dressing made with a little oil, a cream cheese dressing, wine dressing or lemon-honey cream dressing is perfect.

Fruit salads are served in place of dessert at luncheon or dinner; or they may be main dish and dessert combined, at luncheon or supper. In this case, a salad fruit plate is the thing, fortified with mild cheese, or toasted nuts. On grand occasions, as a buffet supper, fruits drenched with dry wine are served as the salad garniture of a cold chicken, or cold meat platter. And delectable they are.

Fruit salads may be made from any combination of fresh fruit, cut bite-size. But with the exception of canned pineapple, cooked or canned fruit should not be used. If prunes or figs are called for, do not cook them. Instead wash and pour over boiling water; let stand 10 minutes; drain, dry on paper towels and chill before using.

LETTUCE AND FRUIT SALAD BOWL
(Serves 2 to 3)

½ *small head lettuce*   ⅓ *cup seedless or seeded*
 1 *seedless orange*   *malaga or tokay grapes*
 1 *ripe banana*   ½ *eating apple*
         3 *tablespoons French lemon dressing*

   1.   Shred lettuce.
   2.   Peel and section the orange; cut each section in

thirds. Slice the banana. Halve the grapes if they are large. Dice the apple, skin on.

3. Arrange in the salad bowl with the lettuce; top with pieces of choice fruit. Dress at the table. Chopped nuts may be added. Garnish with small balls of cream cheese.

FRUITS DRENCHED WITH WINE
(*Serves 2 to 3*)

½ *cup sliced orange*
⅓ *cup diced pineapple*
¼ *cup halved seeded green grapes*
¼ *cup whole or sliced strawberries*

⅓ *cup sauterne or white wine*
Juice ¼ lemon or lime
1 *tablespoon granulated sugar*
Hearts of lettuce

1. Combine the fruits with the wine, lemon or lime juice, and sugar. Chill 10 minutes.
2. Serve on the lettuce.

FRUIT SALAD PLATE
(*Serves 2 to 3*)

Select seasonable fresh fruits; wash and cut in sections. Save a little choice fruit for a garnish. Heap the prepared fruit on a slice of lettuce. Pour over 1 generous tablespoonful of lemon-honey cream dressing; dust with chopped toasted nuts or wheat germ, and garnish with the reserved fruit and water cress.

Fruit Salad Plate Combinations

Winter Fruit Salad Plate: Sections of oranges, grapefruit, sliced red-skinned apple, seeded grapes, and halved dates.

Spring Fruit Salad: Sections of fresh pineapple, orange and halved strawberries.

Summer Fruit Salad Plate: Halved peeled peaches containing lemon-honey cream dressing; quartered plums, sliced pears, blackberries, blueberries or red currants.

Fall Fruit Salad Plate: Diced honey-dew melon, sliced red-skinned apple, seedless green grapes, sliced winter pear and sliced figs.

Pick-Up-and-Dunk Salads

These are generous 1-course vegetable or salad plates, the vegetables or fruits cut in dunk-size pieces or strips, with French lemon dressing in a 2 ounce glass or paper cup, placed on the plate for dunking. Any assembly of seasonable raw vegetables or fruits may be used. They are arranged around a mound of cottage cheese. For example:

Vegetable Pick-Up Salad: Arrange a bed of crisp coarse-shredded lettuce on a large salad plate. Center with chived cottage cheese. Surround with tomato wedges, thick halved slices of unpeeled cucumber, strips of green pepper, carrot sticks, raw cauliflower sections and water cress. Black olives for the garnish.

Fresh Fruit Pick-Up Salad: Crisp lettuce on a large salad plate, preferably glass. Center with cottage cheese mixed with chopped pecans or toasted Brazil nuts. Surround with sections of pineapple, strawberries (with the hulls for handles), and strips of banana and pear. Garnish with mint or cress. Lemon Honey Cream Dressing for dunking.

Salad Dressings

Salad dressings, like sauces, are subject to individual taste. The amounts and proportions of the ingredients here given are standardized, but not inflexible.

FRENCH DRESSING

This is the simplest of all salad dressings. Bottled French dressing may be used, but if you prize individualized flavor, better prepare it yourself. Amounts and proportions of ingredients may be varied to suit your taste.

French dressing may be mixed ½ pint at a time in a jar, covered and kept refrigerated ready to use as needed. Shake thoroughly to blend, as it separates on standing. Use French lemon dressing with fruit salads.

FRENCH DRESSING (PLAIN)
(Serves 2 persons 3 times)

6 *tablespoons salad oil*	⅛ *teaspoon pepper*
⅓ *teaspoon salt*	2 *tablespoons mild cider vinegar or wine vinegar*

Combine the oil and seasonings; gradually beat in the vinegar.

FRENCH GARLIC DRESSING

Add a section of halved peeled garlic to French dressing. Remove before serving.

French Herbized Dressing: Add ⅛ teaspoon mixed dried herbs to French dressing. Let stand 30 minutes before using to bring out the herb flavor.

FRENCH LEMON DRESSING
(Serves 2 persons twice)

6 *tablespoons salad oil*	⅓ *teaspoon salt*
2 *tablespoons lemon juice*	*Few grains pepper*
1 *teaspoon honey or sugar*	

Combine ingredients in a jar. Shake and mix thoroughly before using. Use with any fruit salad.

AVOCADO DRESSING
(Serves 2)

1 *raw egg yolk*	*Few grains pepper*
⅛ *teaspoon dry mustard*	1 *tablespoon lemon juice*
¼ *teaspoon salt*	1 *ripe avocado, sieved*

Combine the egg yolk, seasonings and lemon juice. Beat in the avocado. Spoon over fish, shell fish, tomato or chicken salad in place of mayonnaise.

MAYONNAISE

For the family of 2 it is easier and more thrifty to purchase mayonnaise ready-made. As the flavor is bland, add seasonings to your taste, such as a squeeze of lemon or lime juice, or a little table mustard or Worcestershire.

Mayonnaise Variations

Horse-Radish Mayonnaise: To 3 tablespoons ready-made mayonnaise add ½ tablespoon prepared horse-radish. Use with fish, shell fish or smoked meat salads.

Nutted Mayonnaise: To 3 tablespoons ready-made mayonnaise add 1 tablespoon chopped salted nuts and ½ teaspoon lemon juice.

Russian Dressing: To 5 tablespoons ready-made mayonnaise add 1 tablespoon chili sauce, 1 tablespoon sliced stuffed olives or 1 teaspoon capers, 1 teaspoon each minced parsley and green peppers, a few drops onion juice, half a chopped hard-cooked egg and a shredded anchovy. (For 4.)

SOURED CREAM DRESSING (UNCOOKED)
(Serves 2)

⅓ *cup soured cream*	1 *teaspoon lemon juice*
	Salt and pepper to taste

Beat together and use with potato or tomato salad, raw or cooked vegetable salad or fruit salads of any kind. For fruit salads, add ¼ teaspoon sugar to this dressing.

COOKED CREAM DRESSING
(Enough for 4 servings for 2)

2½ tablespoons butter or margarine
1 tablespoon flour
⅓ teaspoon dry mustard
½ teaspoon salt

¾ tablespoon sugar
¼ teaspoon paprika
¾ cup soured cream
1 egg
¼ cup mild vinegar

1. Melt the butter in the top of a double boiler. Add the dry ingredients and mix to a smooth paste.

2. Add the cream; beat and add the egg.

3. Cook and stir over hot water until the mixture thickens. Slowly add the vinegar, beating with a hand-beater until creamy. Chill before using.

LEMON-HONEY CREAM DRESSING
(Serves 2)

1 teaspoon lemon juice
1 raw egg yolk

1 teaspoon honey
½ cup soured cream

Beat the lemon juice into the egg yolk. Add the honey and the soured cream. Use on fruit salads served on lettuce; over fresh dessert fruit cups (no lettuce); or as a sauce with split cup cakes, fruit betties, short cakes, or fruit pies.

For Gourmet and Gourmette
LOBSTER AVOCADO SALAD
(Serves 2)

1 *medium-sized avocado*	*Russian dressing*
½ *cup chilled diced lobster*	*Lettuce*
fresh, canned or quick-	*Cress*
frozen	*Stuffed olives*

1. Cut the avocado in halves lengthwise; peel; remove the seed.

2. Mix the lobster with dressing to blend.

3. Fill avocado halves with the lobster mixture; serve on lettuce. Garnish with the cress and olives. Nice for the first course at dinner, or for the main dish at lunch or a party supper. And quick to make, no matter how many guests.

CHAPTER XIII

Desserts to Make You Famous

DESSERTS ARE MORE FASHIONABLE TODAY THAN EVER. Be selective. Serve a light dessert after a substantial main course.

We need dessert—that touch of sweet—for energy. And best of all are fruit desserts, for they combine fruit and sugar. Or you can serve a fruit-and-nut bowl. Even eat up the red apples used as the centerpiece.

There are on the market an ever-increasing family of desserts suitable for two—canned, quick-frozen or those that may be quick-readied for service.

For instance, excellent canned rice pudding, Indian pudding and steamed fig or fruit puddings ready for re-heating and sauceing. And several sweet sauces are on the market, including chocolate, butterscotch and hard sauce. Then there are the ready-to-cook pudding mixes, including vanilla, chocolate, butterscotch, lemon; there's tapioca pudding ready to cook, and that excellent Danish dessert, a replica of the famous red raspberry currant pudding of Denmark. There is junket of many flavors, a wide choice of ready-to-make gelatins, innumerable delectable canned fruits, and some fruit desserts; there are even canned Baba rum cakes. Any number of desserts that may be readied by the turn of a can opener, or 5 minutes preparation. Most of these are within the everyday budget, a few are for high days and holidays. Watch the stores for many new items, and try them. Don't depend on one or two types of desserts; vary your dessert repertoire.

If the can or package yields enough to serve 4, use ½ the amount. The contents of the can should be transferred to a refrigerator dish, covered, refrigerated and used in a day or so. The remaining ½ package of a ready-to-cook pudding or gelatin may be carefully rewrapped and used at any time.

Individualizing Prepared Desserts

Commercially prepared desserts are sweetened and flavored to appeal to mass taste. Whenever you serve them they do not reflect your own knowledge of fine flavor, or your cooking personality. So better individualize them by adding interesting flavors, combining them with harmonizing ingredients, and serving them at the right temperature. Remember, hot desserts should really be hot; cold desserts should be well chilled; and always served daintily and attractively with the right sauce, or decoration of fruit, nuts, coconut, candy sprinkles or chocolate chips. This costs little in time or money, and adds that luxury feeling that builds morale both for you who prepare these attractive dishes, and for the fortunate diners who will eat them.

You will soon work out many ways to individualize prepared desserts. Here are a few suggestions as a starter:

Canned Rice Pudding: Heat and serve with hard sauce, or with coarse white bread crumbs fried in butter, and dusted with sugar and cinnamon. Or turn into a freezing tray, and serve half frozen, topped with sweetened whipped cream.

Canned Indian Pudding: Heat with bits of candied ginger and serve with hard sauce or whipped cream. Heat plain and serve topped with scoops of vanilla ice cream.

Steamed Fruit or Fig Pudding: Heat and serve with lemon sauce, sherry hard sauce, or hot rum or brandy sauce; see pages 243, 244.

Danish Dessert: Serve ice-cold with almost defrosted frozen raspberries and whipped cream. Or plain with whipped cream and sliced bananas.

Ready Gelatin Desserts: Make into whips with added bits of fresh or canned fruit; mold with fresh fruits (any kind except fresh pineapple); or mold with fruits, nuts and bits of fruit cake. Make with apple or other non-sweetened fruit juices instead of water for fine flavor—a little passion fruit juice, for instance.

Canned Fruits: Try half freezing these in the freezing tray; especially fine for pineapple gems, nectarines and black Bing cherries.

Prepared Pudding-Mix Desserts

These must be served ice-cold to be at their best.

Fruit Juice Pudding: Make up vanilla pudding mix with any bottled or canned fruit juice instead of milk (grapefruit juice excepted).

Nutted Pudding: When cool, add sliced Brazil nuts, or coarse-chopped pecans, filberts or walnuts to any prepared pudding made with milk. Then chill. Serve with plain or whipped cream.

Sherried Pudding: Add 2 tablespoons sherry to any prepared pudding made with milk.

Pudding with Fruit: Make vanilla pudding and serve with well-chilled canned or defrosted apricots or sliced peaches, Bing cherries, nearly defrosted frozen strawberries or raspberries, or fresh berries of any kind slightly sweetened; or with sliced bananas.

Coconut Pudding: Prepare ½ package of vanilla, chocolate or butterscotch pudding mix, adding ½ cup of canned. dessicated, or defrosted quick-frozen coconut.

Serve with whipped cream and/or sweetened fruit, fresh, canned or quick-frozen.

But you will not want to depend entirely on prepared desserts. Fortunately there are many others that can be made for two which you can serve often. And here they are. Select the recipes you think you'll like best

All measurements are level

FLOATING ISLAND
(2 *servings*)

1½ *cups milk*	*Few grains salt*
2 *egg yolks*	¼ *teaspoon vanilla*
1 *teaspoon cornstarch*	2 *tablespoons powdered*
3 *tablespoons granulated*	*sugar*
sugar	*Any firm red jelly*

1. Scald the milk.

2. Beat the egg yolks; add the cornstarch, granulated sugar and salt. Add the hot milk, a little at a time and cook in a double boiler, stirring almost constantly for about 3 minutes, or until the mixture coats the spoon.

3. Remove at once from the double boiler and cool covered. Add the vanilla and chill.

4. Just before serving, beat the egg whites stiff with the powdered sugar and 2 extra drops of vanilla. Heap onto the custard to form the islands; top each with a bit of the jelly.

Pear or Peach Floating Island: Put ½ a canned pear or peach round side up in a good-sized sauce dish; cover with custard; finish as directed in the preceding recipe.

Soft Custard: Prepare the custard mixture for floating island. Flavor with vanilla, orange, almond or rum extract.

Caramel Nut Custard: Make floating island custard, substituting brown sugar. Beat in 1 tablespoon butter.

Chill; just before using add 4 tablespoons chopped pecans, hazel nuts, or toasted almonds.

Serve over sliced plain or toasted pound, or sponge cake, or in sherbet glasses lined with lady fingers; top with whipped cream and whole nut meats.

BAKED CUP CUSTARDS
(2 servings)

1 *cup milk*	1½ *tablespoons granulated sugar*
1 *egg*	*Few grains salt*
¼ *teaspoon vanilla or nutmeg*	

1. Scald the milk.

2. Beat the egg slightly; add the sugar, salt and vanilla; stir in the milk.

3. Pour into 2 custard cups and set in a pan of hot water.

4. Bake about 25 minutes in a moderate oven (350 degrees, F.), or until a knife when inserted comes out clean.

Steamed Cup Custards: If you do not have an oven, steam the custards. To do this, place them in a deep saucepan, with 2 thicknesses of folded newspaper in the bottom. Pour in hot water half the depth of the custard cups, cover, and boil gently for 30 minutes.

BREAD AND BUTTER CUSTARD
(2 servings)

2 *slices buttered white bread, crusts removed*	⅛ *teaspoon salt*
	1¼ *cups milk*
1 *egg*	⅛ *teaspoon nutmeg*
3 *tablespoons granulated sugar*	

1. Cut the bread in strips or squares, and place in large ramekins or shirred-egg dishes.

2. Beat the egg with the sugar and salt. Add the milk and nutmeg. Pour this over the bread. Sprinkle with sugar.

3. Bake 20 minutes in a moderate oven (375 degrees, F.). Serve warm or cold.

Cake Custard: For the buttered bread in the preceding recipe substitute ½ cup coarse cake crumbs, any kind, or a mixture of cake and cookie crumbs. Best served warm, topped with whipped cream.

APPLE BROWN BETTY
(2 servings)

1½ cups chopped raw apple
1½ cups soft bread crumbs
½ cup granulated sugar

1 tablespoon melted butter
½ teaspoon cinnamon
Few grains nutmeg

1. Combine the ingredients in the order given.

2. Transfer to a buttered baking dish; bake slowly about 35 minutes in a moderate oven (350–375 degrees F.).

3. Serve warm with hard sauce or top cream.

Fruit Cocktail Betty: Follow the preceding recipe using an assortment of fruits, such as chopped raw apple, peaches or apricot, pears and seedless green grapes, or pitted cherries.

PINEAPPLE TAPIOCA
(2 servings)

1 (No. 1 can) grated pineapple
½ cup water
2 tablespoons granulated sugar

Few grains salt
3 tablespoons quick-cooking tapioca
1 teaspoon lemon juice

1. Combine the pineapple, water, sugar and salt. Bring to boiling point and add the tapioca.

2.   Cook over hot water, stirring occasionally, until the tapioca is clear, about 8 minutes. Add the lemon juice and chill.

3.   Serve with extra pineapple or light cream.

APRICOT RICE COMPÔTE
(2 servings)

1 (*No. 1*) *can apricots or*   ⅓ *cup white rice*
  1 *cup cooked apricots*   ½ *tablespoon butter*
  and juice   *Melted jelly sauce* (*page*
½ *teaspoon grated lemon*   245)
  rind

1.   Drain the juice from the apricots and measure it. Save the apricots.

2.   Add enough boiling water to the juice to make a cupful; bring to boiling point in a double boiler top.

3.   Add the lemon rind and rice; cover and cook without stirring until the rice is tender; then stir in the butter. Form into nest shape; heap the apricots in the middle.

4.   Serve with the jelly sauce poured over.

ORANGE SNOW PUDDING
(2 servings)

½ *envelope plain granu-*   ⅓ *cup orange juice*
  lated gelatin   ⅓ *cup boiling water*
½ *tablespoon lemon juice*   ¼ *cup granulated sugar*
           1 *egg white*

1.   Soak the gelatin 5 minutes in the fruit juices.

2.   Add the boiling water; if necessary, place over boiling water and stir until dissolved.

3.   Add the sugar. Chill until beginning to thicken; then beat until white and frothy.

4. Beat the egg white stiff and add. Transfer to custard cups, first dipped in cold water; chill until firm, about 3 hours.

5. Unmold and serve with soft custard, or chilled, sugared orange sections.

PEACHES IN GELATIN
(2 servings)

¾ *cup boiling water*   ½ *package prepared lemon*
 1 *cup sliced peaches*   *gelatin*

1. Pour the boiling water into the gelatin; stir until dissolved and set aside until syrupy.

2. Half fill sherbet glasses with the peaches; pour in the gelatin.

3. Chill until firm, about 2 hours; serve topped with sweetened whipped cream, or half scoops of vanilla, peach or lemon ice cream.

Strawberries in Gelatin: Use sliced fresh or defrosted strawberries and strawberry prepared gelatin.

Raspberries in Gelatin: Use fresh or defrosted raspberries and raspberry prepared gelatin.

Orange Date Gelatin: Use prepared orange gelatin; add 1 teaspoon lemon juice, orange sections and shredded dates. Or make with ginger ale instead of water, in case some is left over.

Grape Gelatin: Make up prepared lemon gelatin, using grape juice instead of water. Half fill sherbet glasses with halved seedless green, or seeded malaga or tokay grapes. Finish as directed for peaches in gelatin.

PEACH COBBLER
(2 servings)

4 halves canned, cooked
   or defrosted peaches
   Granulated sugar
   Cinnamon
1 egg yolk
¼ cup milk

½ cup flour
½ teaspoon baking powder
¼ teaspoon salt
3 tablespoons granulated
   sugar
2 tablespoons melted
   shortening

1. Quarter peaches; put in 2 buttered shirred egg dishes; dust with a little sugar and cinnamon.

2. Beat the egg yolk and add the milk. Beat in the remaining ingredients.

3. Pour over the peaches; bake 20 minutes in a moderate oven (375 degrees, F.). Serve warm, with or without hard sauce.

Cherry Cobbler: Substitute ¾ cup pitted fresh or canned cherries for the peaches.

Cobblers with Prepared Cake Mix: For the batter use ½ package of plain cake mix, made up according to directions on the package. Add 2 extra tablespoons milk or water.

BAKED APPLE DUMPLINGS
(2 servings)

Homemade piecrust or
   piecrust mix
2 medium-sized tart apples

Granulated sugar
Cinnamon
1 teaspoon butter

1. Roll the piecrust a scant ¼ inch thick; cut into 2 5 inch squares.

2. Pare and core the apples. Place an apple on each square of crust; fill the center with granulated sugar mixed with a little cinnamon. Top with butter.

3. Fold the piecrust up over the apple, twisting it into little ears at the top.

4. Brush lightly with milk. Place on a pie plate and bake in a hot oven (400 degrees, F.) for 10 minutes; then reduce the heat and bake 35 minutes longer at 350 degrees, F.

5. Serve plain or with hard lemon or brandy sauce.

Peach Dumplings: Substitute large peeled, stoned, halved peaches or canned peaches, for apples in the preceding recipe.

BAKED APPLES
(4 servings)

4 *large cooking apples*	½ *teaspoon cinnamon*
4 *tablespoons granulated sugar*	½ *cup water or fruit juice*

1. Core the apples nearly to the stem-end. Pare off 1 inch of the skin at the top.

2. Fill the apples with the sugar and cinnamon.

3. Place in a small deep dish, add ½ cup water or fruit juice, cover, and bake until tender, about 35 minutes at 375 degrees, F.

4. When done sprinkle 1 teaspoon sugar on top of each apple; place under the broiler about 30 seconds to brown and glaze.

PRUNE CREAM WHIP
(Serves 2)

½ *cup heavy cream*	¼ *teaspoon vanilla*
½ *cup stoned quartered cooked prunes*	*Sugar to sweeten*

1. Beat the cream stiff. Fold in the prunes and vanilla. Sweeten to taste.

2. Serve piled in sherbet glasses or on thin slices of pound cake.

BISCUIT SHORTCAKE
(2 servings)

1 cup flour
2 teaspoons baking pow-
der
¼ teaspoon salt
½ tablespoon sugar
2 tablespoons shortening
6 tablespoons milk

1. Sift together the dry ingredients.

2. Chop in the shortening with a pastry blender. Moisten with the milk.

3. Toss onto a floured board; pat to ½-inch thickness; cut into 3-inch rounds. Transfer to an oiled pan, and bake 15 to 20 minutes in a hot oven (400 degrees, F.).

4. Split, butter, and put together with the prepared fruit, saving enough to pour over the top.

5. Serve hot with plain or whipped cream, a whipped topping, or hard sauce.

Strawberry Shortcake: Use fresh strawberries, adding ½ cup sugar to 1 pint of sliced berries. Let stand at room temperature until juicy, about 30 minutes. Or use defrosted quick-frozen berries. Make plain shortcake as directed and put together with the berries. In addition to whipped cream, serve with a small pitcher of sweetened strawberry juice if possible.

Blueberry Shortcake: Stew and sweeten fresh or quick-frozen fruit before using, allowing 1½ cups.

Raspberry Shortcake: Slightly crush and sweeten 1½ cups raspberries. Defrost frozen berries but do not sweeten.

Peach Shortcake: Use sliced, fresh, sweetened peaches, or canned or defrosted peaches. Serve with cream or brandy sauce.

Cake Shortcake: Split plain, or sponge cup cakes in two layers. Put together with sliced, sweetened strawberries, oranges or peaches, or slightly crushed raspberries. Top with sweetened whipped cream or Mile-High Meringue (page 269), and decorate with a berry or section of fruit. Serve at once.

Pancakes, Waffles or French Toast for Dessert

Breakfast hurried? Nobody home for lunch? Is Sunday brunch the only convenient time to serve pancakes, waffles or French toast?

Better try them as a dinner dessert, especially if the rest of the meal is on the lean side. They'll taste grand enjoyed at leisure. For recipes, see Chapter VI of this book.

Frozen Desserts
All measurements are level

It is more practical to purchase ice cream for a small family. But if making it, better use a good commercial mix, and freeze it in the automatic refrigerator, according to the manufacturer's directions. Or buy one of those speedy little crank-turning affairs that freeze ice cream in 2 minutes—at the table if you like. It's to the frozen dessert field what the pressure-cooker is to cooked dishes. And as it needs no electric connection, it can be used anywhere a small quantity of ice or ice cubes is obtainable.

Butter Pecan Ice Cream: To a package of vanilla ice cream mix when ½ frozen, add ⅓ cup broken pecans lightly toasted in 1 tablespoon butter (*not* browned), and a few grains of salt. Finish freezing.

Peppermint Ice Cream: A reasonable facsimile. Add 1 teaspoon peppermint flavoring to a package of vanilla ice cream mix when made up. Half freeze, then beat in ½ cup fine-crushed peppermint candy (any kind) and finish freezing. Nice with chocolate sauce.

Coffee Ice Cream: Make up vanilla ice cream mix,

ready to freeze. Add 1½ teaspoons instant coffee dissolved in 1 tablespoon hot water, and freeze.

Ice Cream Pears: Chill large halved fresh or canned pears. Fill each with ½ scoop of vanilla or fruit-flavored ice cream or a sherbet; pour over orange marmalade slightly melted and thinned with orange juice.

Cup-Cakes Luxuro: Buy, or make cup cakes as directed in this book. Cut in quarters almost to the bottom, and spread out like the petals of a flower. Place ½ scoop of ice cream in the center of each; serve with chocolate or butterscotch sauce.

Fruits for Desserts

All solid fruits should be thoroughly washed with cold water before putting into the refrigerator. This includes oranges, lemons and grapefruit.

Apples should be scrubbed with a brush and well rinsed.

Berries keep best if spread on plates lined with paper towels. Wash and drain just before serving.

Bananas should *not* be stored in the refrigerator, as they come from the tropics and cold affects their fine flavor.

Fruit Cups and Cocktails

These are the same with one difference. Fruit cocktails are served in small stemmed glasses, as a first course; fruit cups in larger stemmed glasses as dessert. They almost prepare themselves. Use a pint-size preserve jar for the purpose. In it put ¼ cup water, or sweet wine, and 2 tablespoons sugar. As they accumulate add sections of orange, grapefruit, slices of peaches, plums or apricots, berries, cubes of honeydew melon, or what not, including leftover defrosted fruits. Keep in the refrigerator not more than 24 hours. To serve, add a little cubed red-skinned apple; and if too sweet, a squeeze of lemon or lime. Garnish with a choice berry or bit of fruit and serve very cold.

The following fruit cups are decorative topped with a sprig of mint. Try growing a potful in a semi-shaded window.

Fig and Orange Cup: Combine fresh sliced, canned or stewed figs with sections cut from oranges.

Prune and Pineapple Cup: Combine stewed or canned prunes with pineapple cubes and orange juice.

Melon Cup: Combine diced watermelon or honeydew with equal parts orange and pineapple juice.

Pineapple Mint Cup: Add a little sugar, minced fresh mint and lemon or lime juice to chilled fresh or canned pineapple cubes.

Red Currant Cup: Slightly crush red currants; add tangerine juice to ½ cover, and sugar to taste.

Bananas in Orange Juice: Combine sliced ripe bananas with orange or tangerine juice.

Citrus Fruit Cup: Combine sections of orange, grapefruit and tangerines. Pour over a little lemon juice and mild honey. Chill thoroughly.

Mixed Fresh Fruit Cup: Serve very cold topped with lemon-honey cream dressing (page 225); dust with fine-minced nut meats or with wheat germ.

Strawberry Rhubarb Cup: Combine sliced strawberries, sections of stewed rhubarb and shredded orange.

Grapefruit Cherry Cup: Use canned grapefruit sections and pitted red or Bing cherries.

Fruit Cups with Wine: These are delicious. Use any of the preceding combinations for fruit cups, adding ½ tokay or muscatel wine in place of ½ the fruit juice. Serve as a dessert.

SHREDDED FRESH PINEAPPLE

(2 servings)

½ a medium-sized pine-   *Powdered sugar*
   apple   *Juice ¼ lemon*

1. Use the top half of the pineapple, leaving on the leaves or "crown." Peel the pineapple and remove the eyes with a small sharp knife.

2. Put it on a plate. Hold the top firmly, and with a silver fork, shred down the pineapple. Add the sugar and lemon. Chill in a covered jar.

BANANAS, RAISINS AND CREAM
(2 servings)

2 *sliced ripe bananas*　　　2 *tablespoons small raisins*
Light cream or top milk

1. Slice the bananas into glass dishes; sprinkle with the raisins and pour in light cream to half cover.

2. Serve with or without sugar. Combine with any crisp flaked cereal if desired and serve at breakfast or for a bedtime snack.

Ways with Apple Sauce

Canned or defrosted frozen apple sauce may be used in many ways. Sprinkle with powdered cinnamon or clove; combine with shredded orange, stoned cherries, diced fresh or canned pears, or grated pineapple. Try it over warm, buttered gingerbread, or mixed with whipped cream and served on cake. And for a Swedish relish for pork, add a touch of wine vinegar and grated horse-radish. Uh-huh, it's good!

Poached Fresh Fruit

This is just another name for stewed fruit, coined because we have learned that fresh fruits must be merely cooked through—not stewed to death—and tenderly tended to hold their shape. When this is done we retain both vitamins and color. In any case the fruit should be washed clean. Peeled if the skin is tough. Put 1 cup water

and ¼ cup sugar in a rather wide saucepan and bring
to boiling point. Add thin slices of lemon or lime, or 2
or 3 whole cloves. Slide in the fruit, cover, and simmer
until barely tender.

Berries and stoned cherries .   .   .   .   *5 to* 10 *minutes.*
Halved peaches (peeled) .   .   .   10 *minutes.*
Apricots (peeled) .   .   .   .   10 *minutes.*
Halved pears (peeled) .   .   .   .   10 *to* 15 *minutes.*
Thick slices apple (not peeled)   .   .   .   10 *minutes.*
Plums (prick with a fork in 2 places) .   .   12 *minutes.*

Dried Fruits

These are especially good for dessert, whether they are
dates, apricots, peaches, pears, prunes or figs au naturel or
stewed.

Au Naturel: All dried fruits, unless pasteurized, if
served raw, should be separated, then scalded with boiling water, and dried on paper towels. They taste very well
with cream cheese, Brie, or Bel Paese and crisp crackers.

Stewed: Wash well in tepid water; place in a saucepan. Add boiling water to nearly cover. Put on a lid and let
stand 1 hour. Then stew very slowly until barely tender.
The time varies with the fruit. Add a very little sugar
after cooking. If the fruit is not naturally tart, add a little
lemon or lime juice. Cinnamon harmonizes with prunes,
whole cloves with pears. Prunes and apricots are good
stewed together. It pays to cook 1 pound of dried fruit
for 2 persons. Just put it in a covered dish, refrigerate,
and use as needed. It will keep about 10 days at a temperature of 45 degrees F.

Sweet Sauces
All measurements are level

HARD SAUCE
(To serve twice)

⅓ cup butter
1½ cups sifted powdered
   sugar

1 tablespoon heated top
   milk
¼ teaspoon vanilla or cinnamon

1. Stir the butter until creamy; then alternately cream in the sugar and hot milk until all has been used.

2. Add the flavoring; heap in an attractive dish; chill before serving. Keep the remainder in a covered jar in the refrigerator.

Lemon Hard Sauce: Substitute lemon juice for milk in the preceding recipe. Omit vanilla.

Sherry or Rum Hard Sauce: Follow the recipe for hard sauce substituting sherry or rum for the hot milk. Omit the vanilla.

BUTTERED RUM SAUCE

Method I: Combine 1 cup granulated sugar and ¾ cup water; boil 5 minutes, add 4 tablespoons butter, stir until it melts and add 1½ teaspoons rum flavoring extract.

Method II: Combine 1 cup granulated sugar and ½ cup water and boil 5 minutes. Add 4 tablespoons butter and ¼ cup rum.

BRANDY SAUCE
(4 servings)

3 tablespoons butter
1 egg yolk

1 cup sifted confectioners'
   sugar
3 tablespoons brandy

1. Measure the butter into a double boiler top. Stir to a cream and work in the egg yolk. Add the sugar.

2. Place over hot water and cook and stir rapidly 3 minutes. Beat in the brandy and serve at once.

LEMON SAUCE
(2 servings)

½ cup sugar
¾ tablespoon cornstarch
⅛ teaspoon salt

¾ cup boiling water
½ tablespoon butter
½ tablespoon lemon juice

⅛ teaspoon nutmeg

1. Mix the sugar, cornstarch and salt together.

2. Add the water gradually and boil 5 minutes.

3. Remove from the heat and add the remaining ingredients.

BUTTERSCOTCH SAUCE
(4 servings)

1 cup granulated sugar
3 tablespoons corn syrup
½ cup boiling water

1 tablespoon butter
½ tablespoon vinegar
½ teaspoon vanilla

1. Combine the sugar, corn syrup and water. Boil until a little, when dropped in cold water, forms a soft ball, 238 degrees, F. by a candy thermometer.

2. Remove from the heat; beat in the butter, vinegar and vanilla; stir until slightly creamy. Serve warm.

CHOCOLATE SAUCE
(Keep on hand for service any time)

2½ squares (ounces) unsweetened chocolate
½ cup water or coffee beverage

⅓ cup honey
⅓ cup white corn syrup
1 tablespoon butter
¼ teaspoon vanilla

1. Cut the chocolate in bits; add to the liquid and cook and stir until melted.

2. Add the honey and syrup, and the butter. Continue to cook 5 minutes or until the sweetening dissolves and the mixture is as thick as heavy cream.

3. Add vanilla and serve hot or cold.

MELTED JELLY SAUCE

Put ¼ cup any tart jelly in a small saucepan; add 1 tablespoon hot water. Cook and stir until the jelly melts.

WHIPPED CREAM

Purchase heavy or whipping cream, and chill; (½ pint serves 6 persons). It is impractical to whip less than ½ cup. Pour into a small deep bowl. With a hand beater, beat steadily until it begins to thicken. Then to ½ cup of cream add 1 tablespoon sugar, and 2 drops of vanilla. Continue to beat until the cream stands up in peaks. Use within 1 hour. If it must stand longer, omit the sugar and beat in a heaping tablespoonful of marshmallow cream.

RASPBERRY BAVARIAN CREAM
(3 to 4 servings)

½ package prepared, rasp-   ½ cup fresh, canned, or de-
*   berry gelatin   frosted quick-frozen*
*   raspberries*
½ cup heavy cream

1. Prepare the gelatin according to the directions on the package.

2. Chill, and when the gelatin looks syrupy, stir in the raspberries. Whip the cream and fold it in.

3. Transfer to sherbet glasses and chill until firm, about 2 hours. Serve heaped with additional sugared raspberries, or whipped cream topped with raspberries.

Ice-Cream and Sherbet Specials
ICE-CREAM LOAVES

Unmold 1- or 2-pint cartons of ice cream on a chilled platter. Top and surround with a mixture of sweetened fresh or half-thawed frozen fruit. Garnish with whipped cream if you like. Use the more unusual ice creams, such as butter-pecan, apple, ginger, lemon or black raspberry, or choose 2 kinds of contrasting colors. Fruits with a pleasant color contrast should be chosen. A little curaçao, crème de menthe, or grenadine syrup add "flair" to the fruits.

HAWAIIAN MANGO CUP

Line large shallow sherbet glasses with vanilla ice cream. Fill the centers with chilled canned mangoes. Top with coarse chopped Macadamia nutmeats first heated and slightly browned in ½ tablespoon each honey and butter to ¾ cup nuts, then cooled.

BRANDIED CHOCOLATE MOCHA CUP

Into each sherbet glass measure 1 teaspoon brandy. Fill with alternating half scoops of chocolate and mocha (coffee) ice cream. Spoon over 1 tablespoon brandy. Top with whipped cream and toasted chopped filbert nutmeats.

SAMBÉES

Use iced-tea or highball glasses. In the bottom of each put 1 tablespoon each frozen peaches and strawberries, or use partly thawed frozen-fruit cocktail. Fill with chilled orange juice, or equal parts orange juice and tokay or sweet sauterne. Top each with a scoop of vanilla ice cream. Garnish with sprigs of mint. Serve with iced-tea spoons as an afternoon or evening refreshant.

FROSTED FRUIT CUPS
Serve in fruit-cocktail glasses as a dessert

Use chilled fruit-cocktail mixtures sparked to taste with frozen lemon n' lime syrup or any fruit liqueur. Top with a small scoop of lemon or lime sherbet and a sprig of mint.

CHAPTER XIV

Cakes, Pies and Cookies

IN MANY FAMILIES OF TWO HOME-MADE CAKE IS NEVER served because it takes time to make and often is not a success. I grant it is time saving to buy cake from the baker or grocer, and many such cakes can be delightfully individualized with fillings, toppings or sauces. Or excellent cake mixes may be purchased ready to quick-mix and bake. Try pound, honey-spice, devil's, or angel-food.

But to make a mystery of baking a good homemade cake is ridiculous. Anyone can learn if they use a reliable recipe, and observe level measurements and accurate baking temperature.

Ingredients for Cake Making

Butter or margarine may be used as alternates wherever a butter flavor is desired. Shortening may be used as a substitute. As this is unsalted, add ¼ teaspoon salt for every ½ cup used.

Eggs should be fresh and medium-sized. Good quality dried egg (see manufacturer's directions) may be used in cakes when the egg whites are not beaten separately.

Sugar is granulated unless otherwise specified.

Milk may be whole, homogenized or skimmed, or use equal parts of unsweetened evaporated milk and water, or dried milk reconstituted according to the manufacturer's directions.

Flavorings should be varying and daringly used. Try to accumulate a variety of flavoring extracts—not only vanilla, but lemon, orange, black walnut and almond. They keep indefinitely.

Baking powder of any reliable make gives good results.

The flour may be one of two kinds—all purpose flour, which results in a cake of slightly coarse crumb, or cake flour which makes a cake of fluffier crumb and finer texture. Or a self-rising cake flour may be used. This flour contains the right proportions of baking powder and salt per cup of flour. In using follow this rule:

When using self-rising cake flour, omit all baking powder and salt, and use the self-rising flour in place of the plain flour designated in the recipe.

Mixing the Cake

The most convenient utensil is a round-bottomed saucepan, of 2-quart size, because it can be held firm by the handle.

Have all ingredients at room temperature.

Always sift flour before measuring, then a second time with the baking powder (or baking soda), salt and spices if used.

If an egg yolk is left over, put in a small glass, cover with cold water, cover, and use in scrambling eggs, making French toast, etc. Keep egg whites in a covered jar, and use for a meringue, fruit whip or frosting.

Using an Electric Mixer: Read the manufacturer's directions. Avoid over-beating as this sometimes causes cake to fall.

The Pans: These may be aluminum, tin or glass.

Use shortening for greasing the pans; the salt in butter or margarine is likely to make the cake stick to the bottom.

For cakes needing long baking, line the bottoms of the pans with smooth clean paper cut to fit, or use cake pan linings.

Baking Cake: Put the batter in the pan and make it a little higher at the edges than in the center to insure even rising and a level cake. Be sure the oven is the right temperature (pages 45, 46). Place the cake in the center of the oven. Never put a cake to bake directly on the bottom of a gas, kerosene, or portable oven; put it on a rack, about 3 inches from the bottom. If the cake is browning too fast, cover it with a smooth piece of heavy brown paper.

During the first quarter of the baking time the cake batter begins to rise; during the second, rising continues and the top begins to brown; in the third quarter rising is completed and the cake browns evenly; during the last quarter, the baking is completed and the cake shrinks a little from the pan.

Test for Done-ness: The time factor is a guide. To be sure the cake is done, insert a clean toothpick into the center of the cake, then gently remove it. If the toothpick is clean, with no stickiness, it is done. Otherwise, bake 3 or 4 minutes longer and test again.

Care After Baking: Cool 5 minutes; then loosen around the sides with a spatula and turn out on a wire cake cooling rack, or use the rack from the broiler. Remove the paper lining if used. Then turn the cake right-side up to finish cooling. If by chance it is burned on the bottom, grate off the burned portion when the cake cools.

Sponge cake and angel cake are cooled in the pan which is turned upside down. Remove when cool.

Layer Cakes

Buy or make 2 plain or sponge cake layers; for a small cake use 1 layer, cutting it in halves crosswise.

Put together with the desired filling; spread the top with sweetened whipped cream or whipped cream topping; or cover it with icing; or use jelly meringue topping or a suitable frosting; or sift powdered sugar over the top. To make a very attractive finish, place a lace paper doily on top of the cake; sift the powdered sugar onto this; lift up the doily and the cake will be covered with a lacey design.

The following layer cake recipes make 2 generously thick or 3 thin layers. This is too much for a family of 2, unless guests are expected. In this case, cut one of the layers in half, and use it for the filled layer cake. Serve the second layer the following day as a pudding with lemon or chocolate-mocha sauce.

All measurements are level

ONE-EGG LAYER CAKE
(*Serves 6*)

6 *tablespoons butter or*	1½ *cups flour*
shortening	1½ *teaspoons baking*
¾ *cup granulated sugar*	*powder*
1 *egg*	¼ *teaspoon salt*
½ *teaspoon flavoring*	½ *cup milk*

1. Stir together the shortening, sugar, egg yolk and flavoring until creamy.

2. Sift the dry ingredients together, and add alternately with the milk to the first mixture.

3. Whip the egg white; fold in and transfer to 2 oiled 8-inch layer cake pans.

4. Bake 25 to 30 minutes in a moderate oven (350–375 degrees, F.). Cool and put together with the desired filling.

RICH LAYER CAKE
(*Serves 8*)

⅔ *cup butter or shorten-*
    ing
1 *teaspoon flavoring*
1 *cup granulated sugar*
2 *eggs*

1¾ *cups flour*
2½ *teaspoons baking*
    powder
½ *teaspoon salt*
½ *cup milk*

1. Cream the shortening, flavoring, sugar and eggs until the mixture is very fluffy.

2. Sift together the dry ingredients; add alternately with the milk to the first mixture. Beat 1 minute.

3. Transfer to 2 oiled 9-inch layer cake pans or three 8-inch layer cake pans.

4. Bake from 25 to 30 minutes in a moderate oven (350–375 degrees, F.). Put together with the desired filling and top as desired.

Chocolate Layer Cake: Put together with chocolate filling, plain or mixed with chopped hazelnuts (page 262). Top with rich chocolate icing (page 264). Or sprinkle the top layer with chocolate bits before baking.

Orange Layer Cake: Put together with orange filling (page 261). Top with lime or lemon butter cream; or with confectioners' sugar, or sweetened whipped cream; or sprinkle one layer with packaged coconut before baking for a rich flavorful topping.

Fig Layer Cake: Put together with fig jam. Finish as described for Orange Layer Cake.

Boston Cream Cake: Put together with cooked cream

filling (page 262). Top with sifted powdered sugar. If possible stand in a cool place a few hours before serving.

Coconut Cream Cake: Put together with cream filling (page 262), mixed with ⅓ cup grated coconut. Top with sifted powdered sugar.

Banana Layer Cake: Put together with banana filling. Top with confectioners' sugar or sweetened whipped cream. Just before serving decorate with sliced bananas.

Tokay Cake: Put together with tokay orange filling (page 261). Top with sweetened whipped cream and sprinkle with chopped toasted almonds.

CHOCOLATE LAYER CAKE
(Serves 2 to 3)

¼ cup shortening	1½ squares (ounces) un-
½ cup granulated sugar	sweetened chocolate
1 egg	1¼ teaspoons baking
⅓ teaspoon vanilla	powder
Few grains salt	¾ cup flour

¼ cup milk

1. Cream the shortening with the sugar, egg yolk, vanilla and salt.

2. Melt the chocolate in a double boiler and stir in.

3. Sift together the dry ingredients and add to the first mixture alternately with the milk.

4. Fold in the egg white, whipped stiff.

5. Transfer to 1 oiled 9-inch layer cake pan; bake 25 minutes in a moderate oven (350–375 degrees F.).

6. Cool, cut in halves and put together with rich chocolate icing (page 264), or filling (page 262), or sweetened whipped cream.

Note: To make a 3-layer cake, double the quantities and bake in three 8-inch cake pans.

Applying Layer Cake Fillings and Icings

A few years ago we put layer cakes together with frosting. And by the time we had spread it over the top and on the sides, the cake was indeed a sweet morsel. Too sweet in fact for trim waistlines. As a result came the oh-so-delicious fashion of putting cake layers together with a thick cooked filling, and using icing merely on the top. Result—an even more glamorous cake!

Applying the Filling: One word of caution. Wait until the cake filling is nearly cool before spreading it on the cake, and then spread to within only ½ inch of the edge. The top layer when pressed into place, makes the filling spread way out to the edge.

Icing the Cake: Before putting icing on the cake brush off the crumbs. If you haven't a pastry brush, use a fringed paper towel. The easiest way to apply icing is by means of a long spatula. Otherwise use a table knife. If dipped in hot water before spreading the icing, the job won't be nearly so sticky.

By the way, the cake filling recipes in this book make enough for an 8- or 9-inch layer cake. If covering just one layer, cut it in halves; put the remaining filling in a jar in the refrigerator and use it next day to make sweet cracker sandwiches, tarts or to fill baker's plain cup cakes.

SPICE CAKE
(Makes a loaf 7 by 11 inches)

½ cup melted shortening	3 teaspoons baking
1⅓ cups soft brown sugar	powder
2 eggs	¼ teaspoon salt
½ cup milk	¾ teaspoon cinnamon
1¾ cups flour	¼ teaspoon nutmeg
¼ teaspoon cloves	

1. Melt the shortening and combine with the brown sugar, eggs and milk. Blend thoroughly.

2. Beat in all the dry ingredients sifted together.

3. Transfer to a good-sized shallow oiled cake pan, 7 by 11 inches; bake about 45 minutes in a moderate oven (350 degrees, F.).

4. Serve plain or covered with plain or sherry icing (page 263), or use a broiler topping (page 264).

Save part of the loaf and keep closely covered 2 or 3 days; then serve as a pudding with any fruit sauce or soft custard (page 230).

SPONGE CAKE
(Makes a 9-inch round loaf)

4 *eggs*	⅓ *teaspoon salt*
1 *cup granulated sugar*	1 *cup flour*
½ *lemon grated rind and juice*	1 *teaspoon baking powder*

1. Separate the eggs.

2. Beat the yolks till light and add the sugar, lemon rind and juice; add the salt and whip till lemon-colored.

3. Beat the whites stiff.

4. Mix the flour and baking powder together, and add the whites and flour alternately to the first mixture, folding them in.

5. Transfer to a slightly oiled tube pan, 3 x 9 inches. Place in a slow to moderate oven (325 to 350 degrees F.), and bake about 50 minutes. Turn upside down to cool in the pan. If closely covered this cake keeps moist for several days.

Ways to Use Sponge Cake

1. Serve sliced with sugared fruit.

2. Serve sliced with butterscotch sauce and toasted almonds.

3. Slice, put together sandwich fashion with raspberry or apricot jam, and top with whipped cream.

WARM BANANA NUT CAKE
(*Serves 3*)

3½ *tablespoons shortening*
⅓ *cup granulated sugar*
⅓ *teaspoon lemon or*
  orange extract
⅛ *teaspoon salt*
 1 *egg*
¼ *cup milk*

¾ *cup flour*
 1 *teaspoon baking*
  powder
 2 *sliced small bananas*
 1 *tablespoon sugar*
  (extra)
¼ *cup chopped nuts*

1. Cream the shortening, sugar, extract and salt together.

2. Add the egg slightly beaten and the milk.

3. Beat in the flour and baking powder; transfer to an oiled, medium-sized cake pan.

4. Lay the sliced banana on top. Dust with granulated sugar; sprinkle with nuts.

5. Bake 20 to 25 minutes in a moderate oven (350 to 375 degrees, F.).

Apple Cake: Follow the preceding recipe, substituting ½ cup sliced apple for the bananas. Omit nuts if desired and sprinkle with ½ teaspoon cinnamon. Serve plain or with hard or brandy sauce.

WHITE COCONUT CAKE
(*Serves 3*)

3 *tablespoons shortening*
½ *cup granulated sugar*
⅓ *teaspoon vanilla*
¾ *cup flour*

Few grains salt
 1 *teaspoon baking powder*
¼ *cup milk*
 1 *egg white*

1½ *tablespoons shredded coconut*

1. Cream the shortening with the sugar and vanilla.
2. Sift together the dry ingredients and beat in alternately with the milk.
3. Fold in the egg white, whipped stiff.
4. Transfer to a small oiled loaf pan, or to a 9-inch layer cake pan. Sprinkle the coconut over the top.
5. Bake in a moderate oven (350–375 degrees, F.), about 30 minutes.

BIRTHDAY CAKE

Bake a loaf of sponge cake (page 254), or double the preceding recipe for white coconut cake. Cover with lime or lemon butter cream (page 264), making twice the quantity, and let stand in a cool place until it begins to firm. Decorate with halved candied cherries and whole toasted almonds, or with halved candied tangerines or other crystallized fruits. Put the candles (in candle holders) around the edge; or try this: Surround the cake with cup cakes (any kind) covered with the same or contrasting icing and decorated to match. Put a candle on each cup cake. This arrangement is effective on a paper-doilied tray. Decorate further with flowers.

Cup Cakes

Cup cakes and muffins are two different foods; cup cakes are actually small cakes, baked in individual pans, sometimes called muffin pans. Muffins on the other hand are a kind of individually baked hot bread, and when correctly made are only slightly sweet.

Better bakers and pastry shops sell excellent plain cup cakes, which can be varied in many ways. However, if you want to feature cup cakes as a spécialité of your house, make them by any of the cake recipes in this book. Bake the batter in small cup cake pans that come for the purpose. The pans should be lightly rubbed with unsalted fat, dusted all over inside with a little flour, then tapped smartly upside down to shake out the excess flour. The pans will be lined with a thin film of flour over the fat, which prevents sticking and makes it easy to remove the little cakes. Also easier to wash! Or simpler still, buy the fluted paper baking cups that come for the purpose. Grease medium-sized cup cake pans, put a paper cup in each, fill ⅔ with the cake batter, then bake. Remove the cups while the cakes are still warm. It is not necessary to grease the paper cups.

Chocolate Flower Cakes: Cut chocolate iced cup cakes into 4 sections nearly to the bottom. Open up, like a flower, and fill the centres with ice cream. Pour over chocolate sauce and sprinkle with chopped nuts.

Tokay Orange Cup Cakes: Cut a round from the center of each cup cake, making a shell. Fill with Tokay orange filling. Cut the removed round of cake in halves and stick upright in the filling. In the middle put a dot of whipped cream.

Blueberry Layer Cup Cakes: Split blueberry or date cup cakes in 2 layers. Put together with lime or lemon butter cream (page 264). Then turn upside down and ice all over.

Raspberried Cup Cakes: Turn un-iced cup cakes upside down. Pour over canned or defrosted quick frozen raspberries.

Cottage Cup Cakes: Heat plain, raisin or berry cup cakes. Serve with hot lemon, pineapple or any fruit sauce.

Ginger Apple Cup Cakes: Serve ginger nut cup cakes (page 258) with 1 tablespoon of thick chilled applesauce over each.

GINGER NUT CUP CAKES

(Makes 10)

⅓ cup shortening
½ cup boiling water
½ cup molasses
⅓ cup sugar
1 egg, beaten
1 teaspoon ginger

1½ cups flour
½ cup walnut meats,
chopped coarse
½ teaspoon baking soda
½ teaspoon salt

1. Melt the shortening in the water.

2. Then add the remaining ingredients in the order given, beating thoroughly.

3. Transfer to small oiled muffin pans and bake 20 minutes in a moderately hot oven (350 degrees, F.). Serve warm or cold, plain, or with lemon sauce.

DATE CUP CAKES

(Makes 10)

⅔ cup brown sugar
2 tablespoons shortening
1 egg
¼ teaspoon nutmeg
¼ teaspoon cinnamon
1½ cups flour

½ teaspoon baking powder
½ teaspoon baking soda
½ teaspoon salt
¾ cup dates cut in eighths
½ cup soured cream
1 tablespoon granulated sugar

1. Cream together the brown sugar, shortening and egg.

2. Sift together the spices, flour, baking powder, baking soda and salt. Mix in the dates.

3. Add to the first mixture alternately with the soured cream. Transfer to oiled muffin pans (2½ inches in diameter). Dust with the granulated sugar. Bake 20 minutes in a moderately hot oven (375 degrees, F.).

Date Cup Cakes de Luxe: Cut date cup cakes nearly in halves and stand each cake in a sauce dish. Pour over 1 big tablespoon of lemon-honey cream dressing (page 225). Dust with wheat germ or powdered nuts.

Powdered Nuts: Put nut meats of any kind through a small inexpensive nut grinder that comes for the purpose; or put them in a paper bag, and roll with a rolling pin until powdered.

Pie-Cakes

These are delicious newcomers to the cake field which I call "pie-cakes," as they are a combination of pie and cake, neither one nor the other. They are made in 2 forms:

1.   Round layers of cake, covered with sliced peaches, cherries, strawberries or other fruit cooked for 2 minutes in just enough thick sweetened sauce to hold them together. When cold, the cake is edged with whipped cream or a whipped cream topping.

2.   Two square sweet cookie pastry layers, ¼ inch thick, put together with a thickened fruit filling. No topping is needed. For pastry see page 260.

TOPPING OR FILLING FOR PIE-CAKES

¾ *cup water or apple juice*
2 *tablespoons corn starch*
½ *cup granulated sugar*
⅛ *teaspoon salt*

2 *cups sliced peaches or apricots, blueberries, strawberries or stoned cherries*

1.   Heat the water or apple juice. Combine the corn starch with 2 tablespoons cold water and stir into the hot liquid. Add sugar and salt and cook and stir 1 minute.

2.   Add the fruit and cook 2 minutes. Cool and use as directed.

SWEET COOKIE PASTRY
(Makes a large pie cake)

2 cups flour	Grated rind ½ lemon
½ cup powdered sugar	2 egg yolks
⅓ teaspoon salt	¾ cup shortening
6 tablespoons cold water	

1. Into a bowl sift together the flour, sugar and salt. Heap it up and make a well in the center. Into this put the lemon rind, egg yolks and the shortening.

2. With a pastry blender mix until the shortening is distributed in flakes the size of bran flakes.

3. Gradually add the cold water.

4. Then roll out to ¼ inch thickness. Fit into 8-inch pans; bake 15 minutes at 375 degrees, F. Put together with pie-cake filling (page 259).

When Cake Is Left Over

It's Steamed: In this case, steam the cake until thoroughly hot in a strainer placed over a kettle of boiling water, or else use the pressure-cooker (no pressure). Serve hot with any suitable pudding sauce.

It's Toasted: Or if it's dried-out loaf cake, toast or serve hot with a sauce or stewed canned or defrosted fruit.

Cake Fillings and Icings

Again manufacturers come to the rescue of hurried cooks—or those who bake seldom and do not have room to store a full quota of ingredients. This time it's frosting in jars, or frosting or candy mixes in packages, quick and easy to use. However, you undoubtedly will wish to use oc-

casionally very special fillings and icings. The following
are delicious and not difficult to make.

All measurements are level

ORANGE FILLING
(Covers 1 layer)

3 tablespoons flour	Grated rind 1 orange
½ cup granulated sugar	¾ cup orange juice
1 egg slightly beaten	1 tablespoon lemon juice
½ tablespoon butter or margarine	

1. Mix together the flour, sugar, egg, orange rind, orange juice, lemon juice and butter, in the top of a double
boiler.

2. Cook over hot water 10 minutes, stirring occasionally. When done, the filling should be quite thick.

Tokay-Orange Filling: Follow the preceding recipe,
using ½ cup orange juice, ¼ cup tokay wine and ½
tablespoon lemon juice.

BANANA FILLING
(Covers 1 layer)

4 ripe bananas	½ cup sugar
1 tablespoon lemon juice	

1. Peel the bananas; put into a double boiler top and
mash with a fork.

2. Add the sugar and lemon juice, and cook in the
double boiler 5 minutes. Cool and use.

CHOCOLATE FILLING
(Covers 1 layer)

Use ½ package of any good chocolate pudding mix, but add ½ cup less than the usual amount of milk. Flavor with ⅓ teaspoon cinnamon, or 1 tablespoon sherry.

Hazelnut Chocolate Filling: Add ⅓ cup chopped toasted hazelnuts.

QUICK COOKED CREAM FILLING
(Covers 1 layer)

Use ½ package of any good vanilla pudding mix. Add ⅔ the usual amount of milk, and stir in ½ tablespoon butter or margarine.

RICH COOKED CREAM FILLING
(For layer cake, 8-inch pie or 6 fruit cream tarts)

1½ *cups milk*	⅓ *cup granulated sugar*
¼ *cup flour*	¼ *teaspoon salt*
¼ *cup cold water*	½ *teaspoon any flavoring*
1 *egg or 2 egg yolks*	½ *tablespoon butter or margarine*

1. Scald the milk in a double-boiler. Combine the flour with the cold water and stir until smooth.

2. Add to the scalded milk and cook and stir until the mixture thickens, about 5 minutes.

3. Beat the egg; add the sugar and salt and stir into the thickened mixture. Cook 3 minutes longer, stirring occasionally. Then add flavoring. Cool before using.

Rum Cream Filling: Make rich cooked cream filling and flavor with 1 teaspoon rum extract.

UNCOOKED WHITE BUTTER ICING
(Topping for 1 cake)

2 *tablespoons butter or*   ½ *teaspoon vanilla or*
  margarine   *black walnut flavoring*
1 *cup sifted confectioners'* 1 *tablespoon hot milk*
  sugar

1. Cream the butter until soft.
2. Gradually work in ½ cup of the sugar, the flavoring, salt and hot milk.
3. Add remaining sugar and beat until creamy.
Sherry Butter Icing: Follow the preceding recipe using 1 tablespoon sherry instead of hot milk. Omit the vanilla.

FLUFFY BOILED ICING
(Enough for filling and topping)

1 *egg white*   3 *tablespoons water*
⅞ *cup granulated sugar* ½ *teaspoon lemon juice*
       ½ *teaspoon vanilla*

1. Put the egg white, sugar and water in the top of a double boiler.
2. Place over boiling water; cook and beat the mixture continuously with a hand beater for 5 minutes. Remove from the heat.
3. Beat in the lemon juice and vanilla and spread on the cake, in "swirls."

SHADOW BITTER-SWEET ICING
Cover the top and sides of a cake with fluffy boiled icing. When firm, melt 1 square unsweetened chocolate with 2 teaspoons butter or margarine. Spread nearly to the edge of the cake and let it dribble down the sides.
Peppermint Icing: Flavor plain uncooked butter icing,

fluffy boiled icing, or chocolate icing, with peppermint extract. Do not use any other flavoring.

LIME OR LEMON BUTTER CREAM
(Topping for 1 cake)

2 *tablespoons butter*
Rind ⅛ lemon or lime

1 *cup sifted confectioners' sugar*
1 *tablespoon lemon or lime juice*

1. Stir the butter until soft.

2. Add the lime or lemon rind; gradually stir in alternately the confectioners' sugar and the lime or lemon juice. Cream until very smooth before using.

RICH CHOCOLATE ICING
(Enough for filling and topping)

4 *squares (ounces) unsweetened chocolate*
4 *tablespoons butter or margarine*
⅛ *teaspoon salt*

1 *teaspoon vanilla*
1½ *cups sifted confectioners' sugar*
⅔ *cup light cream or undiluted evaporated milk*

1. Cut the chocolate into bits; place in the top of a double boiler. Add the butter, and melt over hot water, stirring occasionally.

2. Remove from the heat; beat in the remaining ingredients and continue to beat with a hand beater until the icing is thick enough to spread. Beat in more sugar if necessary.

BROILER TOPPING FOR CAKES

¼ *cup butter or margarine*
⅔ *cup smooth brown sugar*

½ *cup chopped pecans or walnuts*

1. Cream the butter till smooth, then blend in the brown sugar. Add the nuts.

2. Spread onto a plain cake not more than 1½ inches thick, while warm: do not remove from the pan. Place under the broiler, 3 inches from the heat, until golden brown. Serve warm. Nice on quick spice cake or 1-egg layer cake.

Pies and Tarts

Pies and ice cream are close runners-up for popularity in desserts. For the family of two an occasional pie or some tarts from the bakery solves the problem if reheated in a slow oven to freshen. But these do not have that flavor and texture we associate with the words "home-made." So bake a pie now and then. Frozen pies are good, too.

Home Pie Making for Two

Better make a whole 8- or 9-inch pie, and serve it twice. Between times keep it refrigerated. Before re-serving, barely heat through in a slow oven to freshen the crust.

Buy a pastry cloth and rolling pin cover set; this is inexpensive and makes rolling the crust easy without a pastry board.

Use a good commercial piecrust mix until you become proficient in making your own.

Use as little flour as possible when making piecrust. To save time bake a piecrust shell or a few tart shells when baking a pie. Keep in a closed container, reheat and use several days later for cream pie, fruit tarts or creamed meat or vegetable pies.

Better practice making piecrust once, and bake a sample to be sure it is flaky and tender, before putting in a filling.

All measurements are level.

PIECRUST

(Makes 1 two-crust 8-inch or 9-inch pie, 1 dozen tart shells or 2 pie shells)

2 *cups sifted flour*	¼ *teaspoon baking powder*
¼ *teaspoon salt*	¾ *cup shortening*

⅓ *cup cold water*

1. Sift together the flour, salt and baking powder. Chop in the shortening with a pastry blender.

2. When flaky, carefully add just enough cold water to make the mixture barely stick together. It should not feel sticky.

3. Transfer to a slightly floured board; roll to ⅛-inch thickness and use in making any kind of pie.

PIECRUST (PREPARED MIX)

Follow directions on the package. If the contents will make too much piecrust, make up half the package.

QUICK FROZEN PIECRUST

Defrost before using. This takes about 3 hours at room temperature.

BAKED PIECRUST SHELLS

1. Roll the pie dough thin, and fit it over a pie plate turned upside down.

2. Press down and fit it on; cut the edges off even with a knife or scissors. Prick the crust with a fork in 6 places.

3. Bake in a hot oven (400–450 degrees, F.) 12 to 15 minutes.

Tart Shells: Proceed as described using inverted large shallow muffin pans.

Nut Piecrust: Add 3 tablespoons minced Brazil nuts,

hazelnuts, pecan or walnut meats to the flour for piecrust, and proceed as directed. This crust is tops for any pie.

Keeping Leftover Piecrust Dough

Press the remnants together, and store in a covered glass dish in the refrigerator. This will keep up to 5 days without drying out.

Using Leftover Piecrust Dough

Piecrust Rounds or Diamonds: Roll to ⅛-inch thickness; cut into rounds or diamond shapes. Bake and use to decorate the top of an open pie, or to top quick deep-dish fruit or meat pies. Store in a covered container. They will keep fresh several days.

Quick Deep Dish Pies: Fill deep sauce dishes with stewed fruit or apple sauce; top each with a baked pastry round.

GRAHAM CRACKER PIECRUST

1 (8- or 9-inch) pie shell

1½ *cups fine graham*	½ *teaspoon nutmeg*
cracker crumbs	¼ *teaspoon salt*
½ *cup granulated sugar*	2 *tablespoons butter*
1½ *teaspoons cinnamon*	1 *egg white*

This is not a real piecrust; but as it is sweet, and bakes to a crisp texture, it may be used for any jellied or cream pie. Serve the day it is made.

1. Combine the crumbs, sugar, cinnamon, nutmeg and salt.

2. Chop in the butter with a pastry blender until the mixture looks like bran flakes.

3. Add the egg white unbeaten. This holds the crumbs together.

4. Rub an 8-inch or 9-inch pie pan with butter. Pack in the mixture evenly.

5. Bake 5 minutes at 350 degrees, F.; then cool and put in the filling.

APPLE PIE

(4 to 6 servings)

Home-made or piecrust mix

5 *medium-sized tart apples*

⅔ *cup granulated sugar*
⅛ *teaspoon salt*
¼ *teaspoon nutmeg or cinnamon*

1 *teaspoon butter*

1. Roll the piecrust a scant ¼ inch thick, and line an 8-inch pie plate with it.

2. Pare, core and slice the apples thin; mix with the sugar, salt, the nutmeg or cinnamon.

3. Spread in the pie plate, dot with the butter, cover with a piece of pastry rolled to a scant ¼ inch in thickness, and press the edges together with a fork. Cut off the rough trimmings.

4. Slash the top crust in the center to allow the steam to escape. Brush over with milk, or dot the pie with a little extra butter, and place in a hot oven (400–425 degrees, F.) for 10 minutes; then reduce the heat to 375 degrees and bake 35 minutes longer.

5. Reheat for second day's service.

Pear-Apple Pie: Follow the preceding recipe, using 2 good-sized firm pears and 3 apples. Omit spice, and flavor with ½ tablespoon lemon juice and the grated rind of ¼ lemon.

LEMON MERINGUE PIE
(4 to 5 servings)

¾ cup granulated sugar   2 eggs separated
2½ tablespoons cornstarch   ¾ cup boiling water
  1 teaspoon butter   3 tablespoons lemon juice
⅛ teaspoon salt   Grated rind ¼ lemon
        1 (8-inch) baked piecrust shell

1. Combine the sugar, cornstarch, butter and salt.

2. Beat and add the egg yolks.

3. Gradually stir in the boiling water. Cook and stir over hot water until very thick; then add the lemon juice and rind. Cool a little.

4. Pour into the baked piecrust shell, top with mile high meringue. Bake 12 minutes in a slow oven (325 degrees, F.).

MILE-HIGH MERINGUE
(Enough for a 9-inch pie)

  3 egg whites   ¼ teaspoon cream of tartar
2½ tablespoons cold water   (measured scant)
⅛ teaspoon salt   ¼ teaspoon flavoring
        3 tablespoons sugar

1. Add water to the egg whites and beat until frothy with a hand-beater.

2. Add the salt, cream of tartar and flavoring; beat until stiff.

3. Add the sugar and beat until stiff enough to form peaks.

4. Pile onto the pie, tarts or cake and bake in a slow oven (325 degrees, F.) for 12 minutes.

UNCOOKED MERINGUE TOPPING—
A Whipped Cream Substitute

Prepare Mile-High Meringue, and use in place of whipped cream. It must be served within 1 hour after making.

LEMON PIE (PREPARED FILLING)
(4 to 5 servings)

Purchase a package of lemon pie filling. Prepare according to directions, but add sugar to taste, about 2 tablespoons sugar, and 1 teaspoon butter or margarine. If equal parts of fruit juice and water are used (any kind except grape fruit, or grape juice), the flavor is greatly improved. Put the pie together and bake according to the directions for lemon meringue pie.

PUMPKIN PIE
(4 to 5 servings)

Piecrust, home-made or mix
2 eggs separated
1 cup cooked sieved, canned or defrosted quick-frozen pumpkin
½ cup granulated or brown sugar
⅛ teaspoon salt
⅔ cup whole milk
½ tablespoon melted butter
¼ teaspoon cinnamon
½ teaspoon ginger

1. Line a small, deep pie plate with the piecrust, and brush lightly with a little of the egg white to keep it from becoming soaked or soggy.

2. Beat the egg yolks until creamy and the whites stiff. Mix the egg yolks with the remaining ingredients.

3. Fold in the egg whites.

4. Pour into the crust-lined plate, and bake in a hot oven (400 degrees, F.) for 10 minutes. Then decrease the heat to 350 degrees, F. and bake 25 minutes longer. The pie filling should not boil. When done, the center will feel firm to the touch. Serve warm or cold.

Pumpkin Tarts: Follow the preceding recipe, using individual tart pans or large shallow muffin pans. Sprinkle with chopped walnuts, pecans, or hazelnuts, and bake.

Pumpkin Tarts à la Mode: Top pumpkin tarts with small scoops of vanilla ice cream.

Pumpkin Tarts Gratinés: Top pumpkin tarts with grated sharp cheddar or Old English cheese. Serve as is or slide under the grill a moment to melt the cheese.

CUSTARD PIE
(5 to 6 servings)

Piecrust, home-made or mix | ½ cup granulated sugar
3 eggs | ¼ teaspoon salt
| ¼ teaspoon nutmeg
2½ cups milk

1. Line a deep pie plate with the piecrust and brush it over with uncooked egg white. (This keeps the filling from soaking into the lower crust.)

2. Beat the eggs until fluffy with the sugar, salt and nutmeg. Add the milk.

3. Turn into the pie plate, place in a hot oven (400 degrees, F.) for 10 minutes; reduce the heat to 375 degrees, F. and bake 30 minutes longer, or until a knife when inserted in the center comes out clean. Do not allow the pie filling to boil. Serve the day it is baked.

Custard Tarts: Prepare as above, baking the pies in individual tart pans or large shallow muffin pans. Serve plain, or topped with strawberries rolled in sugar, sliced bananas or sugared sliced peaches.

CHOCOLATE FUDGE PIE
(*4 servings*)

1 *package chocolate pud- 1 baked piecrust shell
ding mix*   2 *tablespoons chocolate
½ *tablespoon butter*   sprinkles or chocolate bits*
¼ *cup chopped nuts (any*   *Whipped cream or mile-
kind)*   *high meringue*

1. Prepare the pudding mix, using ½ the milk indicated on the package. Cool until tepid.

2. Add the nuts, and 1 tablespoon sherry if desired. Spread in the piecrust shell.

3. Just before serving spread with the whipped cream or uncooked mile-high meringue (page 269), strew on the chocolate sprinkles or bits.

GRAHAM CRACKER CREAM PIE
(*6 servings*)

1 *recipe graham cracker   Cooked cream filling
piecrust (p. 267)   (p. 262)*
2 *tablespoons chopped toasted nuts*

1. Reserve 3 tablespoons of the graham cracker mixture; then bake the piecrust as directed.

2. Meantime make the filling and half cool it.

3. Carefully spoon into the piecrust shell.

4. Combine the reserved crumbs and nuts; sprinkle over the top of the pie.

5. Chill in the refrigerator; serve as soon as possible.

RASPBERRY CHIFFON TARTS
(*4 servings*)

Bake 4 tart shells (pages 265, 266). When cool fill with raspberry bavarian, made according to directions (page

245). Chill until firm. Serve topped with sweetened whipped cream and dotted with raspberries.

PEACH TARTS
(2 servings)

2 *tart shells*
⅔ *cup sliced fresh sweet-*
    ened, canned or de-
    frosted frozen peaches

⅓ *cup apple or any jelly*
Whipped cream or mile-
high meringue

1. Fill the tart shells with the peaches.
2. Melt the jelly and pour over and around the peaches.
3. Cool, and cover or decorate with the cream or meringue.

Apricot Tarts: Substitute drained canned apricots for peaches, in the preceding recipe. Green seedless grapes can be arranged on top in an attractive design.

BANANA-NUT CREAM TARTS
(2 servings)

2 *tart shells*
¼ *package vanilla pudding*
    mix (prepared and
    cooled)

1 *large ripe banana, sliced*
2 *tablespoons chopped*
    toasted nuts or coconut

1. Put a layer of sliced banana in the tart shells.
2. Nearly fill tarts with the pudding mix, made as directed on the package.
3. Cool, and serve topped with the remaining banana; sprinkle with the nuts or coconut.

Strawberry Cream Tarts: Follow the preceding recipe, substituting ½ cup sliced, sugared strawberries for the banana.

Deep-Dish Fruit Pies

These may be made with piecrust and any sweetened fruit, fresh, canned or quick-frozen and defrosted. Peaches, sliced peeled apples, quartered plums, stoned cherries, raspberries, blueberries and strawberries are favorites.

1. Fill buttered shirred egg or meat pie dishes ¾-full of the sweetened fruit mixed with 1 teaspoon flour, first blended smooth with ½ tablespoon cold water. If flat in taste add a little lemon or lime juice, ginger, clove or nutmeg.

2. Dot with 1 teaspoon butter or margarine.

3. Roll out piecrust dough; fit over the top of each dish. Do not draw it tight. Press down the edges with a fork, then cut off the loose bits with scissors.

4. Slash three places in the center with the point of a knife to let the steam escape. Brush with milk. Bake 30 minutes at 350 degrees, F.

5. Serve cold or hot; plain, or with hard sauce.

Cookies

The cookies described in this book are unusual, easy to make, and very easy to eat. All of them keep well if stored in a jar or canister with a tight fitting cover, so it pays to take time out to make several dozen. In storing them, place waxed paper between each layer of cookies. In mixing use all purpose flour. Follow directions exactly. If you have a cookie sheet place the cookies on it for baking. If not, use large pans turned upside down to make it easier to remove the cookies after baking. Cool them on a wire cake rack if you have one; otherwise use the broiler rack. Do not pack into the jar or canister until they are cooled.

Presenting Cookies: In arranging cookies for service, choose a pretty plate with a paper doily on it; place the cookies overlapping in a ring, or pile them in the center of the plate and place thin fingers of fruit cake radiating out to the edge. Or for a party trayful use both, augmented by packaged cookies or specials from the baker. Even a few home-made cookies lend the personal touch that makes party refreshments a success.

All measurements are level

MOLASSES SHORTBREAD COOKETTES

(6 dozen—keep indefinitely)

1 cup fortified margarine	1 cup nuts chopped fine
2 tablespoons sugar	2 cups flour
¼ cup molasses	Confectioners' sugar (optional)
1 teaspoon cinnamon or ginger	

1. Cream margarine, sugar and molasses until blended.

2. Mix and work in the spice, nuts and flour. The dough will be thick and heavy.

3. Form into large rolls ½ inch in diameter. Cut into pieces 1 inch long. Form into balls, and flatten with a fork.

4. Place on an unoiled cookie sheet; bake 10 minutes in a hot oven, 400 degrees, F. Cool and sift over confectioners' sugar.

CHOCOLATE CHIP COOKIES

(4 dozen)

½ cup butter or shortening	½ teaspoon salt
¼ cup granulated sugar	½ teaspoon baking soda
¼ cup light brown sugar	1 cup semi-sweet chocolate chips
1 egg	
1 cup flour	½ teaspoon vanilla

1. Cream the butter; add the sugars; beat and add the egg.

2. Sift together the dry ingredients; gradually beat them in.

3. Last add the chocolate chips and the vanilla.

4. Drop by small teaspoonfuls onto oiled cookie sheets or pans, keeping the cookies 2 inches apart. Bake at 375 degrees, F. 10 to 12 minutes.

BROWN EDGE ICE-BOX COOKIES
(6 dozen)

1 *cup butter or margarine*	3 *cups flour*
1 *teaspoon vanilla*	¼ *teaspoon baking soda*
1 *cup brown sugar*	1 *teaspoon baking powder*
2 *eggs*	½ *teaspoon salt*

1. Prepare dough several hours in advance of baking.

2. Cream the butter and vanilla; gradually work in the sugar.

3. Beat and add the eggs.

4. Sift the dry ingredients and work into the first mixture.

5. Form into a roll 2 inches in diameter. Wrap in waxed paper and place in the refrigerator several hours until firm.

6. Slice very thin. Place on an oiled baking sheet or inverted roasting pan and bake in a moderate oven (375 degrees, F.) 7 minutes, or until brown around the edges.

Rolls of this cookie dough can be kept in the refrigerator to slice and bake when needed. Pretty nice to turn out fresh baked cookies at a moment's notice.

Almond Ice Box Cookies: Follow the preceding recipe. Flavor with almond extract; just before baking brush with unbeaten egg white, and sprinkle over almonds, chopped medium-fine. The egg white is used to bake on the almonds so they will not fall off.

ENGLISH TEA CAKES
(4 dozen)

2¼ cups flour
1½ teaspoons baking pow-
    der
⅛ teaspoon salt
½ teaspoon nutmeg
¾ cup sifted powdered
    sugar

½ cup shortening
1 egg and 1 egg yolk
½ teaspoon vanilla
½ cup milk
½ cup whole nut meats or
    raisins

1. Sift together the flour, baking powder, salt, nutmeg and powdered sugar.

2. Chop in the shortening with a pastry blender until the mixture looks flaky.

3. Beat the eggs; add the vanilla and milk. Beat into the first mixture, and stir until smooth and free from lumps.

4. Drop by large teaspoonfuls onto an oiled pan or cookie sheet. Keep the cakes 1 inch apart to allow room for spreading. Dust with additional powdered sugar, and top each cake with a nut meat or raisin.

5. Bake 12 minutes in a moderate oven (375 degrees, F.). These cakes will keep in a closely covered can for weeks.

CREAM DROP COOKIES
(4 dozen)

½ cup shortening
1½ cups granulated sugar
2 eggs
3½ cups flour
1 teaspoon salt
½ teaspoon baking soda

½ teaspoon baking powder
1 cup thick soured cream
1 teaspoon vanilla
Sugar and cinnamon, or
sugar and chopped nut
meats

1. Cream the shortening and sugar; beat and add the eggs.

2.   Sift together the dry ingredients. Add to the first mixture alternately with the soured cream. Add the flavoring.

3.   Then drop by teaspoonfuls onto an oiled pan, allowing 1-inch space between each cookie.

4.   Dust with a little sugar and cinnamon, or sugar and chopped nut meats, or leave plain. Bake in a moderate oven (375 degrees, F.) about 12 minutes. These cookies keep fresh almost indefinitely in a closely covered can.

GOLD COOKIES
(2 dozen)

¼ *cup butter or margarine*	2 *egg yolks*
½ *cup granulated sugar*	¾ *cup flour*
½ *teaspoon almond, lemon*	¾ *teaspoon baking powder*
or vanilla extract	*Few grains salt*

Whole nut meats

1.   Cream together the butter and sugar. Add the extract and egg yolks, well beaten; then work in the dry ingredients sifted together. Chill the dough.

2.   Shape into balls the size of a marble, using a small teaspoonful for each. Place a nut meat on each cookie and put onto an oiled pan or cookie sheet, keeping 1 inch apart.

3.   Bake about 12 minutes in a moderate oven (350–375 degrees, F.).

For Gourmet and Gourmette

RUSSIAN APPLE PIE-CAKE
(Serves 2 to 3)

¼ *cup butter or margarine*	1½ *large tart apples*
¼ *cup cream cheese*	¼ *cup soured cream*
¾ *cup flour*	⅓ *cup confectioners' sugar*
¼ *teaspoon salt*	

¼ *teaspoon cinnamon*

1. Blend the shortening and cream cheese in a bowl.

2. Blend in the flour and salt, using a pastry blender to make a dough.

3. Transfer to a board dusted with flour. Roll to ⅓ inch thickness.

4. Transfer to an 8-inch oiled pie plate.

5. Peel, core and slice the apples; arrange in rows on the pie-cake dough.

6. Pour over the soured cream. Sprinkle with the confectioners' sugar and cinnamon.

7. Bake 10 minutes at 400 degrees, F., then reduce the heat to 375 degrees, F. and bake 20 minutes.

8. Dust with additional confectioners' sugar and serve warm; for a large hit, top it with ice cream.

CHAPTER XV

What Beverage?

EVERY MEAL NEEDS A BEVERAGE. WATER, OF COURSE, BUT not more than one glassful with a meal, and not iced.

Coffee or tea as an eye-opener for breakfast, and in the late afternoon as a pick-up.

Milk or café au lait whenever the meal is protein shy.

Fruit juices as the first course, at any meal or between times, day or night.

Chocolate or cocoa when a lunch or supper menu needs fortifying.

Coffee with beaten egg or an eggnog when one must eat and run.

Wine at dinner for enjoyment, relaxation and good digestion.

Properly selected, and carefully served, the right beverage is as important to a meal, as the right tie to a man's costume, or the right jewelry to a woman's ensemble. A beverage is not something merely to drink. It is a contribution to flavor and/or food value, and merits careful choice, preparation, and dainty service.

Coffee

Good coffee is fresh and sparkling, full of life, and mellow, the aroma enticing, the color dark golden-brown and clear as crystal.

The essentials for preparing perfect coffee are:

A good grade of coffee of the grind suited to the kind of pot to be used.

The right pot, spotlessly clean.

Freshly drawn water brought to a galloping boil.

The brand of coffee depends upon your own taste. Only experience will prove which you like best. However, it must be fresh, and either packed in vacuum cans or otherwise protected, or freshly roasted and ground. Keep it in a tightly-closed can or canister away from heat and sun. But not in the refrigerator.

Coffee Makers

Four kinds of coffee-making devices are sold—vacuum type, drip, percolator, and the old fashioned coffee pot. The best coffee is made in the vacuum type or drip pot. In any case choose a coffee maker that contains approximately the amount of coffee beverage usually served, for best results are obtained when used to capacity.

All measurements are level

Making Coffee

Allow 2 level tablespoons of medium-ground coffee per half-pint cup of boiling water, no matter what method is used.

Vacuum Type Method: Follow the manufacturer's directions.

Drip Coffee: **1.** Set the pot in a pan of boiling water where it will keep hot.

2. Measure into the drip part of the pot 2 level tablespoons of medium-ground coffee for each cup of coffee to be made.

3. Pour in 1 half-pint measuring cup of rapidly boiling freshly drawn water, for each 2 tablespoons of coffee. (For very strong coffee use only ¾ cup of boiling water.) Cover, and let the water drip through.

Café au lait (Coffee with hot milk): Combine equal parts of hot coffee, and heated whole or homogenized milk.

Coffee with Beaten Egg: For an eat-and-run breakfast. Beat 1 egg in a large coffee cup, and stir in boiling café au lait.

After-Dinner Coffee: Make it ⅓ as strong again as for breakfast, and serve in demitasse cups. Pass sugar tablets or candies, preferably chocolates. It is not customary to serve cream.

Cordials, liqueurs and brandies are passed with after-dinner coffee.

Some hostesses, after serving fruit for dessert, pass small crisp cookies with the demitasse. It is a pleasant custom to bring the coffee service on a tray to the living room as a leisurely finale to a fine dinner. Or barring a real living room, to that portion of a one-room apartment laughingly given that name.

ICED COFFEE

Prepare strong coffee, using ⅓ more ground coffee than when making it for breakfast. Half fill tall glasses with ice cubes or cracked ice; pour the boiling coffee over; then add cream and sugar to taste; or serve with sweetened whipped cream, or scoops of vanilla ice cream. Provide long handled sipper spoons.

To Keep and Reheat Coffee: Pour any remaining coffee into a jar, cover, and refrigerate or keep in a cold place. Reheat in an enamelware or glass double boiler; do not use metal. And do not allow the coffee itself to boil.

Instant Decaffinated Coffee: Serve hot or cold; should courteously be included as an alternate to regular coffee when entertaining.

INSTANT OR SOLUBLE COFFEE

Some of the soluble coffees are excellent in flavor and aroma. When cooking space is limited, or when only 1 or 2 cups of coffee are needed, they have a definite place. Make according to the directions on the package.

Instant Café au Lait: Add the right amount of instant coffee needed to ½ cup boiling water for each service; then fill the cup with scalded milk.

In case there is no cooking equipment at all, a cup of water can be quickly heated by an electric immersion rod; the required amount of soluble coffee can then be added.

TEA

The best method for making tea is the English style, as follows:

1. Scald a heavy earthenware pot, measure in 1 shaken-off teaspoonful of tea, or use 1 tea ball for each cup to be made. Pour in a full ½ pint measuring cup of rapidly boiling water for each teaspoon of tea or tea bag used; set the pot in a warm place 3 minutes for the beverage to infuse or steep.

2. Pour at once into a second heated pot, from which it is served. Or remove the tea bags. Tea should never be allowed to stand on the leaves.

Milk and sugar are the English accompaniments; sliced lemon is Russian style.

Iced Tea: Make tea twice as strong as usual; pour at once from the leaves and cool at room temperature. Do not refrigerate, as this often causes it to become cloudy. If to be sweetened, add the required amount of sugar dissolved in a little hot water. Add lemon juice to taste if desired. Pour into glasses containing ice cubes; and serve a wedge of lemon with each glass. Provide long handled spoons or sipper spoons.

HOT CHOCOLATE
(Serves 2 to 3)

1 *square (ounce) un-sweetened chocolate*	2 *tablespoons sugar*
	Few grains salt
1¾ *cups whole milk*	*Few grains cinnamon or*
¼ *cup boiling water*	*a few drops vanilla*

1. Grate the chocolate; add to the milk and cook in a double boiler until the chocolate melts. Add the water, sugar, salt and cinnamon, if used, and continue to cook in the double boiler 10 minutes longer.

2. If the cinnamon is not used, add the vanilla after the chocolate is done.

3. Beat well with a hand beater. Serve in small cups with or without a topping of sweetened whipped cream.

Bavarian Chocolate: Follow the recipe for hot chocolate, using 1¼ cups milk and 1 cup strong coffee beverage. Serve with whipped cream.

Iced Chocolate: Prepare hot plain or Bavarian chocolate. Pour into a jar, cool and refrigerate. Serve in tall glasses, topping with a scoop of vanilla or mocha ice cream.

COCOA
(Serves 2 to 3)

Stir together 4 teaspoons cocoa, 2 teaspoons sugar and a few grains salt. When blended, add ½ cup hot water; and when smooth, 1½ cups milk. Bring to boiling point; beat until frothy with a hand beater, and serve. If the cocoa must stand, cover, to prevent the formation of a "skin" on top.

Milk

Milk is far more than a beverage; it is a definite building protein, rich in vitamins and containing more essential minerals than any other food. It should always be pasteurized. For use as a beverage, buy homogenized milk, which is blended by centrifugal force, so that the cream is thoroughly beaten into the milk and will not separate. However, if the container of milk is to furnish cream for coffee, and milk for cooking, buy plain pasteurized milk. The cream rises to the top, and can be easily poured off or removed by means of a cream dipper. The remaining milk is a form of skimmed milk, which can be used for any desired purpose. It contains all the food value of the milk except the cream.

Buttermilk: This is that portion of the milk left after the cream and most of the solids have been churned out in making butter. Serve very cold; as a beverage, plain, or combined with ¼ the quantity of any fruit juice. In cooking use in place of sour milk.

Dry Skim Milk: Technically called "non-fat dry milk solids." (See p. 290.) Sold in packages, it may be used for any purpose. It should be reconstituted, that is, mixed with the right amount of water, according to the directions.

Evaporated Milk: This is unsweetened canned milk from which nearly half of the water has been removed. The best evaporated milks have only a very slight cooked flavor, and may be used as is for coffee, or diluted with an equal quantity of water, for making cocoa, chocolate, milk drinks, or for any form of cooking. Diluted and heated it is excellent in café au lait, or for service with cooked cereals.

Condensed Milk: Is canned sweetened milk prepared with equal weights of sugar and milk. It may be used in coffee and in certain types of cooking.

Canned Cream: Is excellent in coffee, and whenever cream is indicated in cooking. It may be whipped.

Yogurt: This is a form of cultured milk, especially beneficial because it is a natural intestinal antiseptic. It may be eaten from the jar with a spoon; or it may be stirred smooth, beaten with ¼ the quantity of fruit juice, and drunk as an enjoyable food beverage. To act as an intestinal corrective, 3 jars a day should be taken over a period of 3 weeks; and 1 each night thereafter for several weeks.

EGGNOG (WITH MILK)

Beat an egg light with 2 teaspoons sugar or honey. Add ⅔ cup cold or hot milk as desired, and flavor with a few drops of vanilla, a dusting of cinnamon or 1 tablespoon sherry or brandy. Serve with sippers.

Eggnog with Orange Juice: Beat an egg light with 2 teaspoons sugar. Add ⅔ cup chilled orange juice.

Vegetable Juices

It is a question whether vegetable juices should be classed as appetizers or beverages, for they are both. As they are often served with the main course as a beverage, I am mentioning them in this section. The most familiar are vegetable juice cocktail, sauerkraut and carrot juice; tomato juice is really a fruit juice. However, other vegetable juices are available—celery, beet (or beet with pineapple), string bean, parsley, etc. Some of these may be purchased ready prepared, but it is a better plan to buy a juicer and make them at home to insure full vitamin value. Tomato juice may be combined with any of the vegetable juices; or add a squeeze of lemon juice or dash of meat condiment sauce to bring up the flavor.

Of a winter's night try a small cup of heated spiced tomato or vegetable juice cocktail before the meal, or to sip with the main course.

Fruit Juices

Fruit juices are natural cleansers and "taste good" either plain, or in combination as the first course at any meal; as an alternate choice on a tray of cocktails or wines, or with carbonated water and ice cubes as a cooling summer drink. A great variety is ready to use in canned, bottled and quick-frozen form. The word "nectar" used in describing them, implies a mixture or blend of fruit juices, such as apricot with peach, or pear with plum.

The frozen juices may be partly defrosted and used instead of ice cubes to chill lemonade or orangeade.

Excellent fruit juice combinations include:

Orange and pineapple *Apple juice with passion fruit*
Grape juice with lemon *Raspberry with orange*
Papaya with lime *Tangerine and raspberry*
Apricot with orange *Grapefruit and orange*
Prune with orange *Plum and apple*

Any of these may be laced with a little sweet white wine. Tomato juice is used plain, with lemon juice or a dash of dry sherry.

After a long day's work it is refreshing and energizing to come home and sip a 4-ounce glass of fruit juice or tomato juice. If dinner is delayed, this allays hunger, without dulling appetite, and is an antidote to irritability traceable to an empty stomach left too long to its own devices.

FRUIT JUICE TODDY

Heat any fruit juice (or combination) with 2 cloves and 1 inch of stick cinnamon. Strain and serve as a refresher any time of the day or night. Excellent for insomnia, too; just forget the sleeping pills. And speaking of insomnia, here are some special suggestions.

Lullabed Beverages

HOP-TEA

No, this is not a typographical error. It is just what it says "hop-tea," a "receipt" from the notebook of an old country doctor who did not believe in sleeping pills. His prescription, prepare hop-tea as follows:

Measure into a scalded earthenware teapot 1 tablespoon dried hops (the kind used in making beer; most druggists carry them). Pour in 2 half-pint cups of boiling water. Cover; steep 5 minutes; then strain and drink with or without sugar and/or lemon or cream an hour before retiring. Tastes bitter I know, but what a safe, good natural sleep, with no hangover! Persisted in, this is usually effective.

Or if nerves need quieting, and the body needs building-up, try the following:

HOT MILK WITH HONEY

Heat a cup of whole milk and stir in 1½ teaspoons honey. Shake over a bit of cinnamon if you like. A grand nightcap.

For a third choice try this:

HOT ORANGE EGGNOG

Thoroughly heat ¾ cup orange juice in a double boiler. Add 1 teaspoon honey. Stir into a well-beaten egg and drink at once.

Wine for the Family of Two

There is usually too little cupboard space in small households for a variety of wine glasses. So choose one pattern and size. Four-ounce glasses in a stock pattern may be replaced if there are breakages. Neither is there room for bottles of many kinds of wine. So select the kind you like best; after it has once been opened keep it cool until used up. A "fifth" provides 8 average-sized glasses; half bottles provide 4 glasses and are a better buy for 2 persons if refrigeration space is limited. Domestic American wines are delicious, inexpensive and offer excellent variety.

Dry wines are not sweet, and are served usually with the entrée or the main course.

Sweet wines are those to which a little grape brandy has been added so they will be suited to dessert and refreshment service.

There are a few simple rules for the service of wines with certain foods:

Dry sherry or an aperitif such as Dubonnet are served before the meal with canapés and appetizers.

Dry red wine as claret, burgundy, and chianti, may be served with red meats and game.

Dry white wine as sauterne, hock and chablis may be served with poultry, oysters and fish. White wines should be cooler than room temperature. Red wines may be served at room temperature. Sparkling burgundy should be iced.

The sweet or dessert wines include port, Madeira, muscatel, angelica, tokay and sweet sherry. These wines do not need refrigeration before serving, and are served with pastry, fruit and nuts, puddings, cake, cookies or cheese and crackers.

Champagne is in a class by itself, and may be served with any course or on any occasion, but always well chilled; if possible in a bucket of ice.

Cordials, liqueurs and brandies are served at room temperature in thimble-shaped glasses and with after-dinner coffee.

Always cork a bottle of wine after using. And remember no matter how small an amount may be left, it will be enough to give flavor-lift to some otherwise dull food.

WINE COOLERS FOR SUMMER

Iced Wine: Pour red or white wine over crushed ice or ice cubes. Use tall glasses with sippers.

Iced Wine with Charged Water: Put 3 ice cubes in a

tall glass; pour in red or white wine to ½ fill, and add charged water. Serve with sippers.

WINE WARMERS FOR WINTER

Hot Wine-ade: Prepare ⅔ of a glass of hot, tart lemonade; add red or white wine to fill the glass.

Hot Wine Cup: Combine equal parts of water and sweet sauterne, muscatel or tokay wine. Add a twist of lemon peel; twisting is necessary to release the lemon oil flavor. Add sugar to taste; heat and serve in a tall glass.

For Gourmet and Gourmette

VIENNESE COFFEE

Make fresh strong, black coffee and serve in small cups with a topping of whipped cream. Pass sugar. Socially correct to serve instead of the demitasse.

A distinguished restaurant in Chicago gained fame by serving coffee Viennese style after a good dinner. You and your guests will like it, too.

WHIPPED DRY SKIM MILK TOPPING

Into a deep pint bowl measure ¼ cup cold water, ½ tablespoon lemon juice, and ¼ cup dry skim milk. Add a few grains salt. Beat steadily with a hand beater until it holds its shape. Beat in 1 tablespoon sugar and 4 drops vanilla. Keep cold. It will stand up 4 to 5 hours. Use as a topping on gelatins and cold desserts, chiffon pies, gingerbread, cocoa, or instead of heavy cream in bavarian creams and gelatin whips.

Whipped Fruit Topping: Just before serving beat in 3 tablespoons grated apple, mashed banana, peach or strawberries, or raspberry jam.

CHAPTER XVI

All-in-One Dinners

THE TITLE, "ALL-IN-ONE DINNERS" REFERS TO THE PREPA-
ration of the main course, when meat or fish, vegetables
and sometimes the dessert are cooked by means of the same
heat. The finest and quickest method to use is pressure-
cooking, fully described in my book, *Pressure Cooking*. All-
in-one meals may also be broiled, boiled or oven-baked.
They may be prepared on any type of stove, in a large
separate electric oven, or roaster or broiler; or on a one-
unit electric plate, supplemented by an electric casserole
or cooker, or even by a small kerosene or solid alcohol
stove, supplemented by a good-sized kettle, and/or an
ovenette.

Broiler Meals

All gas and electric ranges are equipped with broilers.
In addition, there are many adequate separate electric
broilers (or grills) that may be used. The food to be broiled
is placed on the wire rack and set to cook beneath the
direct flame or heat of the preheated broiler. In broiling
foods for an entire meal, start first the food that takes
longest to cook.

Meats that may be broiled include steak, chops, liver,
kidney, sausage, sweetbreads, and small portions of ham,

pork, lamb or veal sliced thin. Chicken, cut into sections and fish fillets are at their best when broiled.

All firm vegetables and fruits that can be sliced or halved, may also be broiled in a broiler preheated for 10 minutes.

All measurements are level

A Sample Broiled Dinner
(Broiling time 18 to 20 minutes)

Spiced Tomato Juice
Thick Mutton or Lamb Chops with Kidneys
Broiled Potato Slices   Clove Apple Rings
Eggplant Paprika
Cake   Coffee

1.   Preheat the broiler. Wash the potatoes; do not peel. Cut lengthwise into slices ½ inch thick. Place on a well-oiled broiler rack; dust with salt and pepper. Start to broil 3 inches from the heat.

2.   Dust the chops with salt and pepper. Place on the broiler and broil 6 minutes; then turn both meat and potatoes; dust again with salt and pepper.

3.   Next start the eggplant to broil; this should be cut in ½-inch slices, dusted with salt, pepper and paprika, and seasoned with French garlic dressing (page 223). Turn once when ½ done and dot with butter.

4.   Last, core and slice unpeeled apples; stick a whole clove in each slice; dust with sugar; dot with butter and broil during the last 5 minutes, turning once.

5.   Arrange for service on a glass or metal sizzling platter. In this case, dot the foods with butter and slip under the broiler until it melts. To serve, place the platter on a heat-proof mat to protect the table.

Boiled Dinners

Chicken or meat with vegetables, cooked long and slowly in a covered pot of water, or in an electric casserole or cooker, make delicious boiled dinners. Actually the only "boiling" that should take place is when the meat is first plunged into the boiling water, for the heat must be turned down at once so the food merely simmers until tender. As boiled dinners take considerable time to cook, choose them when not hurried.

Suitable meats for boiled dinners include: chicken, thrifty cuts of beef from the chuck, brisket, flank and round; corned beef; neck, leg and shoulder of lamb or veal; and the smoked meats, such as smoked pork tenderloin, ham butts and tongue.

New England Boiled Dinner
(Cooking time 2½ hours)

Corned Beef and Cabbage
Turnips   Potatoes   Parsnips
Pickled Beet Salad   Corn Muffins
Apple Brown Betty   Beverage

1. To prepare, cover the corned beef with boiling water and bring to boiling point. Drain off this water; cover with fresh boiling water; cover, and simmer nearly 2 hours or until it can easily be pierced to the center with a cooking fork.

2. Then add the vegetables; the turnips should be peeled and sliced; the parsnips peeled and quartered, and the potatoes peeled.

3. Twenty minutes later, add the cabbage, cut in thick slices; slow-boil 15 minutes longer.

4. To serve, slice the meat; arrange in the center of a heated platter; surround with the vegetables; garnish with parsley, and serve with horse-radish sauce or mustard, pickled beet salad and corn muffins.

Oven Meals

Whether a whole meal is being prepared in the oven, or whether a cake or other food is being baked, full use should be made of the oven heat, to save fuel and "watching time." Baking develops rich flavors in foods. In addition, oven-cooked meals reduce dishwashing, because most foods may be served in the dishes in which they are baked.

Temperature: The time of cooking and the temperature varies with the type of foods selected. In general, a temperature of 350–400 degrees, F. is ideal. Any foods that can be cooked within that temperature range may be oven-cooked together at one time in the oven. And any kind of an oven may be used, the oven of the range, a top-of-the-stove oven, or a separate electric oven or roaster.

Utensils: Any utensil that is not wooden-handled can be used in the oven. Heavy earthenware, ceramics and heat-proof glass retain heat for a long time, and have a way of bringing out fine food flavors. Casseroles of earthenware, glass or pottery, or heat-proof glass pie plates and loaf cake pans may be used in the oven. Custard cups or shirred egg dishes of pottery or glass are very useful. Heavy iron and very heavy aluminum utensils are also suitable. In many cases special heavy paper baking dishes can be used and discarded, leaving no pots and pans to wash. Care should be taken to place protective pads under the baking-dishes when they are put on the table.

Selection of Foods: Baked apple sauce or rhubarb; baked custards; baked stewed prunes or pears; or baked squash or beans for a subsequent meal can often be prepared in advance in the oven; vegetables and cereals can always be boiled in the oven.

One of the best ways to save time and fuel is to make good use of the oven by cooking a whole meal at a time. To learn how to utilize every inch of oven space, first fit the utensils into the cold oven to find out how many kinds of utensils it will hold. Then plan the menu. It might be as follows:

A Sample Oven Meal
(Cooking time 30 minutes)

Baked Shoulder Lamb Chops
Sliced Carrots   Small Onions
Oven-Fried Potatoes   Celery Rolls
Gingered Pears   Beverage

1. Dust the lamb chops with flour, salt and pepper; brown quickly on both sides in savory drippings. Place on a large baking dish or heat-proof platter. Scrape and slice the carrots. Peel the onions. Arrange the vegetables around the chops. Dust with salt and pepper. Add 1 cup water and cover.

2. Peel and slice the potatoes thin; put in a very well-oiled baking dish; dust with salt and pepper; dot thickly with butter or margarine.

3. Light the oven and set it at 375 degrees, F.

4. Peel, halve and core 3 pears; sprinkle with grated lemon rind and a little chopped candied ginger; put in a baking dish with one cup boiling water in which ⅓ cup sugar has been dissolved. (Baste the fruit occasionally with this syrup while baking.)

5. Put all the food in the oven at one time; bake ½ hour.

Casserole Dinners

There are 2 kinds of casseroles, open and covered. Open casseroles are used for foods to be browned on top, such as macaroni au gratin, or glacéed sweet potatoes. Covered casseroles are used for foods that are bake-stewed, that is, stewed slowly in the oven (or on top of the stove) in a small amount of liquid, as any ragout, stew or pot roast. However, casserole cooking is slow, so choose this type of dinner when there is ample time to cook it. It needs almost no watching.

A Sample Casserole Dinner

(Cooking time 2 hours)

Anchovy Appetizer Salad
Casseroled Chicken Fricassee   Casseroled Sweet Potatoes
Onions cooked en casserole
Baked Apples   Beverage

1. Prepare the fricassee ready to cook (page 160). Bring to boiling point. Transfer to a casserole, cover and place in a slow oven (325–350 degrees, F.).

2. At the end of 1 hour, peel mild onions and put in a casserole; add salt, pepper, butter, and boiling water nearly to cover. Place in the oven. Also put in a casserole containing the sweet potatoes, and one with the prepared apples. Cook 1 hour longer. Serve from the casseroles.

Two-Burner Meals

Many apartments and dwelling places are equipped only with a two-burner table stove. By planning ahead, appetizing two- or three-course dinners can be prepared almost as easily with this limited equipment as with a regulation range. And not only for families of two, but even four or six.

A heavy iron kettle with a cover, of the Dutch oven type, insures delicious pot roasts and stews. Two or more vegetables at a time may be cooked in a 3-sectioned utensil, or they may be wrapped separately in moistened parchment paper, tied up, and boiled in one large utensil. A top-of-the-stove oven that fits over one burner may be used for baking cakes, muffins, biscuits and desserts, or a whole oven meal. Or a whole meal may be steamed or boiled, over one burner. An electric Dutch oven is helpful.

A Sample Two-Burner Meal

(Cooking time about 1¼ hours)

Chilled Tomato Juice   Crusty Bread
Chicken Fricassee   Parslied Potatoes
Fresh Lima Beans   Radishes
Fruit Cup   Beverage

1. Prepare the fruit cup.

2. Make the fricassee (use a tender chicken). Cook 35 minutes. Meanwhile, peel and add the potatoes.

3. Pod and cook the lima beans. Keep hot by standing on the inverted cover of the kettle of chicken fricassee.

4. Set the table; make the coffee on the free burner; assemble and serve the meal.

Hurry-Up Dinners

The menus that follow make full use of fresh, quick-frozen and canned fruits, fruit juices and vegetables. Thirty minutes is allotted for preparation. This may be scaled down, by substituting more canned or frozen fruits or vegetables for fresh varieties; by eliminating an appetizer or a salad; or omitting a special dessert and substituting assorted fresh fruits. Or serve crackers and cheese, cheese and fruit, or cream cheese and preserves (see pages 99 and 100).

Thirty-Minute Dinners for Two
(*Starred recipes are in this book)

I

Cream of Spinach Soup (Canned)   Croutons*
Ham and Fruit Platter*   Broiled "Sweets"*
Tossed Salad Bowl*   Heated Rolls
Floating Island*   Beverage

II

Melon Fruit Cup
Broiled Kidneys and Bacon en Brochette*
Parslied Diced Potatoes   Corn Heated in Broiling Pan
Apple Betty* with Lemon-Honey Cream Sauce*
Beverage

III

Hot Vegetable Juice   Crisp Crackers
Beef Burgers* on Toasted Buns
Broccoli* with Butter   Scallions
Orange and Grapefruit Cup
Beverage

IV

Coleslaw* with Chived Cottage Cheese   Dark Bread
Broiled Fillet of Flounder*   Sauce Remoulade*
Broiled Sliced Potatoes*   Shredded String Beans
Fruit Short Cake* (with sponge cake)   Beverage

V

Split Pea Soup (canned or dehydrated)   Melba Toast
Garden Plate of Quick Baked Potatoes with Soured
Cream and Chives* or Crisp Bacon
Asparagus*   Buttered Carrots*
Radishes*   Scallions*
Bread-and-Butter Custard*   Beverage

VI

Stuffed Egg and Tomato Appetizer
Creamed Tuna* on Flaky Rice*
Sliced Beets (canned)   Whole Wheat Rolls
Sliced Bananas with Tart Cherries
Beverage

VII

Vegetable Soup (canned) with Soured Cream
Sautéed Luncheon Meat   Noodles with Tomato Sauce*
Fried Eggplant*   Rye Bread
Assorted Fruits   Cheese   Crackers
Beverage

Frozen Food Combination Dinners
VIII

Shrimp Bisque (frozen)
Chicken Pies (frozen)   Mixed Vegetables (frozen)
Tossed Lettuce-Tomato Salad
Sliced Oranges with Coconut
Beverage

IX

Chilled Vegetable Juice
Broiled-Liver Platter
Cole Slaw   Whipped Potato (dehydrated)
Lemon Sherbet   Raspberries (frozen)
Beverage

X

Clam Chowder (canned or frozen)
Celery   Radishes
Lamb Chops   Browned Sweet Potatoes (canned)
Broccoli (frozen)
Sliced Elberta Peaches (canned)
Beverage

CHAPTER XVII

Your Good Eating Insurance

THAT PHRASE "THE BALANCED RATION" MAY SOUND A BIT boresome, unnecessarily scientific, or as if meals planned by rule could not possibly taste good. But quite the contrary is true. To balance meals, a wide variety of foods is used, so balanced meals cannot be boresome. Because they are scientifically planned to meet every need of the body, they are satisfying; and because they are made up of the world's most delectable food products they cannot taste grim. In fact it is only when meals are *not balanced* that they are boring, unsatisfying and unappetizing. Let's take that phrase "the balanced ration" and think through its meaning. Ready? **The balanced ration is the combination into three meals a day of several types of essential foods planned to meet every need of the body and literally keep it going.**

The Essentials

In this group of foods we have:

Protein: Necessary to build and repair muscular tissues in children and replace worn-out cells and tissues in adults. To assist in regulating body processes, and for general good condition.

The proteins include meat, fish, poultry, game, milk, cheese, eggs, nuts and the legumes.

Energy Foods: Necessary to furnish fuel to the body. These foods consist of three groups:

1. The Starches: Include cereals, breads, the spaghetti family, and potatoes.

2. The Sweets: Include sugar, honey, syrups, candies, and all sweetened foods and sweetened beverages.

3. Fats: Include cream, butter, margarine, meat fats, vegetable oils, mayonnaise and shortening.

Water: Essential to good digestion, and the absorption and transportation of food to different parts of the body. Everyone needs plenty of water each day; cool, but not iced, in addition to the tea, coffee, fruit juices, milk and other beverages included in the menu.

Minerals: Important as builders for bones, teeth, blood, tissues and all organs. They are also body regulators, affecting heart, nerve and muscular activity and gland action.

The mineral-rich foods include milk and eggs, cheese, whole grains, salad plants, and fresh, canned, quick-frozen, dried and brined fruits and vegetables.

Vitamins: Essential to general good health, normal growth—repair and reproduction. They are catalysts that help many foods to function efficiently. Vitamins A, B Complex, C and D are best known to most people, but there are many others.

Vitamins of various types are present in all natural foods, including fruits, vegetables, milk and milk products, eggs, meat, nuts, salad plants and whole grains.

Protecting the Foods You Cook

A balanced diet results in balanced food values if foods are cooked to conserve them. But only too often this is not done. Soluble proteins and minerals are wasted if foods are boiled and the cooking water is drained off and discarded. The potency of vitamins is lessened by contact with the oxygen of the air. So foods should be cooked so there will be as little contact with air as possible. These losses or wastes can be largely prevented by observing a few simple, sensible rules.

1. Use as little water in cooking as possible, unless the liquid is to be served with the food, as in making a stew or chowder.

2. Always start vegetables to boil in boiling water, and bring back to boiling point rapidly.

3. When possible use short-time methods of cookery in place of long-time methods.

4. Fry food seldom, as the high temperature necessitated impairs the efficiency of Vitamins A, B_1 and C.

5. Cover closely all boiling or steaming foods—no exceptions.

6. Except by special directions in the recipe stir foods as little as possible while cooking, to avoid stirring in air and therefore oxygen.

7. Avoid putting hot foods through a sieve unnecessarily.

8. Save all water in which vegetables have been cooked; use in making vegetable cocktails, gravies, sauces and soups, or in cooking meat, fish or vegetables.

9. Cook vegetables with the skin on when possible to assist in holding in the minerals, vitamins and soluble proteins.

10. Prepare chopped, diced, or sliced fresh fruits or vegetables just before serving.

11. Squeeze fruit juices just before serving.

12. Keep foods and all fruit and vegetable juices closely covered in the refrigerator or in a cold pantry.

13. Start cooking quick-frozen foods while they are still frozen if possible.

14. Serve raw quick-frozen foods immediately after thawing so they will not be exposed to the air.

15. Never use baking soda while cooking fresh or dried vegetables, as it destroys vitamins.

16. Do not let fresh vegetables stand in water before cooking; when this is done, valuable food elements seep out and are lost.

17. Learn and practice pressure cooking, the best of all methods to conserve vitamins, minerals and soluble proteins.

How to Balance Meals

"But what foods do balanced meals include?" you ask. This can be summed up in a single sentence.

Each meal must include 1 protein food, 1 or 2 starchy foods, 1 sweet, 1 fat, one or more vitamin-rich foods of the right kind, plenty of bulky food and liquid.

This may sound both complicated and expensive. In reality it is neither. The simplest meals can be balanced. For instance, entire wheat bread and butter, a baked apple and milk is a well-balanced meal, vitamins and all. The reason this is so is because almost all foods contain more than one type of essential vitamins. However, it is difficult to memorize all the elements of each food, so let's take an easy method. If you will read through and mentally digest the following Round Dozen Rules you will be able to plan three meals a day that contain the food essentials and therefore balance.

Round Dozen Rules

1. Include 1 pint of whole milk a day for each person; more for children and expectant or nursing mothers. Use in the form of a beverage, with cereals and/or in cooking other foods. All forms of whole milk may be used, fresh, evaporated or dried.

2. Use only whole grains or fortified cereals and whole grain or enriched breads. Serve 1 or 2 at each meal.

3. Provide butter or fortified margarine at each meal.

4. Serve oranges, grapefruit, tangerines or tomatoes at least once every day. Whole fruit is preferable to juice as it provides roughage.

5. In addition provide each day an apple, pear, peaches, grapes, banana, berries, or other seasonable fruit, melon, or stewed, dried, canned or quick-frozen fruit.

6. Use a choice of a green-colored or yellow-colored vegetable once a day, and add any other vegetables you like.

7. Serve a leafy green salad or coleslaw once a day either in addition to, or in place of a green-colored vegetable.

8. Provide a protein food, or a made dish based on a protein, at each meal.

9. Use at least 3 eggs a week, or better still at least 1 a day in the form of plain egg dishes, or in cooking other foods.

10. Introduce one sweet at each meal—dessert, a sweet spread, syrup, and/or sugar on cereal or in a beverage.

11. Be sure that each meal includes enough bulky or roughage food to induce adequate intestinal action.

12. Furnish not more than one glass of water at meals (or none at all); but be sure a glassful is taken on rising, and at frequent intervals during the day and early evening.

Shall We Balance Each Meal?

I believe you'll agree this can all be painlessly understood. But you still have a question, and it's this: Is it really necessary to *balance every meal?* Can't we have juice, coffee and toast for breakfast, a sandwich and a coke for lunch, and a big dinner at night? Do this if you like, but you won't like the result. You will feel tired by 10:30 A.M. Strike a low fatigue point by 4 P.M. because the supply of fuel food is low, and feel stuffed and sleepy during the evening, because you ate more at one time than the digestive system can easily manage.

Every split second of the day and night the body works. And it is necessary to balance that output of work with the intake of balanced food at regular intervals, to furnish energy (fuel), replenish constantly wearing tissues, and to regulate and control body functions. This is why we need three regular balanced meals each day.

The quantity of food each person requires varies with their type of activity. Outdoor workers need more than indoor workers. Those doing active work need more than those whose work is sedentary. For practical purposes estimate the necessary foods by average-sized helpings. Remember that men usually eat more than women, and like robust foods. So be sure to provide enough. However, when meals are balanced, overeating of any one type of food is unlikely.

How About Snacks

If it is difficult to tuck in enough milk or fruit at meals, use them for snacks during the day or even at bedtime. Yes, I approve of these if the evening has been active, the hour is late and if the snack consists of easily digested food and relaxing beverages.

Breakfast Is Important

Many doctors consider breakfast the most important meal of the day. The reason so many persons skip it, or take breakfast on the run, is because it is usually dull and monotonous. But this is easily remedied. Shop for interesting fruits, cereals and breads for breakfast. Introduce interesting principal dishes. It is easy to produce good breakfasts with little work if you plan in advance.

Pattern for Breakfast

Fruit, 1 protein food, 1 or 2 starch foods, sugar in some form, one fat, coffee, a coffee substitute, tea, cocoa or milk.

Sample Menu

Oranges
Eggs in Any Form
or
Whole Grain Cereal Cooked in Milk
Toast with Butter or Margarine   Choice of Beverage

Vary Breakfast Dishes

Use a variety of fruits, cereals and breads; cook eggs in different ways. Alternate bacon and fried ham and sausages with chopped beef toasts, stewed kidneys, creamed dried beef, corned beef hash, or apple rings with sausage cakes. Fishcakes, kippers, broiled fish and grilled sardines are all appetizing breakfast dishes.

Luncheons for Two

Whether luncheon is to be prepared for two persons or only one, it must be appetizing and balanced. Even if you are a stay-at-home and alone, and it scarcely seems worth while, stop to prepare and eat a good lunch, not a snack snatched standing up in the kitchen. Arrange the food on a tray; relax and eat it leisurely. Such luncheons bring big dividends in good health.

Pattern for Luncheon

A protein food, 1 starchy food, 1 fat, a vegetable and/or fruit, a sweet and a beverage.

Sample Menu
Bouillon
Choice of a Cheese, Fish, Egg or Meat Dish or Salad
Whole Grain Bread   Butter or Margarine
Fresh or Stewed Fruit
A Beverage (Preferably Milk)

Lunchbox Meals

Remember that the lunchbox meal is one of the three balanced meals needed each day, so follow the pattern for luncheon in planning it.

A balanced lunchbox meal could include whole grain bread sandwiches with meat, poultry, cheese or egg filling (no fish, as it spoils too easily). A tomato, celery stalks or carrot sticks. A fruit tart, or a cut of pie, cake or cookies, and fresh fruit; coffee with hot milk or tea or cocoa in the thermos bottle, or better still, a glass of milk.

Pattern for Dinner

A protein food, 1 or 2 starchy foods (no more); 1 fat, 2 vegetables and/or a green salad; a sweet, a beverage.

A dinner based on this pattern could include for the protein, any meat, poultry, game, fish, egg or cheese dish; or use a meat or fish hors d'oeuvre or soup, and a main dish based on dried beans; have potatoes and a yellow vegetable; coleslaw or tossed salad; any dessert and a beverage.

Legumes, nuts and cereals are all known as secondary proteins. But if a small serving of a primary protein such as milk, meat, fish, cheese or eggs is provided in the same meal, full protein requirements will be met.

Sample Menu
Vegetable Soup
Broiled Chopped Steak   *Broiled Sweet Potatoes*
Rolls with Butter or Margarine
Peas   *A Tossed Green Salad*
Baked Custard   *Choice of Beverage*

Remember you can go all out on fancy cooking if you like, provided you practice the Round Dozen Rules each day. In any case, no matter how average or how generous the food budget may be, it is possible to produce appetizing balanced meals. Future health security depends on the success of your effort.

How to Plan Your Own
At this point I might continue with a large number of menus for two planned to cover the whole year. But you have your own tastes, food favorites and food dislikes. So instead of planning your meals, I suggest that you read and re-read this chapter and the Round Dozen Rules until they become actual working knowledge. Meanwhile, plan your meals in advance for a week. Each time it will be easier and quicker. You'll find it a pleasant way to spend an hour.

Making Menus: This is the way to proceed: Sit down for an hour's quiet session with yourself, armed with a newspaper giving the weekend specials of your favorite store. Have ready a sharp pencil and a big sheet of paper marked into 3 columns, which are in turn ruled across to make 21 squares—1 for each meal of the week. Label one column "Breakfast," a second "Luncheon," and the third column "Dinner."

Then, with this book beside you for guidance and suggestions, and keeping in mind the amount of money you wish to spend, roughly figure out the menus for the week, working in your favorite dishes from the hundreds given in this book. Better start with Sunday's dinner. Then plan how you'll use the oddments from this meal. Next plan (in turn) the remaining dinners of the week, utilizing the probable oddments for breakfast or luncheon. Plan to use the most perishable meats and vegetables first. Follow with foods which are less perishable and can be bought in advance, such as smoked pork tenderloin, tongue or ham, cabbage, young turnips, beets, and so on.

After the dinners are scheduled, plan the luncheon menus, and last the breakfasts. Next, make your marketing list. Jot down the quantities of each food needed for the week, keeping the various types separate to make shopping easier.

Food Shopping: Friday or Saturday, buy all the groceries, fats, cheese and eggs for the week, together with enough bread, meat, fish, fruits and vegetables to last through Tuesday's breakfast. On Tuesday sally forth again to buy what perishables you need through Wednesday or even Friday, when it will be time for another food shopping jaunt. If you do not have a good refrigerator that is quite large and sufficiently cold, daily shopping may be necessary.

Twosome shopping is fun, quicker, too. Many men go on the weekly shopping tour and enjoy it. They are fast learning to cook, too, as a hobby. But don't let them overdo it. Men love to have women cook. Better make it a gracious, graceful appeteasing specialty.

CHAPTER XVIII

Let's Have a Party

THE TREND IN ENTERTAINING IS TOWARD INFORMALITY. IT is only on formal occasions that maid service is required. And frankly, it is impossible to be formal without it. But the family of two can entertain delightfully in a casual way that everyone, even the hostess, will enjoy. By way of caution, keep all menus and foods simple; save elaborate planked steak and fancy desserts for the two of you; do not attempt to serve dishes calling for last-minute preparation, such as soufflés; plan foods that can stand before serving if guests are late; and above all, do not experiment when guests are expected.

There are two ways of serving—the guests seated at table, or in buffet style when they serve themselves and enjoy the food seated at small tables put in convenient places. The number of guests expected determine the choice. If serving more than six, buffet service is best for the small household. If there is a shortage of dishes so that unmatched designs of several kinds are used together, buffet service is a "must."

Buffet Service

Arrange the foods and eating equipment in the order of service, so each guest can obtain them in sequence. Buffet service should move as smoothly as an assembly line. This depends merely on thoughtful planning and table setting.

Although guests are supposed to serve themselves they seldom do; so the host or hostess can serve the main dish, and someone should be appointed custodian of the coffeepot. Someone else should be reponsible for picking up soiled dishes and taking them to the kitchen, or its reasonable facsimile.

Now to start with the top of the morning and go through till midnight.

BRUNCH

This is a combination breakfast and luncheon, served any time between 10 A.M. and 1 o'clock P.M. of a Sunday or holiday morning. Use simple colorful doilies and napkins, with a fresh fruit bowl for decoration. If the weather is warm, serve on the porch, terrace or in the patio if possible. In this case an electric coffee maker, and a hot plate plugged in near the table for keeping foods warm is a big help. Or it might be a barbecue brunch; seat the guests at the table if there are not too many. Otherwise serve buffet style.

Menus for Brunch
(Starred recipes are in this book)

Fall or Winter
Fresh Fruit Bowl
Broiled Chicken* with mushrooms
or
Wined Beef Burgers* on Toasted Buns
Creamed Potatoes*   Heated Rolls with Marmalade
Tea and Coffee

Spring or Summer
Pineapple and Strawberry Cup
Escalloped Eggs*   *Canadian Bacon**
Hot Corn Muffins   *Potato Chips*
Tea and Coffee

Barbecue Brunch
Assorted Fruit
Frankfurters Grilled with Bacon*
Grilled Potato Slices*
Heated Rolls   *Heated Sugared Doughnuts*
Cheese   *Coffee*

THREE INFORMAL LUNCHEONS
Luncheons are almost always for "the ladies," and as the fashion trend is toward a slim and youthful silhouette, menus have become a bit slim, and less elaborate. Two smart courses are quite enough. For example:

An Hors d'Oeuvre Luncheon-Buffet
First Course:
Hot or Cold Tomato Juice
Canapés, with Hors d'Oeuvres or Toasts such as
Buttered Crab Meat
and Cheese in Wine* Toasts
with fresh Vegetable Nibblers* and Olives

Second Course:
Fresh Fruit Cup* with
Lemon-Honey Cream Dressing*
Coffee

A Dessert Luncheon

When an extra delicious dessert and coffee make up the entire menu. For example:

1. Raspberry bavarian cream, sponge cup cakes and coffee.

2. Date Cup Cakes* split, filled with diced fresh fruit, and topped with lemon-honey cream sauce and nuts. Serve coffee.

Sit-at-the-Table Luncheons

(Can be served on a bridge table)

I

Hot or Chilled Consommé   Tiny Cheese Biscuits
Lobster Avocado Salad   Melba Toast*
Fruits in Wine   Hot or Iced Coffee*

II

*Chili Con Carne in Rice-Lined Bowls**
*Corn Muffins   Mixed Greens Salad Bowl**
Baked Custards with Strawberries   Coffee*

III

*Fresh Fruit Pick-Up Salads**
Small Chicken Sandwiches   Coffee

COCKTAIL PARTIES

The service is always buffet style, with help-yourself-bowls of savory nibblers such as crisp potato chips, coconut chips, raw vegetables, and dips placed conveniently.

Allow 4 or 5 canapés, and 2 or 3 drinks per person. With cocktails the accompaniments should not be sweet. Cake, cookies, or sweetened biscuits, are served only with dessert wines or sherry. But either sweets or savory tidbits harmonize with tea or coffee.

With cocktails serve canapés (see Chapter V) and/or open sandwiches (Chapter VI); a hot cheese appetizer, such as cheese balls on picks, vegetable nibblers and olives. As an alternate to cocktails, coffee or chilled fruit juice may be provided.

LITTLE DINNERS

Every family of two occasionally gives a little dinner. A first course of appetizers is served casually as the guests arrive, by the host or hostess from a tray or hospitality wagon—a selection of simple canapés and hors d'oeuvres (see Chapter V), together with a choice of dry sherry or cocktails—with chilled tomato or orange juice as alternates. The main course and dessert are served at the table. A tossed salad may be served with the main course, in place of a second vegetable. Coffee and liqueurs follow in casual service in the living room. All foods should be of a kind that can be prepared in advance.

A Spring or Summer Casual Dinner
(Starred recipes are in this book)

Before the meal service:

Assorted Canapés   Choice of Beverage
Vegetable Nibblers*

At the Dining-Table:

Chicken Platter: Broiled Chicken
Asparagus Tips and Corn Fritters*
Chef's Salad Bowl of Greens*
Strawberry Shortcake**

After dinner service:
*Demitasse with Brown-Edge Cookies**

Fall or Winter Casual Dinner

Before the meal service:
*Smoked Turkey Canapés**   *Choice of Beverage*
Olives and Celery Sticks

At the dining-table:
Shrimp Curry with Flaky Rice**
Mixed Greens Salad Bowl
*Baked Apple Dumplings**   *Hard Sauce**

After dinner service:
*Viennese Coffee**   *Chocolate Candies*

BUFFET DINNERS

Set card tables for four, just as for regulation table service. But arrange the foods for casual buffet service in assembly-line fashion, on any large enough table. This should be covered with an attractive cloth matching or harmonizing with those used on the card tables. Guests serve and group themselves at the small tables. I attended a most graceful yet inexpensive dinner of this type in—of all places—Hollywood.

The spécialité de la maison was Boston baked beans, so the menu was built around that dish. A carafe of red wine was placed on each table.

Baked Bean Casual Dinner

*Liver Pâté and Mushroom Hors d'Oeuvre**
Dry Sherry
*Olives   Vegetable Nibblers**
*Boston Baked Beans in the Bean Pot**
Hot Sliced Boston Brown Bread   Red Wine
*Chef's Salad Bowl with Juliennes of Ham**
Grilled Mince Pie   Cheddar Cheese Topping
Demitasse   Benedictine

Instead of baked beans any spécialité may be starred as
the main dish: For instance, a curry, ragout, stew, shrimp
creole, chopped beef-burgers, or spaghetti with meat balls.
It is not the money cost of the food, but perfect cooking
and attractive and friendly presentation, that makes a
dinner party a success.

SUPPER PARTIES

Supper parties on Sunday evenings or holidays are de-
lightful and an easy way to pay up social obligations. If
not more than six are invited better sit-at-the-table; for a
larger group plan assembly-line buffet service. Two courses
are ample if supplemented with tidbits and nibblers.

Cold Weather Supper
(Starred recipes are in this book)

*Chef's Salad Bowl with Julienned Ham**
*Savory Cheese Puddings Individual**   Heated Rolls*
*Pickles   Vegetable Relishes**   Salted Nuts*
*Spice Cake with Sherry Icing**   Coffee*

Warm Weather

Lobster Salad Molds*   *Rolls*
Olives   Carrot Sticks   Raw Caulifleurettes
Crisp Potato Chips
Peaches in Gelatin*   *Brown Edge Icebox Cookies**
Chilled White Wine   *Hot or Iced Coffee*

Midnight Buffet

Hot Bouillon in Cups
Chicken Salad Platter*   *Devilled Eggs*
Crisp Potato Chips   *Heated Buttered Rolls*
Tokay Orange Filled Cake*
Chilled White Wine   *Coffee*

EVENING SNACKS

To serve snacks after cards, or after the movies is an easy way to entertain a few friends. Have the foods all ready beforehand. If a hot dish is to be served, it should be ready for quick cooking, reheating on the electric grill or plate or in the chafing dish. The service is always buffet style. One or at most two courses are ample.

(Starred recipes are in this book)

I

Grilled Devilled Cheese Sandwiches
Or Cheesed Frankfurters*
Coffee or Beer

II

Nut Waffles*   *Coffee*

III

Chicken-Nut Saladettes*   Buttered Rolls
Date Cup Cakes*   Coffee or Tea

IV

Welsh Rabbit on Toast*
Fruits in Wine*   Coffee

V

Cheese Board* with Various Cheeses
Pumpernickel   Crisp Crackers   Beer
Fresh Fruit Bowl   Coffee

HOLIDAY DINNERS

I

(For 2 to 4)
(With a small range available)

Hot Crab-Meat* Toasts   Dry Sherry
Roast Broiler Halves* with Herb Stuffing*   Gravy*
Asparagus*   Chef's Salad Bowl* with Cheese
Mince Pie (Baker)   Hard Sauce*
Demitasse

II

(For 2 to 4)
(With 2 burners and no oven)

Antipasto Salads*
Fricassee of Chicken* or
Turkey on Toast* with Mushrooms
Buttered Peas   Crusty Rolls
Grapes in Gelatin*   Whipped Cream
Mixed Nuts   Demitasse

III
(For 6 to 8)
(With a 2-burner plate and small oven)

Mushroom Anchovy and Ham Canapés*   Dubonnet
Roast Whole Chicken or Turkey Legs*
Herb Stuffing*   *Gravy**
Franconia Style Potatoes*   *Baby Limas*
Cranberry Jelly   *Celery*   *Heated Rolls*
Hot Plum Pudding (canned)
with Sherry Hard Sauce*
Demitasse

HOLIDAY OPEN HOUSE

Of course your friends will be welcome on Christmas
and New Years. So have pleasant refreshments ready to
serve.

Guests in the Morning

I

Coffee Cake   *Viennese Coffee**

II

Molasses Shortbread Cookettes*   *Orange Juice*

Guests in the Afternoon or Evening

Assorted Cookies   *Fingers of Fruit Cake*
Holiday Eggnog*

HOLIDAY EGGNOG

(About 2½ quarts or 36 servings)

6 *egg yolks*	1 *pint milk*
1¼ *cups confectioners' or powdered sugar*	3 *cups heavy cream*
	4 *egg whites*
1 *pint rum, brandy or equal parts brandy and sherry*	¼ *teaspoon salt*
	Grated nutmeg

1. Beat the egg yolks light and cream in the sugar.
2. Slowly beat in the rum, brandy and/or sherry. Stir in the milk and cream. Cover and chill at least 1 hour.
3. Whip the egg whites and salt, and fold in.
4. Dust with grated nutmeg.
5. Serve in punch cups.

LASTWORD

Let good food and good cookery
Bring you cheer and harmony.

Index